L.W. NIXON LIBRARY
BUTLER COUNTY COMMUNITY COLLE
901 SOUTH HAVERHILL ROAD
EL DORADO, KANSAS 67042-3280

W9-AGV-768

SHAMANS, HEALERS, AND MEDICINE MEN

SHAMANS, HEALERS, AND MEDICINE MEN

HOLGER KALWEIT

Translated by
Michael H. Kohn

SHAMBHALA
Boston & London
1992

Shambhala Publications, Inc.
Horticultural Hall
300 Massachusetts Avenue
Boston, Massachusetts 02115

Shambhala Publications, Inc.
Random Century House
20 Vauxhall Bridge Road
London SW1V 2SA

© 1987 by Kösel-Verlag GmbH & Co., Munich
Translation © 1992 by Shambhala Publications, Inc.

All rights reserved. No part of this book may be reproduced in any form or by any means, electronic or mechanical, including photocopying, recording, or by any information storage and retrieval system, without permission in writing from the publisher.

9 8 7 6 5 4 3 2 1

First Edition
Printed in the United States of America on acid-free paper ∞
Distributed in the United States by Random House, Inc., in Canada by Random House of Canada Ltd, and in the United Kingdom by Random House UK Ltd

Library of Congress Cataloging-in-Publication Data

Kalweit, Holger.
[Urheiler, Medizinleute und Schamanen. English]
Shamans, healers, and medicine men / Holger Kalweit; translated by Michael H. Kohn.—1st ed.
p. cm.
Includes bibliographical references and index.
ISBN 0-87773-659-6 (alk. paper)
1. Shamanism. 2. Spiritual healing. 3. Medicine, Magic, mystic, and spagiric. I. Title.
BL2370.S5K35813 1992   92-50127
291—dc20   CIP

291 KAL 1987

Kalweit, Holger.
Shamans, healers, and
medicine men.

For my father,
whom healing did not reach in time

Being conscious
Is an illness
A real
Downright illness.

—FYODOR DOSTOYEVSKY

CONTENTS

INTRODUCTION: HOLY MEDICINE

There are three things our culture has forgotten: basic health, healing, and holiness. All three words have the same linguistic root, and the concepts have same goal: sanity, integrity, completeness, salvation, happiness, liberation, magic.

Healing has little to do with the surgeon's scalpel or antisepsis. Wholesomeness and basic health are attained, rather, only through inner purification. This means removing impure elements and going through suffering. It has nothing to do with the gentle ethos of our softened culture; it means physical and psychic transformation on all levels. The healer, the holy man, and the person who is healed all go through a spiritual reshaping. Their nature is bent, broken, reduced to worthlessness, then immaculately fashioned afresh. At that point, they enter a hale and wholesome world that is free from sickness and that has been purified through suffering. This is the first shamanic paradox.

- Basic health and well-being mean the panoramic perception of all levels of being.
- Healing means healing culture first, then people, and finally sickness.
- Holiness means feeling many—all—spheres of existence within oneself.

We have lost this triad with its qualities of wisdom, happiness, and magic.

Medicine people do not heal patients first. First they heal themselves, then all else. This is the "vision of knowledge," the vision of a new kind of medical practitioner. This book tells of how primal healers experience being, how they give themselves over to the energies of life and act in sympathy with them. They do not, as our culture does, seek trumped-up novelties. They seek to bring themselves into harmony with nature's laws, with the cosmic Logos.

Shamans were the earliest creators of knowledge, and they will be the future ones as well. Thus, this book is in no way a description of archaic and outdated things. It is, rather, an anticipation of ways of healing that we will once more come to esteem in the future. What is it that we as doctors, psychologists, therapists—as people—can learn from shamans?

Primeval medicine and primal healing methods travel the inner way, in a quest for wholeness and health beyond the ego. The medicine of the shaman knows no pills and shots, does not seek to eliminate symptoms—that would go against nature. Rather, it revives life and heals our relations with the world—for is illness not the clogging of our spiritual pores, a blockage of a global perception of the world, and "illness" only in our limited sense?

Our bureaucratized and materialistic medicine—this mechanical model with an active therapist and a passive patient that reduces the patient to an object and relegates healing to the long corridors of the hospital—has failed. This kind of healing belongs to the mechanical age. Today, however, we are already daring to make the transition to "organic" medicine, "spiritual healing" through personal transformation, through the transformation of consciousness on all levels.

If we are seeking classical models for this kind of healing, they exist: the masters of basic health—shamans, primeval healers, primal physicians, wise men and women. Their secrets are now being unveiled by our awakening consciousness; yet so far, only timid forays have yet been recorded.

My first book on shamans, *Dreamtime and Inner Space,* gave an account of the forms of initiation and the psychic process that makes a person a shaman. This second book is a book for everyone, providing an alternative to the ongoing desacralization of the powers of human consciousness. It is not a rough-and-ready guidebook for self-helpers in a hurry, of the kind that are currently so popular. Instead, the reader will find indications of the complexity and enigmatic nature of basic health. These indications themselves may contribute toward self-healing by way of disillusionment, by eating away Western-centered attitudes and outlooks and vain, ego-oriented hopes. Before healing is possible at all, our false conceptions must be shown up in all their unholy confusion. Healing here always means daring to step over boundaries. The notion that ego gratification and stability are the goals of life has to be given up if we are to enter into spheres of consciousness that promise healing arising out of ourselves, that are in themselves healing. From this point of view, healing is a change in the level of consciousness, a change in the spiritual time-space structure. The primal medicine man lives in a universe of many worlds: this world is one world, the realm of the dead is another, and then there are the worlds of other beings in other spaces and other times. Healing for the primal healer is a voyage beyond time and space into other dimensions of existence. What are these voyages like? Consciousness is the traveler, and today we can say that consciousness is an autonomous unity, independent of the brain, that belongs to a higher order altogether than the brain, than the physical substance that produces it and that is its bearer. Consciousness is the origin and the future of all that is living, an expression of a higher order of space and time, of a limitless essence.

Shamanic therapy means the healing of an entire life rather than just healing failing functions and disruptive pains. For shamans, healing involves philosophy, a view of life. In this regard, giving a careful account of ways of healing is only one aspect of our task. The other is to depict the shamanic manipulation of energies of a higher dimension that for us are invisible and even unthinkable. Penetrating into the shamanic way of healing is instructive for researchers into energy, because through it they find their attention directed toward the existence of higher force fields. Still, this is not enough. In the near future we will be applying these healing energies in all areas and will thus be able to bring about a new quality of life beyond anything we have hitherto hoped for and imagined. Shamans are not only the precursors of science; as seekers of knowledge, they embody living science in quest of the way to the future. Gaining knowledge of new energies is inextricably bound up with the dimensions of time and space. Thus, shamans are time travelers. They travel beyond our familiar time boundaries into the past and the future, into other states of being and other universes of time. Time—which in one way or another is the single essential quality of everything existing, because it creates and destroys everything, gives birth to it all and causes it all to die—is alpha and omega. Our human nature itself is a temporal one; we ourselves are beings of time. Shamans penetrate into a kind of hyperspace, whose energies and paradoxical nature they somehow take on themselves. Their wisdom of life, their suprapersonal knowledge, are of a higher space. This higher space remains inconceivable, but this does not mean that it cannot be entered. An initiation into shamanic healing means a devaluation of all values, an overturning of the profane world, a peeling away of inveterate handed-down notions of the world, liberation from everything preconceived. For that reason, shamanism is closely connected with suffering. One must suffer the disintegration of one's own system of thought in order to perceive a new world in the higher space.

Merely occupying ourselves with shamanism inaugurates a kind of healing. I believe it stimulates us to think in a new way, shows us entirely differently constituted ways of living and thinking. It relaxes us and opens us up.

Just one warning before we begin. We often call shamans sorcerers. We are about to enter a realm of deceptions, of miraculous reflections, of absurdities and paradoxes, where things are inverted and mercurial. The point of view connected with either/or, yes/no, and light/dark here gives way to an outlook in which everything is possible. That is why we today associate magic with deception, delusion, and the arts of deceit. In truth, however, these illusions are but illusions of our truncated consciousness. What seems like paradox to us is actually the myopia of the Western way of thinking. All the same, it is a bizarre land we are entering. Those who journey to this gleaming and fabulous realm are in danger of going astray, of drowning: the mirror dupes us with what we project onto it. But if we succeed and are able to return, it gives us a picture of the world whose fruits we have tasted. The journey there may be a journey of healing, and one may return a sorcerer. Or it may be a journey of deception, and we may return bewitched ourselves: salvation or disaster, the Janus face of existence, a walk on the razor's edge. . . .

PART ONE

THE BIRTH OF
THE HEALER

He had the soul of a child and the mind of a philosopher.

—THEODORA KROEBER
about Ishi, the last survivor
of the Yahi of California
(1961, 238)

1

THE FIRST SHAMANS OF
THE GOLDEN AGE

More and more people are beginning to realize *that the "modern experiment" has failed.* It received its early impetus from what I have called the Cartesian revolution, which, with implacable logic, separated man from those Higher Levels that alone can maintain his humanity. Man has closed the gates of Heaven against himself and tried, with immense energy and ingenuity, to confine himself to the Earth. He is now discovering that the Earth is but a transitory state, so that a refusal to reach for Heaven means an involuntary descent into Hell.
—E. F. SCHUMACHER,
A Guide for the Perplexed (1977, 139)

In the very first times there was no light on earth. Everything was in darkness, the lands could not be seen, the animals could not be seen. And still, both people and animals lived on the earth, but there was no difference between them. They lived promiscuously: A person could become an animal, and an animal could become a human being. There were wolves, bears, and foxes but as soon as they turned into humans they were all the same. They may have had different habits, but all spoke the same tongue, lived in the same kind of house, and spoke and hunted in the same way.

That is the way they lived here on earth in the very earliest times, times that no one can understand now. That was the time when magic words were made. A word spoken by chance would suddenly become powerful, and what people wanted to happen could happen, and nobody could explain how it was. (Rasmussen 1931, vol. 8, 208)

Now we know nothing more than that the human mind and human speech once had mysterious powers (ibid., 211).

This is the origin story told by the Netsilik Eskimo woman Nâlungiaq to Knud Rasmussen.

In the distant past, in mythical times, a paradise existed. People lived in happiness and peace, and all the supernatural forces were theirs for the using. In that golden age, people communicated effortlessly with the gods. They could fly and even assume whatever forms they wished and wander between the worlds, for heaven, earth, and the underworld formed a whole. Every one of our earliest ancestors posessed these gifts. There were no distinctions between people; they were all equal. Movement between the three worlds was unobstructed; the universes were not separated from one another, as we are accustomed to regarding them today. Death was unknown; people lived in a state of freedom; sickness and suffering were nonexistent. Animals were trusting and friendly. Unlike today, when spirits, animals, and people live in separation from one another, in the primordial time they formed a unity.

The first races of the world consisted of beings of the most various origins and characters. They came from very different dimensions of existence. Beings traveled effortlessly in the sky and met God face to face. Crossing a bridge that joined heaven and earth, they reached the upper spheres. But through some mysterious misdeed, this connection was disrupted, the bridge broken. Little by little, after this world-shaking event of the primordial time, sentient beings lost their original wisdom, so that what was then accessible to everybody is today reached only by individuals—shamans. Today, the possibility of experiencing this state of paradise exists only by means of the soul's departure from the body. Only in spirit do a few people dare to cross over. The fall, the mysterious event of the primordial time, brought about the end of the relationship between gods and human beings, the end of interspecies communication, the end of the exchange between levels of existence. What is possible only for a few chosen ones today through paranormal powers or spiritual concentration seems formerly to have been a general condition of life.

In the primordial time, the Australians say, it was possible to live beyond time and space, to transform oneself at will, and to accomplish supernatural things. As a result of the current decay of this tradition, only medicine people now reenter the dreamtime. According to Mircea Eliade, myths of the degeneration of shamans recall the times when shamans actually flew physically in the heavens rather than "flying" only in a state of ecstasy. In the primordial time, the ascent took place not in spirit but actually in the flesh. Then the primordial cosmic catastrophe destroyed the harmony and unity of humanity; death entered the scene, and soul and body became alienated from each other.

According to the traditions of many peoples, the first powerful shamans descended directly from heaven. They were divine beings with supernatural gifts. Often the first shaman appeared as a culture hero and god who brought humanity knowledge from beyond the world. But this knowledge has been continually deteriorating since the culture hero's first appearance. Since the violent break between heaven and earth, which was perhaps the most important event of the primordial time, only the shaman has been capable of ascending to heaven; and since contact with Western civilization, flying to heaven has been denied even to many shamans. In short, in the view of many cultures, shamanism is in full decline.

The traditions of primordial shamans reach back to a realm of mythical revelation, to the golden age when the gods reigned on earth and supported humanity's endeavors through word and deed. The gods helped the first human cultures build their civilizations and societies. They are the classical authors of culture, for they instructed human beings in everyday things, in all matters of life and knowledge.

In many traditions, the first shamans, who very often were identical with the founders of the culture, provided the model for later human shamans. The Australian heroes of the primordial time traveled in the "dreamtime" through the country while "dreaming," and they created the first beings through "dreaming." The tribes of northwestern Australia in the Kimberley Division speak of dreams when they refer to the mythical beginnings of the world, the primordial time, or the *lalai,* the creative primordial state per se.

But *lalai* means not only the state of things in the primordial time or its heroes; present-day shamans can also reach the *lalai*. While they are "dreaming," they heal, fly to distant lands, or descend into the underworld. In Australia, the shaman still returns to the sacred epoch. He returns to the origin, to the creation itself; he voyages back in time to the source of power. Today still, by "dreaming," he maintains the spiritual connection between the present and the primordial time. Through an alteration of consciousness, he enters the primordial time: there, transpersonal consciousness and the primordial mode of existence are unified (Lommel 1951). Whereas according to other traditions, the power of the shaman has been constantly declining since the golden age or the beginning of creation, the aborigines of Australia have preserved the possibility of returning to it at any time.

The Nepalese Magar, too, tell of a primeval golden age that contrasts with the "blind land," the dark age of today. Then there was neither sickness, nor old age, nor bad qualities. In the following, second age, sacrifices and rituals developed. In the third age, conflicting views and contradictory ideas emerged, resulting in the appearance of passions and illness. In the fourth age, bloodthirsty rulers took over; greed, servitude, suffering, and materialism gained the upper hand. In that iron age, death, danger, war, pain, and material craving dominated humanity, but the first shaman, Rama Puran Tsan, also appeared. He immediately recognized that evil spirits and sorcerers were the cause of poverty and sickness. After major battles with the nine witch sisters in which they were unable to harm him, he concluded a pact with them: the witches could continue to bring down illnesses on humanity, but in exchange for payment and blood sacrifices, the shaman would heal them (Oppitz 1981, 8ff.).

The Magar shamans still enact the myth of the first shamans today in all detail. Nothing in this has changed since time immemorial. Each cure, each initiation of a shaman into his function, is an invocation of the primordial time. This blending of the sacred time and the present, of myth and reality, keeps the tradition alive.

The Indonesian Miau were in direct communication with the supreme spirit in the primordial time; they traveled back and forth freely between heaven and earth. We encounter related traditions among the Tibeto-Chinese peoples. In the primordial time, spirits and humans lived in harmony together; but through a trespass on the part of humanity, this connection was lost. Today, few have access to the spheres of the spirit world (Hermanns 1970, vol. 2, 68).

On an *olopatte,* a golden disk, humanlike beings of the primordial time flew down from heaven and landed on earth, according to the legends of the Cuna, who live on islands off Panama in the Caribbean. After Ipeorkum, the mythical culture hero, taught all his heavenly knowledge to humans, he departed again, and white, yellow, blue, and red mists came floating down. Ipeorkum had scarcely disappeared when the Cuna found a child in a treetop lying on an *olopatte* like the one on which Ipeorkum had descended from heaven. Later, ten more children came to earth in this fashion. They were raised by virgins and were called *nele,* or shamans. They became the *saila,* the rulers of the Cuna (Holmer and Wassén 1958, 156ff.).

The saga of the first shamans among the Buryats tells us that at the beginning there were no people, only the gods, the Tengri. The western, good Tengri made human beings, who lived happily and at first knew neither suffering nor sickness. But then the eastern, evil Tengri made people suffer. The western Tengri held conferences on the moon and the Pleiades where they discussed how to help human beings. They decided to send a shaman to humanity and chose for this purpose an eagle. But the eagle came from the eastern Tengri. The first time he flew down, he was unable to fulfill his mission, since he was incapable of speaking the human language. So the gods decided he should fly down a second time and confer the shamanic power on the first person he met. When he arrived on the earth, the eagle saw a woman sleeping under a tree and had intercourse with her. Soon she bore a son, who became the first shaman. According to another variant, this woman became the first shaman (Agapitow and Changalow 1887, 286).

The Alaskan Eskimo tell the following about the first two shamans, who descended from heaven. Two brothers wanted to be reborn through a woman. The woman could not have anything dark about her, and no shadow could fall on her body or bones. They searched for a long time for a clean, good woman. Then one of the brothers caught sight of a nearly gleaming woman. Before he crawled into her, he shouted, "I'm coming!" Soon after his birth, he was recognized as a great shaman who could fly through the air in his seances. In the meantime, his brother had also found a nearly gleaming woman, but after birth he forgot his brother. The first brother, however, searched for him and finally came upon him. The second brother was unable to fly through the air, but he consulted the spirits through the use of amulets and a spirit wand. These two were the first shamans, from whom all those of the following generations learned their art (Rasmussen 1952, 165).

The Iglulik Eskimo have a particularly detailed story concerning the origin of the first shaman:

> In the very earliest times, men lived in the dark and had no animals to hunt. They were poor, ignorant people, far inferior to those living nowadays. They travelled about in search of food, they lived on journeys as we do now, but in a very different way. When they halted and camped, they worked at the soil with picks of a kind we no longer know. They got their food from the earth, they lived on the soil. They knew nothing of all the game we now have, and had therefore no need to be ever on guard against all those perils which arise from the fact that we, hunting animals as we do, live by slaying other souls. Therefore, they had no shamans, but they knew sickness, and it was fear of sickness and suffering that led to the coming of the first shamans. The ancients relate as follows concerning this:
>
> "Human beings have always been afraid of sickness, and far back in the very earliest times there arose wise men who tried to find out about all the things none could understand. There were no shamans in those days, and men were ignorant of all those rules of life which have since taught them to be on their guard against danger and wickedness. The first amulet that ever existed was the shell portion of a sea-urchin. It has a hole through it, and is hence called itEQ (anus) and the fact of its being made the first amulet was due to its being associated with a particular power of healing. When a man fell ill, one would go and sit by him, and, pointing to the diseased part, break wind behind. Then one went outside, while another held one hand hollowed over the diseased part, breathing at the same time out over the palm of his other hand in a direction away from the person to be cured. It was then believed that wind and breath together combined all the power ema-

nating from within the human body, a power so mysterious and strong that it was able to cure disease.

"In that way everyone was a physician, and there was no need of any shamans. But then it happened that a time of hardship and famine set in around Iglulik. Many died of starvation, and all were greatly perplexed, not knowing what to do. Then one day when a number of people were assembled in a house, a man demanded to be allowed to go behind the skin hangings at the back of the sleeping place, no one knew why. He said he was going to travel down to the Mother of the Sea Beasts. No one in the house understood him, and no one believed in him. He had his way, and passed in behind the hangings. Here he declared that he would exercise an art which should afterwards prove of great value to mankind; but no one must look at him. It was not long, however, before the unbelieving and inquisitive drew aside the hangings, and to their astonishment perceived that he was diving down into the earth; he had already got so far down that only the soles of his feet could be seen. How the man ever hit on this idea no one knows; he himself said that it was the spirits that had helped him; spirits he had entered into contact with out in the great solitude. Thus the first shaman appeared among men. He went down to the Mother of the Sea Beasts and brought back game to men, and the famine gave place to plenty, and all were happy and joyful once more.

"Afterwards, the shamans extended their knowledge of hidden things, and helped mankind in various ways. They also developed their sacred language, which was once only used for communicating with the spirits and not in everyday speech" (Rasmussen 1930b, 110f.).

Today many shamans assure us that not only were the very first shamans much more powerful than their contemporary colleagues are but that their great-grandfathers and grandfathers and fathers possessed more comprehensive powers and more wisdom than they themselves do. From all sides, one hears that shamanism is now in a state of total decay, and many shamans consider themselves less gifted than their predecessors. With the disappearance of the mythical first shaman, the prototype of the hero, the demigod, and the enlightened one who transcended all material attachment, the systematic degeneration and gradual decline of the magical tradition began.

The Eskimo shaman Najagneq explained to Knud Rasmussen:

I searched in the darkness, I was silent in the great silence of the dark. That is how I became an angaqoq, through visions and dreams and meetings with flying spirits. In the days of our ancestors, the angaqoqs were solitary men; but now they are all priests and doctors, weather prophets, or magicians who produce game, or clever merchants who sell their skill for money. The ancient ones dedicated their lives to the work of keeping the world in balance; they dedicated it to great things, immeasurable enormous things. (Rasmussen 1925, 116)

And another *angaqoq* of the Netsilik Eskimo told Rasmussen: "I am a shaman myself, but I am nothing compared with my grandfather Titqatsaq. He lived in the time when a shaman could go down to the Mother of the Sea Beasts, fly up to the moon or make excursions out through space." (Rasmussen 1931, 299).

Similarly, the Eskimo of St. Lawrence Island believe that endless years ago, all old men and women became shamans, and that it was only in recent times that special people were chosen for this (Murphy 1964, 73).

Among the tribes of Tierra del Fuego, the early shamans are considered to have been incomparably more powerful than their successors, who were infected by the unwholesome habits of the Europeans and who ate European food, which weakened them and made them soft. The new customs also made the shamans unsure of themselves, until they finally acknowledged that they had been beaten. The Yamana believe that the indomitable early *yékamus* (shamans) were wiped out in the great upheaval, the great flood Yaiaasaga and were changed into stars and animals. After this catastrophe, the few surviving spirits taught the later generations of humanity (Gusinde 1931, vol. 2).

The first shaman of the Siberian Yakuts possessed extraordinary powers, but he rebelled against the supreme god of his people, who condemned him to eternal flames. The body of this primordial shaman was entirely composed of a variety of reptiles. Only a frog escaped the deadly fire. From this frog stem the shamanic demons who still today provide the Yakuts with celebrated shamans (Mikhailovskii 1895, 64).

According to the beliefs of the Buryats, in the primordial time, the spirits chose the shamans, whereas nowadays, with the general decline of shamanism, they are determined only by their ancestors (Sternberg 1924, 474).

The Buryats of Balagana have a legend of the first shaman Khara-Ghyrgen, who possessed unlimited power. Because God wanted to test him, he stole away the soul of a rich girl. She became ill; eager to heal her, Khara-Ghyrgen roamed the heavens in search of her lost soul. He spied it in a bottle, which God was holding closed with a finger of his right hand. Khara-Gyrgen changed himself into a yellow spider and stung God on the right cheek. Frightened by this bite, God dropped the bottle and hit himself in the cheek. Now the soul was able to escape. Angered by this trick, God henceforth limited the power of shamans (Mikhailovskii 1895, 63f.).

According to another Buryat version of this legend, God punished the shaman by compelling him to jump up and down on the top of a mountain, on its northeast side, until the mountain in all its massive rock was trampled to dust. It is said that the shaman still has not fulfilled this punishment and is still hopping up and down on the same spot today. Since this tragic event, the power of shamans has continually diminished in comparison with that of the primordial shaman. The heavenly father withdrew their knowledge and cut their powers. Once upon a time, shamans could travel as fast as rifle bullets from one place to another, shifting their positions like lightning. They could reach anything with their hands, and their eyes saw everything; no impure souls remained hidden from them, for they were far-sighted, seeing even into the world beyond. With their ears, they heard the conversations of the dead, and they foretold the future with great precision. Today, as the first shaman uses up his power in his ceaseless jumping, the prestige, power, and knowledge of all present shamans wanes. If the first shaman ever becomes completely incapacitated and collapses utterly, the power of all shamans will be broken, and their end will be nigh.

Since the beginning of time the number of shamans has increased, but their importance and their powers have faded. The first shaman's legs have been worn down from so much jumping, so the shamans of today no longer fly as far or as fast as rifle bullets, for over time, the legs of their souls have also become shorter. The first shaman has lost his entrails from his continuous jumping, so present-day shamans are always hungry and greedy. As a result, they lack inner firmness and resolve. The heart has been taken from the first shaman, so his present-day successors are heartless toward their clients. The first shaman lost his hands in the course of his unremitting jumping up and down, so the shamans of today have crippled hands that can no longer truly gain a grip on the things of life. For this reason, libations of alcohol given to the spirits have no effect on them. They are no longer open to being so propitiated. The sick must therefore die, and evil spirits capture human souls. The first shaman today no longer possesses lips or a mouth, so living shamans speak incoherently and forget their prayers. The first shaman has worn out his eyes, so contemporary shamans have lost the eyes of their souls and the knack of real "seeing." The first shaman has lost his mind, so today's shamans have no more memory and have lost track of the names of the spirits; they have forgotten the sacrificial rites, and even the method of reading auspices with the shoulder blade of an animal. It is said that only the crown of the skull of the first shaman is still intact. The crown of his skull is still dancing up and down on top of the mountain, but when even this falls to dust after aeons of bouncing up and down, there will be no more shamans among the Buryats. Each shaman is less able than his predecessor. Though the first shamans still had mastery over the art of awakening the dead, though they were lords of heaven and earth, with their successors, all original knowledge has unfortunately passed into oblivion (Diószegi 1968, 110ff.).

For us, these stories seem no more than bizarre myths, primitive fantasies. But is that what they really are? Don't these primordial events—disruptions of contact with heaven, losses of connection with all living beings, the introduction of death, and punishments of human beings and shamans by God—actually determine our world? Is this last legend of the primordial Buryat shaman and the slow dwindling of his power not a drastic reality? Isn't the spiritual power of human beings really on the decline? Certainly that of nature peoples and shamans is—but isn't ours too? The "myths" of many peoples recognize a connection between the definitive degeneration of shamanic power and the end of the world. They speak of a planetary catastrophe; the Hopi call this the "great purification." The demise of shamanic power thus expresses of the demise of the human wisdom of survival as well. We must ask, Do tribal cultures possess a knowledge, a foreknowledge, concerning the course of planetary evolution? The first shaman of the Buryats and thus of humanity as a whole is described as greedy now and lacking in resoluteness, as heartless toward others, as ineffective, and as spiritually muddled and blind since he has lost the eyes of the soul. The cruelest fact is that he has also lost his mind and forgotten his original wisdom—only the crown of his skull still dances the mad dance of the world—for how much longer? Are these myths? Fantasies? Myths are fantasies—that is the modern myth, which has lost contact with the great knowledge of earlier generations.

So much for the primordial history of healing, the primordial history of the loss of holiness and health. A person who is capable of reading such legends properly—and perhaps they contain the key to knowledge as yet scarcely conceived—begins to have an inkling that healing and holiness fit together within a framework of the mysterious earliest times of humanity, a framework broader than the contemporary doctor-patient relationship could ever guess.

2

SHAMANIC SCHOOLS AND MEDICAL SOCIETIES

Though the gods give shamans their miraculous powers, shamans must learn the technique of invoking them.　　　　　　　—KOREAN PROVERB

I come to you because I want to see.

—Traditional words of an Iglulik Eskimo
who wants to become the student
of a shaman (Rasmussen 1930b, 111)

It is true that from the time of our birth, we can all physically see. But the question remains: What kind of seeing is it? It is the perception of the world through the prism of concepts, which are in turn based on a given culture's color vision—as well as the color blindness. No matter what societal tradition has influenced our world, it is a subjective creation of the human mind. We have devised all our theories and views in order to understand this world better; many believe that these theories are genuine representations of the laws of nature, summaries of what nature offers us as principles. This naive realism in its haste mistakes the map for the territory, but it is unfortunately still king in our kingdom of the blind.

Shamans participate in two worlds. Their sense of sight is double, their feeling world is split, their thinking runs constantly on two tracks. Their physical mother is responsible for their first birth; for their second, the godfather may be a cosmic life-giver, a god, or the spirits. These powers summon shamans irresistibly.

They give them the strength to lead a new life as a shaman and see behind the scenes of life. But shamans' cosmic, transcendental, or superterrestrial parents are not their only teachers and masters. Old, experienced shamans may support and guide them in bringing their visions and their spirit helpers under their power and who pass on to them all the ideas of their culture about matters of transcendence.

There are as many forms of shamanic training as there are cultures with shamans; here we shall present only a few, representative examples to convey a few main principles. Certainly, some shamans develop the entire range of paranormal perceptual abilities and transpersonal insights without teachers. But after their inborn or acquired powers are manifested to them and the mystic dimension or the spirit world is revealed to them, most of them have supramundane or transcendental teachers who painstakingly transmit power to them step by step and accompany them along each stage of the spiritual path. Many have only one or a few masters, from whom they learn privately in secret. This highly personal master-student relationship often arises between father and son as well.

After his education, a shaman still holds in his hands only a small proportion of the strings that will enable him to direct cosmic forces. Each individual has different talents and specializes accordingly. Each has his own orientation and passes through various stages of mystical consciousness expansion; thus, many cultures have strictly regulated hierarchies of spiritual standing up which students must work their way. Almost everywhere, the process of gaining spiritual knowledge is understood as a graded incrementation of insights into sacred wisdom.

Thus, the Hawaiians have a highly complex ranked order of *kahunas*, or shamans, who pursue quite specific goals and, as priests, are closely enmeshed in the structures of political power. During their training, they perform no ordinary work; they are relieved of all worldly responsibilities. They are *kapu*—sacred. Not only does taking on a spiritual role and office require knowledge of another world; the ceremonies, chants, and rituals of a rich tradition also lie in the hands of these spiritual leaders (Fornander and Thrum 1919).

In earlier times, the Irish bards mastered more than one hundred primary and a hundred and seventy-five secondary stories in six years of training. In the seventh year they were capable of writing poetry in complex metric forms. Then they had to learn legends and traditions, and after fifteen years, having become powerful magicians, they were capable of calling forth storms and directing the winds (Moray 1965, 34).

Among the Zulus, there are twelve stages of training, twelve "vessels," or types of spirits. Only a few *sangomas,* or shamans, reach the last and highest stage. The education of a *sangoma* consists first in developing his ability to find objects hidden by the teacher at any time of the day or night. Later on, the student must be able to determine by telepathic means whether the teacher has hidden anything for him at all (Boshier 1974).

Similarly, the Blackfoot novice must pass through seven "tents" to become a fully accomplished medicine man. Every year he must must undergo an examination in which his master questions and tests him to see if he has mastered both intellectual knowledge and spiritual exercises. To the first five "tents" are added two "tents" of "bad medicine," in which he learns to pronounce curses and kill people through the power of thought (Long Lance 1928, 22).

Let us now look at the various shamanic schools and forms of education for medicine people.

In Japan, various ascetic techniques are indispensable to become a medium. In winter, novices stand under ice-cold waterfalls or immerse themselves continually in cold water, often for up to a hundred days. After a time, they become accustomed to the cold and emerge from the icy water refreshed and warm (Blacker 1975, 91ff.). In this way, paradoxically, cold becomes a means of invoking a magical inner heat. This is a typical trance phenomenon: through cold, inner heat is developed, and amid external heat—as in walking on coals—the skin remains cool. Such paradoxical reversals of physiology are a general sign of a well-developed state of trance.

During her initiation in 1918, Nara Naka, from the Tsugaru region of Japan, passed through the typical stages of trance experience. She lived for a week in a small, unheated hut that had been built for her by her teacher. She had to follow certain dietary prescriptions and was not permitted to sleep for the entire week.

During the nights she had to recite texts that she had had to learn by heart. It was wintertime, no fire warmed the hut, and three times a day she had go down to the river and pour thirty-three buckets of ice-cold water over her left and right shoulders while uttering incantations. She was alone day after day, night after night, yet her master might appear at any time to check her progress. So she could not let herself go even for an instant. In the middle of the week she entered a trancelike state, exhausted by lack of sleep, cold, and insufficient food. At that point, the figure of the creator appeared before her eyes. And at the end of the week, all at once she was overcome by an unexpected strength, her feeling of exhaustion disappeared, and a force filled her that seemed to come from outside. In this way she was well prepared for the morning of her initiation and for the testing that followed (Blacker 1975, 145).

From many similar accounts from northeastern Japan, we gather that after a certain time an overflowing life-giving force touches the would-be initiate. At that point he gives himself over fully to his goal, pain and exhaustion disappear entirely, and a sense of inspiration triumphs.

A Korean shaman must not only learn divination and how to make amulets but must master dancing, the playing of musical instruments, many chants, the preparation of food offerings, and the fashioning of paper flowers and figures. According to whatever deity is supposed to appear in a particular divination, he dons appropriate robes and prepares a specific set of offerings (not an easy task, considering the large number of gods). Then he dances with gestures appropriate for that particular god, while continuously intoning shamanic chants that sometimes go on for more than four hours. He also has to learn a certain interrogation technique called *todum'i*. Should the gods, against all expectation, fail to appear during a particular divination, the shaman still has to tell something to the person who is seeking help. This he can do only if he has acquired sufficient information about the person's family situation beforehand, through a skillful interrogation. This enables him to provide a satisfactory answer. The shaman's teachers *(sinbumo)*, lead and guide the novice *(simjasik)*, during his training. The student aids his godparents when they perform ceremonies with other shamans. Later, he may join other shamans and take over particular tasks within a complex ceremony, until he has learned everything and is able to work independently. Before being accepted as a shaman, the Korean novice must undergo a test to ensure that he is not possessed by evil spirits. At the same time, an attempt is made to ascertain which gods express themselves through him. This will determine his status in the shamanic hierarchy (Hung-Youn 1982, 33).

A novice of the Wurajeri in Australia is allowed to become a doctor only after his completed initiation, after he has been "made a man." Even as a child, he must show signs of a potential capacity to be a doctor and must cultivate a relationship with a teacher, who trains him and transmits his power to him. This role is usually taken on by a father or grandfather, from whom the novice learns religious and mythological ideas that he must keep strictly secret. During nocturnal excursions, the spirit of the teacher leads the spirit of the novice into the other world. When the novice reaches the age of ten or twelve, the doctor conducts him to a hiding place, where he gives him a *bala*, a helping totem, and sings into him the *yarawai'yawa*, the spirit companion. King Dick, for example, had an oppossum "sung into" his chest by his father, a shaman. This process caused him no pain, although he felt a slight burning sensation in his chest. In other cases, the spirit animal enters the back, arms, and legs of initiates. In this way a *bala* is handed down from grandfather to father to son to grandson and remains with the family for generations. During the "singing" transmission, the helping totem duplicates itself without being divided or losing power, so that the father and son are filled by it equally. Through chanting, the totem can be made visible; it comes out of the body as a material form. Naturally, the novice must learn the necessary rituals and acquire the powers of concentration to be able to bring forth the totem. Thus, a prerequisite to becoming a doctor is having a vision of the tribe's patron and traditional protector. Only through him does the would-be doctor receive permission to become a "clever man."

The real source of magical power, however, is Baiami, the creator; it comes from *kating-ngari,* "the other side of the ocean." When Baiami left humanity, he summoned all the doctors together and called upon them to continue practicing their magic. But thenceforth, he said, in order to avoid unnecessarily wasting their power, they must refrain from conflict with one another.

The final phase of the novice's education is a public event. Teachers and students assemble in a holy place, sacred to Baiami. Here the students are definitively "made." They sit next to each other on a row of leaves. The teachers sit facing them and behind them. Soon the chanting that invokes Baiami begins. When Baiami appears in the form of a "clever man," living and corporeal, those present must avert their glance from the light rays emanating from his eyes. Baiami then proceeds to "make" one student after the other into a "clever man." From his mouth foams *kali,* holy water, from liquified quartz crystals. He makes this flow over the students and enter their bodies in a process called *ku'rini,* "penetration into them." The liquid flows at once into the body without even a drop touching the earth. As a result, the initiates soon sprout feathers from their arms, which later grow into wings.

After several days, during a second ceremony, Baiami shows each student how to fly with these wings, and he "sings" a piece of quartz crystal into each of their foreheads. This bestows on them a kind of X-ray vision. Then Baiami takes a flame out of his own body and, while intoning a song, places it on the chest of each novice, into which it gradually disappears. Afterward, the novice talks over all these overwhelming experiences with his teacher. After all the initiates have learned to fly and both crystal and fire have "penetrated into them," they summon Baiami a third time with their chanting. Now the last phase of the initiation begins. Again Baiami appears as a living person before their eyes, but this time he lays a string over every student that reaches from his legs to his chest. Through singing, the string becomes part of the novices' bodies. This is the string that the "clever men" use for many of the feats of their art—they are able to work with it like a spider with its net. When Baiami disappears again, the students practice doing magical feats with the string; but their performances are far less accomplished than those of the elder "clever men." After the students have learned all this, their *warajun,* souls, and their *yarawai'yawa,* helping animals and spirit animals, can flourish freely, and the students can take nocturnal travels through space and time (Berndt 1946–47, 330ff.).

The term that the Dunne-za of North America use for a prophet is *naáchi*, "dreamer." The *naáchi* possesses a profoundly penetrating dream power that goes far beyond that of normal dreaming. In the dream state, the dreamer's shade, his soul, wanders about like a spirit. At night, when the soul leaves the body, it is believed that it follows in the tracks of its previous existences. For this reason, as early as childhood, one must gain control over one's dreams, so that the soul does not leave the body against one's will. Vision quests are conducted even before puberty to prevent this and to acquire medicine power, or control over the ego shade. Every person must have his shade in his power, but only the *naáchi* has comprehensive knowledge in this area. He knows the secret of how consciously to visit the realm of the dead with his soul and return. Moreover he knows songs *(naáchi yine)* that connect the realm of the dead with that of the living.

The Dunne-za call mastery of the dream shade *me-yine.* It can be acquired only through a vision in which the child becomes acquainted with the gigantic animals that humans hunted in mythical times. The child's shade travels back over his life path and encounters the huge animals of prehistory. The fruit of this dream journey into the past is the acquisition of a power song, the sacred song of the giant animals. In the vision, taboos are laid on the dreamer and advice given for his quest for a medicine bundle. The power does not appear, however, until the dreamer has grown to adulthood, and he does not speak of his possession of the various giant animals during the vision quest until he has become an elder. This is because the Dunne-za believe that the complete mastery of the dream and a successful existence as an adult are bound up together. This is not improbable; the vision experience makes it possible for him, for example, to hunt better with the help of his shade since he traveled in the dream the path he would take in the hunt. Since the animals have already surrendered themselves to the hunter in the dream, the hunt that later takes place in reality is actually only an acting-out of the dream hunt (Ridington 1978).

There is an interesting account of an *ayikomi,* a medicine maker of the Florida Seminole. At the age of fifteen, Josie began to take an interest in healing. He sought out the *ayikomi* whom he had befriended and asked them about herbs for treating various illnesses. In this way, his education, which lasted many years, began. Josie tells us:

> When I was about 15 years old I went to a doctor and asked him for instance about coughing—what kind of a song do you use for coughing?—and he told me. . . . I asked him what kind of medicine is used, and he gave me the medicine and the songs. . . . For about two years I talked to him this way. If somebody cuts his foot with an axe, how are you going to doctor him?—and he gave me a song for that. I asked him a lot of times. The doctor said, he wants to know something, that's all right, and he gave me different songs, different medicines and told me about different sicknesses. How to cure fever, he told me that too. He just gave them to me, taught me without pay or anything; it didn't cost me anything. There were several doctors I talked to this way: Tommy Doctor, Old Doctor, there were a lot of doctors around at that time that I talked to. Then, when I was about 17 or 18 years old, Old Motlow knew that I wanted to know things. He said, all right, you fast for a while, maybe by yourself, maybe with two or three boys with you, and you'll learn. I said all right, and got three boys and we went out and camped by ourselves, without any women. We built a little shack and stayed there.

During the four-day fast, they were taught by Old Motlow. Every morning, he gave the students emetics—his way of preparing them for their lessons. Fasting and vomiting, it was believed, heighten personal, moral, intellectual, and religious strength. Every day he taught them something different. The first day he spoke of various illnesses and sang the songs needed for them. On the second day he talked about living creatures, the origins of things, life after death, the destiny of the soul, and the sources of illness. The third day was devoted to repetition of what had already been learned and spoken about. On the fourth day the students received further secret and efficacious songs, curses, and magical formulas for personal protection or for black magic. School ended with a four-day hunt, during which the students talked everything over again. In the following years, they regularly held this school again and again, and after the last time, Josie went to stay with Tommy Doctor and observed him daily in his work. He watched how Tommy Doctor diagnosed patients by gathering information about dreams and physical symptoms from their families; he learned about herbs, watched the medicine-making process, and practiced the sacred chants, whose power was thought to go into the medicine.

After his teacher's death, Josie took over his practice and thereby became an independent practitioner after at least seven years of education. In addition, he had received a medicine from his teacher with which he could either harm or help others. A drug—his teacher had worked a plant into a medicine and administered it to him—came to life in his body and continued to live there, in his heart, Josie thought. Today when he prepares medicines, this special power gives off a characteristic odor that enters into the patient and has an essential healing effect. In order to keep this medicine from degenerating, Josie has to fast and vomit once a month. If his treatments fail, he blames this on a weakening of this inner power. Then he at once prescribes a fasting cure for himself. In treating people, he must pay heed never to treat menstruating women or women who have just given birth. This would destroy his "living medicine" and his healing power as a doctor. He can also use his "living medicine" for negative ends. He can use it to summon the soul of a person so that he can maltreat it once it is in his power, or to make a gun go off by itself in such a way that the shot hits its owner, or to make lightning strike others. But he can also use it to make rain or a love potion, which he often did in his younger years (Sturtevant 1960, 505ff.).

Nanabush, the great culture hero of the Central Algonquian, was charged by the Great Spirit to found the Midewiwin society. This secret society of the peoples of the Great Lakes—Ojibwa, Menomini, Winnebago, and others—developed a strict, hierarchically structured training for medicine people. Its great medicine hut, the *midewigan*, is a representation of the cosmos; its origin is sacred. The traditions of the medicine hut are passed on orally, as well as in a symbolic script written on birch bark. Every Ojibwa tries to become a member of the medicine society. There are four levels of medicine people (in some accounts eight are mentioned), and each level requires particular initiation rituals that transmit to the initiate a precisely determined body of knowledge suited to that level. The higher the level of initiation, the greater the price that must be paid for it. Initially, everyone with healing gifts or certain knowledge of plants was permitted entry, but later new persons were invited only after careful testing, and they could only enter if they had been healed by a Mide member. The central ceremonial object of the *midewigan* is the sacred mussel, a representation of that mussel that long, long ago had guided the Ojibwa from the east to the west.

At their ritual assembly, the highest-placed medicine people "shoot" the initiates with a white mussel shell *(migis)* by touching their bodies with a medicine bundle. Later, they are brought back to life the same way. When they awaken, they vomit the mussel and begin a life enriched with new values—they have been resurrected from death and born again. When a participant has been "shot" four times, he possesses all the supernatural powers: he can fly, can change himself into an animal, is clairvoyant, can prophesy, can find lost objects, can perform love sorcery, is fireproof, and can suck illness out of bodies.

The four training levels of the Ojibwa can be roughly described as follows.

First stage. In the first year the student learns from a mentor the lore of plants, songs, and prayers and must provide the offerings for the Midewiwin ceremony in the spring. He fasts for four days before the ceremony and spends time in a purification hut. In the test itself, he is not allowed to make a single mistake. The presiding *midewiwinini* (medicine man) then "shoots" him with a *midemigis* (mussel). The student collapses as if dead, and in the death state he experiences a vision and receives a sacred chant. Then the *midewiwinini* reawakens him with the breath of life. At this, the novice is considered new-born; his status and existence have changed. Now he must prove his powers publicly. Afterward, as a sign of his inner transformation, he is given a medicine bundle, in which he keeps the objects that symbolize his personal powers.

Second stage. The second stage very much resembles the first. The candidate emerges from the "shooting" ceremony with expanded perception. He can now see further than the eye, hear things beyond the range of the ear, sense good and evil, read the future, touch people from a great distance, and overcome time and space.

Third stage. After the "shooting" with the mussel and the acquisition of the supernatural powers, he becomes a *yeesekeewinini*—

someone capable of invoking higher beings and communicating with the other world. He can know hidden things, and since he embodies the power of thunder, which comes from heaven, he is able to move and shake things.

Fourth stage. Now he acquires the power to awaken in others the same abilities he himself has. He is permitted to instruct and test new candidates. He has died, been resurrected, and been tested four times. As we see, even within this organized framework, the entire initiation ritual follows the pattern of a spontaneous birth-and-death experience. The training is now considered complete; but the student must return every year to regenerate his power. As a sign of his status, every member of the Midewiwin receives the symbol of the society: a mussel that protects him against sickness and misfortune (Johnston 1979, 105ff.; Hallowell 1936; W. J. Hoffman 1891).

An unusual project in Rough Rock, Arizona, supported by the National Institute of Mental Health, finances the training of Navajos as medicine people. They are taught, according to tradition, by older, experienced medicine people. Along with their traditional education, they also receive instruction from Western psychiatrists. The reason for this unusual approach was the belated recognition that native medicine people could help considerably to alleviate the physical and psychological sufferings of their people. The program was devised when the tribal leaders called attention to the fact that the old medicine people were dying out and the young people were unable to meet the costs of the expensive training (Bergman 1973; Steiger 1974, 161ff.).

All schools for medicine people and shamanic paths of learning end, as shown by the examples I have given, with a more or less formal test. Of course, the entire path, on which one has to pass through a number of stages, is in itself a test. But here we are speaking of a final ritual test—either at the end of a specific stage of development or a definitive test that permits the student to become a medicine man and practice on his own. This kind of test is indispensable. Only for shamans who are trained from the "beyond" by spirits of the dead, or who for some other reason do not have a teacher, is there no test.

Generally, representatives of the local society of medicine people are present at magical performances that the candidate must present as part of his test. They critically examine the neophyte's capabilities, and in doing so they themselves seemingly enter another state of consciousness; this way they can better perceive the helping spirits or "power lines" of the new shaman and suitably judge his purely spiritual feats.

When the Birartchen (Tungus) of the middle Amur River area acquire a helping spirit, for example, a trial period follows during which the student is trained through conversations with his shamanic teacher. During this time, the student is called, not inaccurately, *asaran,* "the persecuted one." When the time is ripe, the testing of his knowledge begins. He is asked what the shamanic spirits look like, when and where they lived, what shamans they served, and when these shamans died. Such a test can last up to nine days. If the novice passes the test, great animal sacrifices are made, and the trees—symbols of the breakthrough into other levels of existence—are rubbed with blood (Wassiljewitsch 1963, 375ff.).

The Maori of New Zealand also have a school for priests, the *whara wananga* (among the members of the Ngati Kahungunu tribe). The Maori priests, or *tohunga,* were prohibited in the year 1907, a serious blow to the Maori religion. But the religion began to flourish again when this prohibition was lifted in 1963. In the *whara wananga,* students are given power over the lives of humans, animals, and plants through *karakia,* or prayer and ritual chanting. During the final testing, the candidates must demonstrate their parapsychological knowledge; through *karakia,* they must split a stone or a tree and kill a bird or a human (Greschat 1980, 106ff.).

Before the shaman-in-training of the Tenino, of northern Oregon, can begin his practice, he must prove his gifts before a committee of older shamans. They bring him to a steep precipice, where he must prove his mastery over the spirits. The Tenino believe that the souls of the dead, particularly of departed shamans, are "hungry" and seek a master who will "feed" them. While normal people possess only five supernatural helpers, shamans like John Quinn, for one, can possess fifty-five or more. Most of the helping spirits are animals; grizzly bears, rattlesnakes, and eagles give the Tenino the most power. Every shaman has a number of helping spirits; for example, a spirit who performs diagnoses and, when emanated into the body of the patient, localizes the focal point of the illness; or the spirit of a dead infant, with whose help lost souls are captured. The way the neophyte sends his spirits on missions and the extent to which he exercises a guiding influence over them can of course only be perceived by shamans. No charlatan can pass these tests. The committee of shamans closely scrutinizes the character of the candidate, his strengths and weaknesses, his honesty, his control over aggressive impulses, and his sense of moral responsibility. Whether he is accepted or not depends on their collective decision (Murdock 1965, 166ff.).

To conclude this chapter, I would like to examine in some detail the institution for educating medicine men of the Yamana of Tierra del Fuego. Their school for medicine men is called the *loimayeka-mus*. Not an ongoing establishment, this school is held at intervals of several years during the long winter months and often lasts for half a year. In a chosen place that will likely be free of disturbance, a large hut is built. This *loima* house is not a secular building; it inspires great veneration and awe, for here dwell the *haucélla*, wrathful and dangerous spirits. Even entering the house requires a particularly alert mind. After the students have mentally prepared themselves for several hours in their own huts, they move with bowed heads and half-closed eyes, cautiously placing one foot before the other, toward the *loima* house. As they go along, they maintain a religious frame of mind, now and then casting a timid glance at their goal. This slow groping toward the medicine hut, which is often only a short distance away, can last up to five hours. Each student feels that he will be helplessly at the mercy of the spirits in the hut; only an earnest and awe-filled state of mind will secure him the favor of these beings.

The student knows that in the *loima* house, months of the strictest concentration and practice lie before him, during which he will have to call upon all his spiritual powers. Experienced masters supervise and guide the novices. They are not permitted to spend any time outside the *loima* house; any and every form of distraction is excluded. Communication with family or wife is kept to a minimum. Sexual relations are forbidden. The daily regimen fosters inwardness and contemplation. The students sit in their places almost without interruption and without moving. Group chanting begins at twilight, about four in the afternoon, and continues until long after midnight. After a short period of sleep, practice is resumed at dawn. The students remain quietly in their places until the sun passes the zenith. At that point the small group undertakes some work, such as gathering firewood and mussels. Three hours later, all resume their motionless position. The meals are extremely meager; they consist at the most of three mussels a day. If a student shows good progress, his daily ration is reduced to two mussels or even one, for the less he heats, the faster his spiritual development will progress. It is well known that fasting is a favored means for bringing about altered states of consciousness. This is because debilitation of the body weakens the mind's habitual structures.

Students sit on the floor with their legs extended in front of them. Their upright torsos press a chunk of wood behind their necks against the wall of the hut. This position causes considerable strain over a long period of time and soon worsens into an indescribable torment. In certain circumstances the legs can be temporarily crossed in the tailor's position. The discomfort this position causes is intensified by the fact that the students are not allowed to break it during sleep; they are allowed only to bring their knees up against their chest. The chunk of wood remains behind the neck.

This training process is an attempt to shake the daily experience of the apprentice loose from its foundations. All the patterns of action that reinforce stable habits are disrupted. Fasting, motionlessness, continuous monotonous chanting, the ongoing fear of the *haucélla* spirits, and the long separation from the daily activities of the rest of the tribe lead the student into a new sphere of consciousness. He lives in the magical atmosphere of the *loima* house; his body and mind are in a kind of vacuum that provides no reference point by which he can orient himself, an emptiness in which he feels helpless and confused. All the tribal customs and moral precepts, indeed his entire behavioral code, have been taken from him. But slowly a new world dawns in his experience in which he cautiously attempts to gain a foothold.

The intention of this school for medicine men is the transformation of the body. Aspirants rub their cheeks with wood shavings that have been dipped in white pigment. The pressure on the skin is quite gentle, but the purpose is to bring out a complexion that is finer than the original one. Further constant rubbing continues over weeks, which brings a second layer of skin to the surface. Finally yet a third layer of skin is exposed, which is so sensitive that it cannot be touched without causing great pain. When all the candidates have reached this stage, the training is considered completed. Obviously, this treatment of the cheeks is not carried out for cosmetic reasons. Apparently, this monotonous rubbing reinforces the process of transforming consciousness. The exposure of three layers of skin could also well be symbolic of the students' progressive awareness of the "inner body"—that is, the soul. This cheek-rubbing technique is reminiscent of the stone grinding of many Eskimo peoples, who rub two stones together for weeks until finally a helping spirit appears.

When the third layer of skin appears, the goal of all the previous efforts has been achieved: the formation of a "second body." This new body is made out of a "light material, like down," the Yamana say. The body of the *yékamus* (shaman) appears to ordinary people to be a normal body; but actually the body of the sorcerer is many hundred meters larger, and nothing within this range is hidden from him. If he gets a wound on his body, it is only in the limited vision of normal people that blood flows, for in reality the shaman's down-feather body contains no blood. Because of the subtle material of his body, the Tierra del Fuegans regard the shaman as no longer a human being.

The most important goal of the shamanic education is to acquire the *waiyuwen* of another medicine man. *Waiyuwen* means "power" or "energy"; it is a part of the nonhuman body of the medicine man. The student either requests an old, experienced master to transmit his *waiyuwen* to him or gets hold of it secretly from a dead sorcerer.

The Yamana say that the *yékamus* loses his personality through "dreaming," and then his *kespix,* his soul, begins to go into action. The *kespix* carries out everything that the medicine man requires of it. Through intensive singing, the medicine man puts himself in the state of "dreaming." This singing is an indispensable requirement for the activity of a *yékamus;* only through singing are the *waiyuwen* and the *kespix* activated. To learn "dreaming" is the most heartfelt wish of every aspirant in the *loima* hut. The more advanced a shaman is, the more trouble-free his entry into the "dream state." Through singing, contact is made not only with the *kespix;* the *yefacel,* the protecting spirit possessed by every medicine man, also makes its appearance then. Moreover, in this way the medicine man also assures himself of the goodwill of the wrathful *haucélla* and of the *cowanni* spirits that come from the creatures of the sea.

As the conclusion of the training approaches, if there is a candidate who has not yet established contact with the world of the spirits and his own *kespix,* the teachers make use of a more rigorous method. At this point the master tells the student: "I'm going to try to strangle you!" He takes a leather thong, puts it around the student's neck, and chokes him with all his might until the student falls over. At that point his *kespix* goes to join the spirits. After this torturous event, the student will no longer have any trouble emanating his soul.

On the last evening of the school, many spectators are invited. There is more chanting and more vigorous chanting than usual in order to summon the *cowanni* spirits. The students emanate their *kespixes* to lure the *kespixes* of herring, penguins, whales, swordfish, shore birds, sea lions, or other sea beasts into the *loima* hut. There a great ceremonial reception awaits them. As the *kespixes* of the sea animals arrive in canoes, the students distribute their paddles and harpoons among the spectators. Everyone now imitates the beast *kespixes'* tumultous boat journey and chants to provide a background for the spectacle. The moment the participants' movements subside, the *cowanni* travel back out to sea, and vigorous stamping by the students drives the *haucélla* back into the interior of the earth. This is the crowning finale of the *loima* training for the *yékamus* (Gusinde 1931–74, vol. 2, 1, 399ff.).

The educational processes for healers and shamans that have been briefly sketched in this chapter unfortunately convey only a crude impression of a transpersonal psychotherapy. We may hope that in the not-too-distant future, parapsychologists and transpersonal anthropologists will provide detailed studies of the psychological procedures and of the related consciousness-developing techniques. In this way we may one day be able to arrive at a real

transpersonal theory and representation of the higher consciousness of shamans. The procedures and the view of humanity and the
cosmos hinted at here seem in any case to be incomparably richer
than Western psychology ever dared dream they might be. We may
hope that the anthropology of the future, in investigating the higher
potential of humanity through the example of the shaman, will
develop a genuine understanding of the "other world" rather than
persisting in the antiquated "charlatan theory."

3

HEALING POWERS FROM
THE REALM OF DEATH

A long way to go
A long way to climb
A long way to heaven
—Chant of the Gitksan shaman
ISAAC TENS (Barbeau 1958, 48)

The Winnebago shaman Thunder Cloud believed that he had lived on earth twice before and was now here for the third time. He had been reborn in this life as a holy man, reincarnating the spirit of the north. At a healing ceremony for his brother-in-law, he recounted his otherworld experience of vocation and supernatural shamanic training, which was produced by a long period of fasting.

Brother-in-law, this is how I learned to cure human beings. I was carried up to the spirit-village of those who live in the sky, a doctor's village, and there I was instructed as follows. A dead and rotten log, almost completely covered with weeds, was placed in the middle of the lodge. This log I was to treat as though it were a sick human being. I breathed upon the log and the spirits in the lodge breathed with me. Twice, three times, four times, we did the same. Finally the log that had seemed dead was transformed into a young man who arose and walked away. "Human being," said the spirits, "you are indeed a holy person!"

Brother-in-law, from the middle of the ocean, the spirits came after me, from a shaman's village situated there. They, too, bestowed their powers upon me and they, too, made me try my powers. They asked me to blow upon waves they had created, all of them large as the ocean, and I blew upon them and they became as quiet as water in a small saucer. Three times I did this and three times I succeeded. Then the spirits created a choppy ocean, where the waves piled one upon the other furiously, and I was told to blow upon it. I did so and that ocean of waves, mighty as it was, subsided and became quiet.

"Human being," they said, "thus will you always act. There will indeed be nothing that you cannot accomplish. No matter what illness one of your fellowmen may happen to have, you will be able to cure it." (Radin 1945, 2ff.)

Thunder Cloud learned healing, which, as we see, is nothing but exhaling the breath of life on the person to be healed. The spirits in this village of the beyond blessed him with their power. He also told of grizzly bear spirits that made him the gift of a sacred song and the power of spiritual vision. As they danced, the bears "would tear open their abdomens, then, making themselves holy, heal themselves." In this motif of self-mutilation followed by self-healing, the spirits demonstrate the real art of healing.

Genuine healers can injure themselves without a second thought: if they are holy, then their wounds heal by themselves. In this way they test their capabilities and provide proof of their healing ability—a process that has completely fallen into disuse in modern medicine. In tribal society, the healer experiences the illnesses that he cures, often initially in his own body: he takes on the ailments of his patients and then heals *himself.* It is of the essence of the primal healer that through a deepening of his inner consciousness, he is linked with his body and the illness, with himself and the patient. Our modern culture has little understanding of this extraordinary receptivity; for us, the blazing reality that predominates in the consciousness of the natural healer has been lost.

An old Australian Wurajeri doctor recounted the story of his vocation as a *wulla-mullung* to researcher Alfred Howitt (1887, 48f.). When he was a young boy, his father took him into the bush and pressed two quartz crystals into his chest, where they disappeared. As this was happening, he experienced a pleasant warmth.

He also had to drink water, which, enriched by the addition of crystals, had a sweet flavor. After this initiation experience, he began to see things that his mother did not see. He began to glimpse *yir,* spirits. During his initiation into the tribe in his tenth year, he had to live for a period of time alone in the bush. His father visited him, showed him a piece of quartz crystal, and demanded that he bring a similar crystal forth from his body. Although he was frightened, he succeeded. He acquired a number of crystals from a dead man into whose grave he descended with his father. In the grave, they met Gunr, the tiger snake, which was the *bujan,* the individual totem, of both father and son. On its tail was fastened a string of the kind that doctors produce from their innards. The father took hold of the string, and they followed the tiger snake. It drew them through tree trunks and down into the earth. They ended up inside a hollow tree. Later, they came to a cavity in the earth, where many snakes rubbed themselves against the son so that he would become a capable *wulla-mullung.* The father said that they should now climb up to Baiami, the god of heaven. They took hold of the doctor's string, on the other end of which Wombu, Baiami's bird, was waiting. They traveled up through the clouds to heaven. On the way they passed a place that was constantly opening and closing. The father explained that this was a necessary device: if the spirit of a doctor was crushed here, things would soon go badly for him on earth. Soon they met Baiami, an old man with a white beard. On his shoulders were two great quartz-crystal pillars, which towered into the heavens. They were surrounded by all kinds of animals and birds as well as his relatives. After this encounter, the son was able to bring things forth out of his body. But later, when he became quite ill, he lost this ability again.

This journey by the father and son into the beyond contains many transpersonal motifs. Just as later they flew to heaven on the father's magic string, they were initially pulled on a string by the tiger snake into the earth, apparently through all kinds of obstacles—the hollow tree trunk, the cave in the earth. These are all important symbols of initiation. The episode in the cave in which a number of snakes, the lords of the power of the earth, rub themselves against the initiate, has great power as a poetic image. It is a perfect allegory for the acquisition of regenerative, creative capacity; beyond that, it is an expression of praise for the fertility of the earth, the basis of our life. But the journey to heaven has yet to begin. Next, accompanied by Baiami's bird, the bird of the soul, they fly into the clouds and successfully go beyond the dangerous passage—the symbol of one's own fear and uncertainty. Then they reach the realm of the creator, who is clearly at the same time the lord of the animals, since he is surrounded by them. This contact with the source of life transforms the student completely. He becomes a shaman who from then on is able to see spirits, the invisible, and produce crystals out of his body.

But flying on the end of a string into the realm of the dead and the realm of the creator is not the only version of this kind of journey. Among the Unambal, Worora, Ungarinyin, and Forrest River tribes of Australia, medicine people ride to heaven on the snake of the rainbow; in the Kulin tribes, they fly like eagle hawks; among the Kurnai the corroboree poets climb into the beyond on a ladder (Petri 1952). The medicine people of the Dieri climb on a cord or a hair into the miraculous world of heaven and drink water there from which they acquire strength to annihilate their enemies (Elkin 1977, 108). A shaman of the East Yakuts of Siberia sang the story of his journey into the other world: He recounted how he had been pulled up to heaven on a rope that was let down for him, how he pushed aside the stars that got in his way, traveled through heaven in a boat, and later sailed it down a river back to earth with such speed that the wind blew right through him (Mikhailovskii 1895, 67).

We learn of an entirely different kind of experience from Catherine Ogee Wyan Akweet Okwa, a medicine woman of the Ojibwa. At the age of twelve or fourteen, she was encouraged by her mother to seek spiritual power by fasting. For many days she stayed alone in a small shelter of spruce branches, peeling bark. She tells us:

> During the night of the sixth day, I thought I heard a voice calling to me that said: "Poor child! I feel sorry for you. Come, follow me on the way that I will show you!" I thought the voice came a certain distance from my hut; it seemed to me to lead straight ahead and upward. After I followed it a little way, I stood still and saw to my right the new moon, which was crowned with flame, like a candle shining a very

bright light around itself. But on the left the sun appeared, near the place where it sets.

I went on and saw to my right the face of Kanggegabesqua, the Immortal Woman, who told me her name and said: "I bestow my name on you, and you may bestow it further! I bestow on you also everything I have—immortal life! I bestow on you also long life on earth and the gift of sustaining the lives of others! Go, you are being summoned from above!"

I went on and saw a man with a big round body and light rays coming out from his head like horns. He said: "Don't be afraid. My name is Monedo Wininess, the little human spirit. I bestow this name on your first son. He is my life. Go to the place to which you are being summoned!"

I followed the way further until I saw that it led to the clouds. I stood still and saw the form of a man standing on the way, whose head was surrounded by a bright glow and whose chest was covered with animal teeth. He said to me: "Look at me! My name is O Sha wa e geeghick, the light blue ether! I am the veil that hides the entrance to heaven. Stand where you are and pay heed! Don't be frightened. I am going to provide you with the gift of life and arm you with powers of resistance and endurance." Immediately I saw that I was being surrounded by countless shining light rays that seemed to penetrate into me like needles, without causing me any pain, then fell at my feet. This was repeated several times, and each time they fell to the ground.

He spoke: "Wait without fear until I have said and done everything that I intend!" Then I felt various instruments, first like sharp knives, then like needles, penetrate my flesh, but again none of them caused me any pain; they just all sank to my feet like the needles. Then he spoke: "It is good!" He meant the test with the needles. He continued; "You will see many days! Now step a bit further forward!" I did that and was standing on the threshold of the entrance. "You have arrived," he said, "and can't step over the threshold. Look around you! There is someone to accompany you! Don't be afraid to climb on his shoulder, and when you are back in your shelter, you can once again take to you that which preserves the human body."

I turned around and saw a kind of fish swimming in the air. I climbed on it as I had been instructed, and I was carried back with such speed that my hair fluttered in the wind. As soon as I was back in my hut, the vision faded.

On the sixth morning of my fasting period, my mother brought me a piece of smoked trout. My receptivity to sound was so great and my power of smell so sensitive that I heard her long before she came, and as she came in, I could barely tolerate, not only the smell of the fish but her own. . . . My abstinence had so refined my senses that all animal food had a disgusting and unpleasant smell for me.

Seven days after my fasting period, as I lay in the wigwam I suddenly saw a round object come down from heaven, something like a round stone. When it got close to me, I saw that it had little hands and feet like a human body. It spoke to me: "I give you the gift of seeing into the future; you must use it for yourself and the Indians, your kin and fellow tribespeople!" Then he left, and as he flew away, he acquired wings and assumed the appearance of a redheaded woodpecker.

Endowed with the "gift of life," made holy by her encounter with *manitou* and the Immortal Woman, having undergone a strange kind of dismemberment in which razor-sharp instruments and needles penetrated her flesh, she awoke once again in her little hut. Her senses had been sharpened and made hypersensitive by a long period of fasting and solitude. Then heaven, in the form of an anthropomorphic stone, bestowed on her the gift of reading the future. Catherine Ogee soon became a famous medicine woman, through whom the spirits prophesied. On those occasions she seated herself in a specially constructed skin-covered hut. The little hut bent and shook under the onslaught of the spirits with whose help she answered the questions of those present, who were assembled outside the hut (Kuhlenbeck 1909, 28ff.).

I have presented these stories of journeys to the beyond in an effort to make clear the effect of the realm of the dead on the human psyche. Whoever travels in the other world comes back transformed. In the realm of the dead, shamans receive power objects or are at least shown possibilities of what they can find on the earth. Their powers of healing and their paranormal faculties are also acquired in the realm of the dead. The near-death experiences of modern Westerners do not have this characteristic; in the West, only in people gifted as mediums do we see a similarity with shamans, and they too are for the most part trained in the other world. What factors distinguish the two, we are not currently able to ascertain, but in the case of shamans an inherited psychic proclivity as well as a culture that recognizes such experiences play an important role. Western healers and mediums must face the resistance of the outer world. Shamans of tribal cultures have every step in their development made easier for them, and they are trained by relatives or specialists. Spending time in the other world alters a person's biological constitution. He becomes a knower and seer; his philosophy of life and his way of behaving change fundamentally.

Here I would like to turn to the experiences of ethnologist Patrick Gallagher, who in 1982 published an essay entitled "Over Easy: A Cultural Anthropologist's Near-Death Experience." Gallagher had been all but fatally injured in an auto accident. The doctors had practically given him up and indicated to his family that, if he were to regain consciousness, he would not be able to speak or move. Gallagher did wake up again, but he was paralyzed on one side. Later, amazingly, he regained his speech, and today he is largely healed and is once again teaching. Only one thing has decisively changed: He has given up many habitual cultural behavior patterns and lives now entirely for the moment. He writes:

> The first vision, that of my own dead body, was a far clearer view of death than the typical one seen on television. My body was inert and totally prone. I was floating in the air, but not in some kind of a room, as is often reported. I viewed the body from above at a diagonal angle, with great interest but without any consternation. I cannot recall if I was clothed or not. But soon thereafter, so to say, I noticed I had something else to think about in addition to the bereaved body. Not only was I freed from gravity but from all other human restrictions as well. I could fly, and fly so adeptly that I felt transformed. . . . Next in the sequence was the sight of a dark area ahead, void of all light, which I saw to be the entrance of a tunnel. Flying into the tunnel at once and so moving very, very rapidly . . . finally I saw a circular light in the distance. As I continued to roar along, the light began to look somewhat like the sun on the horizon. . . . The end of the tunnel was

an incredible sight, with an illuminating marvel of yellow-orange color of total beauty, which also seemed at once a marvelous place to be.

When I left the tunnel, I entered a dazzlingly beautiful area, where like time, space was so abundant as to provide no reality for considering parts of it as compartments as we normally tend to do. It was complete space, that is, as totally and perfectly illuminated as the end of the tunnel, with the same ideal colors and radiance. I also saw within this space of space certain surprising creatures, such as lions and other marvels, all wondrously proportioned and replete with grace and beauty beyond imagining. I saw as well a number of people, some of whom were clothed and some of whom weren't. The clothing, which seemed transparent, was adornment but not the sort of shielding safeguards more familiar; it appeared that waving a hand close to such garments would allow it to pass through without disturbance of any kind. The people themselves, also of graceful beauty, all seemed to be those that I have long been interested in, such as my father (who had been dead for some twenty-five years) and Sigmund Freud and Charles Darwin (whom I had written, read, and lectured about for many years). But everyone there, as I knew the very moment I was there, seemed to possess a knowledge as radiant, transfiguring, and ideal as the luminous light. And I possessed it, too. (Gallagher 1982)

Gallagher did not become a shaman; nevertheless, he seems to have changed. He gave up his competitive thinking, stopped accumulating possessions, lost his fear of death, and began to devote himself entirely to the present moment. He was now aware that we are always radiant with light, that from birth on we are radiant beings, endowed with perfect knowledge, and that it is only earthly conditions that prevent us from becoming conscious of all that.

To conclude this chapter, I would like to present the story of Nikolai Markov, a Siberian shaman, that reveals to us a further dimension of holiness and healing.

While gathering firewood on the east bank of the Lena, Markov caught a cold. Once he returned home, he developed a fever. He felt as if he were a wheel being rolled back and forth; his head was spinning. Suddenly he saw that he was standing on the ice of the Lena. Then the shaman Süödärkä appeared and demanded that he climb a fir tree with him. "I'm going to make you a shaman," said Süödärkä. "I will lead you three times nine *olochs* upward." At a certain point they heard a bang above them, and the shaman Küstäch, who had died many years before, landed on the fir. Küstäch demanded that Süödärkä give Markov his shaman's robe, which Süödärkä did without resistance. Now Küstäch intended to raise Markov three times nine *olochs* upward. Markow recounts:

Then I also walked, as it occurred to me to do, in the footsteps of the shamans over the island in the Lena, and suddenly I was next to Küstäch. . . . Then the two of us began, dancing, to raise ourselves up into the upper country, at first as though we were going upward away from the earth. . . . Then I tried to catch up with the shaman, first from the left, then from the right. I asked him, "Don't you have the strength to go any faster?" It seemed to me he was moving more slowly than I could. The shaman answered, "I can't go any faster. If you want, go on ahead and stop in front of the fire of my gaze!" I caught up with the shaman. Far ahead, two fires were shining. We were going toward them, dancing.

It seemed we were flying. Soon I arrived at the ninth *oloch*. Hitherto, I had been flying through a dark country; now suddenly I was in a landscape bright like paradise. From here and there, people came and asked: "Where are you headed?" I replied: "The shaman Küstäch is taking me to the three-times-ninth *oloch*, so that he can make me a shaman in his stead. He wants to get the consent of his people there." These people praised me and said: "You are on the right track, you excellent man!"

I turned around and saw: there came the shaman Küstäch. His eyes were blazing and flashing like fire, like hot crucibles. He approached and sat down next to me. Then he turned to the people assembled there and said: "The shaman Süödärkä wanted to take this child, whom I have long nourished, away from me. I grabbed him, and now I have him here with me. Do you consent to my making him a shaman?" The people all answered: "Just travel on! Why should we withhold our good wishes from a person who surpasses even you?"

Dancing, we continued on our way. Once again we flew through nine *olochs* and arrived in a pure country pervaded by light. It was like our earth; around us was snow and paths. Again, people came from all sides, all of them of extraordinarily tall stature. Again they asked where we were traveling. The shaman answered them: "Here is a person born on middle earth. I intend to set him in my place." The people said to him: "Then you must hurry to the place where you were born." Again we began to raise ourselves up nine *olochs*.

When finally, in the three-times-ninth *oloch*, a wonderful, radiant country, they reached Küstäch's home, the people gathered there proclaimed the following:

Sins and trespasses have proliferated on the middle world to an incredible degree. Over the nine lowest *olochs*, a thick darkness has spread. The middle world has been spoiled and infected through and through. Both of you go back and stay at the level of the ninth *oloch*. We will send a great number of shamans there. On the ninth level, they will purify the middle earth of sins and violations and renew it. For the sight of it has been so ruined. (Ksenofontov, in Friedrich and Buddruss 1955, 124ff.)

So they went back to the lowest level above the middle world. It was dark and shrouded in thick smoke. Many shamans came from above and consecrated the middle world with their prayers, purified its crust from corruption. The shamans went down to the middle earth to heal illnesses. But before Markov had reentered the middle world entirely, the shaman spirits forced him to fly around this world. He described America, where there were great ships, and China. Then he awoke again in the earthly world. During his journey to heaven, he had lain there and whispered to himself continually. He then told those who shared his house that he would now take over the office of the shaman Küstäch so as to remove the sins of humanity from the earth. In heaven, a shaman's robe and drum lay in readiness for him. But his clan thwarted his attempt to become a shaman—that is, to get his robe from heaven. A shaman was summoned to draw the spiritual power out of him. Thus his career as a shaman was prematurely ended.

In this account, we once again encounter shaman spirits who take responsibility for making sure that there continue to be shamans in the earthly realm. Their interest in our world seems not to be extinguished by death; they remain attached to their clan, and they even help persons from other clans gain initiation into higher consciousness. This example shows that conflicts can arise between the spirits of different shamans. Another classic motif here is the three cosmic levels that have to be flown through, level by level. In each of them there are people. What changes is the brightness; on the highest level an extraordinary brilliance is reached.

The journey beyond the confines of time and space is reserved for only the great shamans. For this journey the soul must leave the body, which is possible only through deep-concentration techniques. For Westerners for whom there is no soul, no realm of the dead, and no life after death, this experience is hardly conceivable. In my first book about shamans, I went into these questions in detail. Here let me only point out that since then, researchers into death and dying have compiled thousands of near-death experiences of modern people who have left their bodies as a result of accidents or severe illnesses. All these accounts of revived patients exhibit the same patterns and motifs that characterize shamanic odysseys to the beyond. This can no longer be disregarded. We are dealing with a psychological and spiritual phenomenon that is still far from being acknowledged and processed by our science. It is the most elemental and primordial experience of which humans are capable. For thousands of years, it has drawn our attention; it is the core of many religions and certainly of all tribal religions.

I have shown how the journey of consciousness to the realm of the dead entails a spiritual transformation. Numerous people—overnight, so to speak—have returned from "heaven" with extraordinary powers of healing. Modern research into death and out-of-body states is now following in the footsteps of the shamans. The goal is, in systematically controlled experimental conditions, to separate this something—soul, consciousness, bioplasmic body, whatever we want to call it—from the body. When will we attain the ability to let human beings intentionally travel to the "realm of the dead"? One thing is certain, and this has been conveyed by all the accounts of those who have "come back": The journey to the realm of the dead is the ultimate step in all therapies, the source of health and healing power, the highest goal of all the old religions as well as of our modern transpsychic and transphysical consciousness research.

4

LIGHTNING SHAMANS

S urely the most dramatic form of shamanic initiation is initiation by lightning bolt. What psychic and physiological experiences do people go through when they are struck by lightning? Does everyone who is struck by lightning become a shaman, or are additional circumstances necessary? Presumably there are other circumstances—otherwise people in our culture would also acquire mediumistic abilities from being struck by lightning. Lightning descends from heaven, the locus of holiness, and whoever it touches also becomes holy, a microcosmic representation of heaven. As early as the ancient Greeks, lightning was venerated as a manifestation of holiness, as an epiphany of heaven. The Greeks believed a person struck by lightning was in possession of magical powers, and in tribal cultures throughout the world lightning shamans are often venerated and feared as the mightiest of shamans.

Among the Buryats, the *nerjer utxatay,* the lightning shaman, is imbued with the power of the lightning bolt (Krader 1975, 118). He is similar to the *budal-utcha,* who puts a stone fallen from heaven in fermented milk, drinks this liquid, and in this way causes the power of the stone to work into him (Agapitow 1887, 287).

Among the peoples of the Andes, the appearance of *chukiilla*—lightning or "spear light"—is an initiation experience for the shaman and the *curandero.* It is believed that people who have been struck by lightning three times and survived have been blessed by the gods with miraculous powers. It is said that the first lightning bolt kills, the second separates the head from the body, and the third awakens new life (Hargous 1976, 98f).

A person struck by lightning not only dies but is often outright dismembered. The following was told of the shaman Bükäs-Ulla-jään, later a Nasleg prince (Ksenofontov, in Friedrich and Buddruss 1955, 175f.): Once Bükäs-Ullajään was crossing in a boat with some others to the island of Tojon-Arvy to reap hay. They were over-taken by a storm and heavy cloudbursts and had to draw their boat up on land. Bükäs-Ullajään was hit by lightning and torn to little pieces. His companions gathered the pieces of the body together and rushed to get help. As they were returning to the place where they had left the remains, they saw from a distance a plume of smoke. Sure enough, when they got there, there was Bükäs-Ullajään on his feet, putting a kettle on the fire. He recounted how Süülä-Chaan had come down from heaven and cut him up. Now he had revived and could see everything around for a distance of thirty versts. His brother Bagarach underwent dismemberment at the same time. They are both now shamans.

During a storm in the Sudan, lightning struck the hut of the Kuni shaman Harib. Electricity coursed through him as he was sleeping, and for two days he lay there as though dead. When he woke up, the family spirit had taken possession of him. In this state of possession, he screamed and his entire body shuddered (Nadel 1979, 468ff.; see also Schlosser's [1972] biography of the Zulu light-ning sorcerer Laduma Madela).

A Haida woman was helped by a lightning bolt. Her husband had often beat her, and when she once again made an impertinent remark, he was just about to beat her again. At that moment, lightning struck their house. It was as bright as moonlight and almost set the house on fire. The woman fainted. The husband was frightened and just left her lying there. The next morning, she was still lying motionless on the floor. Later, after she recovered, she had the power of the moon. From that point on, she could influ-ence the weather—hold off the wind or make rain—but only for as long as she sat outside on the beach. As soon as she set foot over the threshold of her front door, she was no longer mistress of the natural forces (Swanton 1905).

The Navajo medicine man Hosteen Klah was rendered uncon-scious by a lightning bolt, which also split a nearby cedar and killed two sheep. Later, he was put through the hail ceremony because it was thought that the hail, rain, and lightning spirit was angry at him. For a time, he lost the power of speech, but shortly thereafter, he became a powerful medicine man (Newcomb 1964).

Long Lance (1976) tells us of Mokuyi-Kinasi, or Wolf Head, a medicine man of the Blackfoot nation. He was one of the most celebrated medicine men of the northeastern plains. He was feared and venerated because he was thought to possess the power of thunder. His initiation, triggered by a profound spiritual experience, took place during his early years when he was on a journey with three friends. As they were crossing the flat, treeless prairie, a storm broke over them with tremendous force. Lightning shot down from heaven and struck all around them. They took shelter in a nearby thicket, cowering in the underbrush. The next thing Wolf Head remembers was red and blue lightning bolts that bathed the scene in gleaming light. Hours later, he awoke from a strange dream. He jumped up and in his distress began running around in circles. He was bleeding all over, and his whole body hurt. Looking down at his body, he saw that he was stark naked. The lightning had hit them; one of his companions was dead. Here he recounts his dream:

> All I remember of it was that after we saw the lightning I fell asleep and dreamed that I was in a tepee. I was sitting with a woman, the one who had tried to kill me. She said she was Thunder Woman. She sang different songs and gave them to me as medicine songs. After a while, the woman's son, Boy Thunder, came in. He sang a war song and let me have it. Then the woman told me I shouldn't be afraid in war, since I would reach a great age. And she said I would do many things that would amaze people. She said, "I will give you seven 'rifles' (enemies)." I had killed five of these "rifles" when we made peace with the Canadian government, and I couldn't fight anymore.
>
> When the sun went down, she gave me a sun song. Then I woke up. I carried on like a crazy man.
>
> After she had dragged me back to camp that night, I felt tremendous pains. I again lost myself in a dream. Boy Thunder appeared to me and said, "I'm the one who strikes. I'm going to make a great medicine man out of you. You will do things that will amaze your tribal brothers and sisters. I will come to you often when you are sleeping, and every time

I come to you, I will teach you something new."

Over the years, Boy Thunder came to me again and again in my sleep, and every time he told me how I had to do something that I had never heard of before. He taught me everything about Indian medicine, and in that way, soon I became a great medicine man. (Long Lance 1976, 101)

After this near-death experience, Wolf Head developed extraordinary abilities in the truest sense of the word. Shortly after Archdeacon Tims, a white missionary, came to the Blackfoot to teach them the alphabet for their language that he had just finished devising, Boy Thunder appeared in a dream. In the morning, Wolf Head stunned the missionary and his tribal brothers by being able to write Blackfoot. The missionary had not yet shown his achievement to any of the Blackfoot, let alone taught any of them how to use it, so he was all the more astounded. He was never able to explain this event. Another time, it is told, Wolf Head woke up with the gifts and skills of a sculptor and began to chisel in stone two life-size busts of King Edward and Queen Victoria, whose likenesses he had seen on a medallion. They were perfect representations of Their Majesties, and it is said that they could only have been executed by a sculptor of genius. In a further anecdote, one night Boy Thunder sought out Wolf Head again and revealed to him how one becomes an engineer. The following day Wolf Head left for the coal mines and there designed a complete system for coal mining, which according to the agency and the government authorities could not have been improved upon by the greatest mining engineers. Like so many other shamans, in later years Wolf Head gave up his activities as a medicine man and converted to Christianity, at which point he lost all his unusual powers.

In Peru I met a number of shamans who had been struck by lightning. This event inaugurated their careers as healers. I would like to present here three of these initiations by lightning.

SIMON QUISPE TITO FROM CHOQUPATA

Simon is a seventy-five-year-old farmer in a typical campesino village. At the age of nineteen or twenty he became a *curandero* by chance. As he was riding on horseback through a thunderstorm, his horse was struck by lightning and killed. He fell to the ground and remained unconscious for three days. Afterward, he was ill for a very long period. His body was very hot to the touch. Three months later, he was nearly injured a second time when lightning struck very close to him. This time he had a vision of Saint James riding on a horse, which he took as a sign. Saint James is the Catholic saint who replaced the ancient Inca goddess of lightning and is presently venerated in her stead. Thus it was natural for him to have a vision of this saint, who he believes empowered him as a "lightning shaman." Besides being engaged in psychological diagnosis and therapy, he also practices pulse diagnosis and coca-leaf reading and functions as a village midwife. Psychological therapy is given through ceremonies. The rituals, which make use of accepted cultural symbols, merely provide a focal point for his healing power, or "positive thoughts." He gives "mental injections," as it were.

Don Benito of Huasao

Don Benito was born in 1901 and did not become a *curandero* until the age of forty. His father was also a *curandero* and worked spiritually with a very high *apu*, a goddess called Chilinchile, to whom he offered his newborn son as a present. Thus Don Benito has lived from childhood on in the presence of a high spiritual entity, and this entity, he believes, can manifest through his human body. While he was living in Q'ero, one of the last Inca refuges, the experience of his *apu* came over him during a mass. The *apu* made itself known to Don Benito and talked to him.

The process that Don Benito underwent is another well-known way of becoming a healer. The basic idea is that the vital energy of the father, himself a *curandero*, was transmitted like electricity to his son and successor. All over the world it is believed that shamans work with invisible energies. Besides the usual ceremonies, Don Benito does coca-leaf readings, rituals to protect against sorcery, and heals with herbal medicines.

Augustin Canahuiri of Huasao

Augustin is a farmer and a *curandero* of the third degree who is now very old. When he was younger, lightning struck near him, and as a result he was ill for about a year. He cannot recall his experiences during the unconsciousness that followed this event. His brother found him lying on the ground and brought him home. He was brought back to life and healed by a village *curandero*, who was himself a lightning shaman. This *curandero* had lost consciousness after being struck by lightning. He was cut into pieces (that is, psychologically—he suffered severe ego loss), but the parts of his body reassembled themselves afterward, forming a new body and mind. As a result of this experience of dying, he is now able to perform the "high mass," a very effective healing ceremony. Augustin himself, on the other hand, was not struck directly by lightning. The lightning bolt struck the earth near him. Thus he became only a third-degree *curandero.* The underlying idea here is that the more drastic the experience of initiation into a new state of mind, the better and more powerful the healer becomes.

5

WHITE SHAMANS

In tribal cultures and the high cultures of Asia, the transformation of human consciousness is regarded as holy and worth striving for. In our culture, inner vocation and the transformation experience take a special path, the only one available in a culture that has lost its spiritual vision and its connection with primal sources—the negative way. For the most part, Western mediums and healers live in a culture that regards their experiences as unnatural, if not pathological, and mediumistic activities are looked at from the point of view of standard psychological norms and are therefore regarded as hallucinatory. A typical example of this situation is found in the story of the famous American medium Olga Worrall.

> By the time I was three years old it became very apparent to my parents that they did indeed have a child with a frightening and undesirable trait that caused her to claim the ability to see and hear those who had died. . . .
>
> To further complicate matters I would describe people whom my parents had known in the old country and who, unknown to my parents, had died. These phenomena greatly disturbed my parents. . . . I was the one child of the eleven who saw things that no one else could see, and made prophecies that were laughed at, but that came to pass, much to their consternation and alarm.
>
> My visions of discarnate entities caused father to have Mass said so that these departed souls could rest in peace, but they continued to appear to me and did not seem to be unpeaceful in these appearances. Candles were burned and prayers offered to free me from this

disturbing and even embarrassing peculiarity. But instead of release, this gift only appeared to be developing more strongly and with greater meaning.

After a time my parents decided that there was nothing they could do to change me or to get rid of these aberrations and notions of seeing things at night. They accepted me for what I was to them—an enigma. (Worrall and Worrall 1965, 85)

The distortion and misrepresentation of transpersonal experience within the framework of our everyday culture is also seen in the attitude that mediums take toward their own experience. They struggle to fend off their own transformation, seek meaningless commonsense explanations, adopt the current psychological and psychiatric interpretive grids to explain it, and in general close themselves off from any alteration of consciousness that deviates from the norm. In all cultures such defenses arise from fears of being overwhelmed and devoured by supranormal experiences, but the Western view of these experiences as pathological aberrations intensifies the defensive reaction enormously. Those unfortunates who come to the attention of psychiatry and become entangled in the snares of psychological professionals have dim prospects of getting a fruitful explanation of the transformation they face.

Typically, many believe that they are the only people to whom anything of this nature has ever occurred. They feel hopeless and lost, and they cling to any theoretical explanation that comes along—which only aggravates their situation. If such people are fortunate enough to come in contact with esoteric traditions or some expression of a magical-natural understanding of the world, they have gained an inkling that may soon lead to their psychological symptoms appearing in a positive light. Of course, a rocky path then has to be traveled, one on which they must cope with the desacralization of intuitive knowledge in this culture and run the gamut of hostility and sarcasm that relegates any superconscious experience to the realm of neurosis and psychopathology. Most accounts of spontaneous spiritual self-realization reveal a fear of madness, the suspicion of which is very much fed by society. When parents, relatives, or a spouse take a person undergoing transformation to a neurologist to get an electroencephalogram or to a psychoanalyst whose diagnosis is based on narrow conventional views—in such situations the person is thrown back on his or her own resources. Various cases show that such people are capable of developing unconscious healing patterns that arise spontaneously from the psyche and that intuitively accord with spiritual traditions.

The path of initiation is branded in the West as degenerate; by contrast, in tribal society the initiation of the shaman is accepted, even encouraged and supported by everyone; and the teacher helps the student to decipher his experiences by means of cultural symbols. But in our culture the symbols of transformation are negative: they include hospitalization, schizophrenia, brain-wave tests, stupefying psychotropic drugs, and ostracism from society. How many unrecognized shamans, mediums, and saints fill the madhouses of rationalism? How many powers have been mangled and cut off during the long history of psychiatry? How many people has psychology reduced to mindless robots through its abasement of the psyche? The spiritual climate of our society shuts down shamanic experience in its incipient stages, distorts it and desacralizes it as neurosis and psychotic deception. But psychic transformation cannot be extirpated by societal taboos. Spiritual experience is a transhistorical, transcultural phenomenon and can break through in individuals at any time.

In the following pages I would like to present the experiences of some of these Western shamans. My objective in this is to show that there is no distinction between shamans and mediums or other supernormally endowed individuals of our culture. The process of spiritual transformation, the expansion of inner vision, is always the same.

PRENATAL SILENCE

The treatment of an enigmatic illness through drumming therapy, which we shall now describe, is not part of a shamanic experience of vocation. Carl Levett, an American psychologist, developed painful physical symptoms as a result of a spiritual experience with an Indian master: "Suddenly a series of uncontrollable vibrations and electric currents erupted powerfully out of me. It was as though a mountain had been hurled into the center of a quiet village." This energy was clearly trying to find a way to release itself from his body. A muscle cramp appeared in his stomach area, spasms consumed his energy reserves, and when his teacher advised him not to cling to these phenomena conceptually but just to let the energy flow happen, he could not. He found himself compelled to eat unusual foods at the most impossible times. But he avoided food as much as possible, since eating caused the pains to increase. By chance, in order to distract himself from the pains, he bought a drum and played it every day. During the drumming, a strange experience began to take place after a time:

> But one day while practicing I was shocked by the sudden realization that the drumming was coming not from me, but from somewhere else. I double-checked in disbelief, but it was a fact. The drumming continued in perfect rhythm, yet completely out of my control. Immediately my body began to convulse and energy surged from deep within me, becoming a liquid radiance which saturated every cell of my body. All conceptions I had of myself vanished as I dissolved into this flow. Suddenly I realized that the spasm had disappeared. A voice inside me was yelling *No more pain! It's gone! You've licked it!*
>
> As the drumbeat became wilder, my meddling intellect kept trying to tell me this was impossible, even though it was clear my hands were plugged into an endless absolute stream of energy. I knew this, not through logic or from past experience, but as pure feeling, convincingly real. *It* was drumming, and it was incredible—an all-knowing, ever-present and inviolable force. I felt no apprehension, only total submission. The beat became more subdued as the energy ebbed briefly, but it soon began to build again and gradually turned, moving back toward my center. I sensed what was to come and knew that I was powerless to stop it: the spasm was beginning to reappear.

In the rhythm of the drum, through the classic instrument of shamanic trance, Levett's cramps relaxed, just as his teacher had predicted: "*It* was drumming," or "the drumming came out of him." For the first time, he let himself be driven by the rhythm— the feeling of "letting things flow" arose, an ecstatic peak experience (see also Csikszentmihalyi 1957).

> I was obviously on the right track, for as the energy intake increased, tingling and shiver sensations began to careen through me. Shock waves surged through my nostrils, mouth, ears, eyes, and genitalia—

eventually even through the pores of my skin—pushing, shoving their way through myriad internal crevices, prodding my stiff muscles and joints into spontaneous and illogical movement.

Images began to appear like slides as compensation for my lack of total release—pictures of leaping, hurdling, racing down rapids; sunburst motifs, and roman candle explosions of blossoming spinoffs in sparkling colors; my being pulverized into tiny golden nuggets parading in long columns.

The drumming and the rhythm relaxed his musculature. At the same time, a release also took place in the form of visual phenomena, an indication of liberation and relaxation on all levels. The energy current broke through the armor of his personality, displaced his inhibitions, and caused them to explode in a fireworks display of muscular, visual, and psychological energy sparks. The result was ecstasy, a classic example of the liberation of blocked energies.

I reasoned that whittling down the intensity of energy penetration to a tolerable level might allow for an eventual collapse of structured-me through the slow-but-sure approach. I experimented with repeating various phrases while continuing the drumbeat and finally settled on, My life is in your hands. The syllables fell into perfect cadence with the drum's rhythm.

My life
My life
My life is in your hands

When I practiced drumming and chanting the phrase, an unusual merging of mind and feeling took place, drawing me downward to a beginning of something. As I trusted its vertical pull, it took me to the fundamental elements of life.

I became one with water—a glacier; the tides and waves; the rain, quenching thirst, nourishing life. I was the sun—a molten fireball, warming the solar system; the light of day; the moon's glow. I was air—the breath of life, sustaining flight; the wind off the ocean. And then I was earth—minerals, rocks, sand; the soil for flora; minuscule in an infinite universe.

Losing myself in the nuclei of these elements was bringing me to the essence of being, but there had to be more. I knew it would be unproductive to try to think of the something that escaped me, but I tried anyway. I had no recourse—I thought. When I stopped trying, the thinking stopped too. It was suddenly crystal clear. I was afraid to risk sacrificing structured-me to a state of nothingness.

Then it erupted from him: a chant that fused into a unity with the vibrations of the drum. This is the classic shamanic power chant, the chant of the freedom of the superconscious from consciousness. We find this power chant, as I have dubbed it, in many accounts of initiation. The rhythm of the song is an expression of inner relaxation, of evenly flowing energy currents, pulsing life. In the song, the existence of the moment is condensed into an all-encompassing formula. All the power songs are characterized by great simplicity and emotion. We are not dealing here with examples of poetic virtuosity or baroque verse with polished rhyme schemes. By contrast, Levett's "My life is in your hands" represents the core of a new philosophy and wisdom of the body. Through these words, he allied himself with all natural forces and manifestations of life and realized the experience expressed by Gustave Flaubert's Saint Anthony:

> I want to fly, swim, bark, bleat, roar, would like to have wings, a shell, bark, would like to belch smoke, have a muzzle, coil my body, divide myself and dissolve into everything, emanate myself in odors, exfoliate like plants, flow like water, vibrate like sound, shimmer like light, take on every form, penetrate into every atom, be absorbed into the fundament of matter—become matter.

Of prime importance in Levett's ecstatic journey through the forms and structures of being is a dissolution of ego that is far greater than even the one that carried him through the rhythm of everything living—total annihilation into nothingness. At that point he dropped his fascination with forms, and the fear of definitive extinction evoked the last vestiges of egoistic self-feeling. Nonetheless, he kept beginning afresh, daring to move forward into the unknown. Step by step he groped forward. . . .

Then I noticed, after an extended round of drumming, a profound silence pervade the room. The contrast between the vigorous beat and the quiet that immediately followed produced an eerie emptiness. I was drawn to that silence. I again brought the drumming to a maximum tempo and volume and stopped and waited. The longer I waited, the deeper and more pervasive the silence became. It reached the nadir of purity and I plunged into its amorphous field. An icy chill ricocheted through me; I suspected death was hovering in the background. I lost all sense of dimension. Then I heard a vague sound which very slowly became audible, becoming separate sounds and then forming into words:

> ee, ell, ey, ee
> pee, bell, bey, bee
> pre-belly baby!

I was at the origin of life, a fetus spinning in a whirlpool. The motion caused a peeling away of the layers of my form, revealing a seed. The action slowed and time came to a halt at ground-zero. I was drifting, suspended. There was no thought, only a sense of pure formlessness. A pulsing, like a heartbeat, floated nearby. Although noise and movement surrounded the flow-space, I remained free of its influence and profoundly at ease.

Without warning, I began tumbling in a vastness, with no up or down. Then I exploded, my atoms flying in all directions. In a flash, I was in pure stillness again, except for tracings of light as if from falling stars.

Finally, after two years of pain and torment, Levett's suffering was resolved by his return to the origin of life. Before reaching that point, however, he had a vision of a woman enveloped in a pulsating aura. She slowly grew into a kind of cosmic mother, while he was transformed into the "pre-belly baby," the pre-womb child. The cosmic mother bore a cosmic father; the two embraced each other with great affection and fused. Levett glided into the belly of the Great Mother. A powerful magnetic field sucked away his cramp affliction: devotion, abandoning himself to the transpersonal figure, opened him up to an ineffable feeling of freedom.

While his colleagues—the shamans and saints of all peoples— return to the mother of animals, the archetype of the Great Mother, Carl Levett returned to the origin of his own life, back to existence at the level of the fetus. The husks of his ego history fell away, and the very core of his existence, the primordial seed, was revealed, as time stood still and sacred time took over.

When Levett stopped playing the drum, the experience of silence continued and deepened until it reached the very boundaries of death. The coordinates of the physical world disappeared, and out of nothingness a sound arose that grew into a new chant. The song was as an acoustic expression of prenatal existence. The drum brought him near death, and his rigidified personality structure fell away layer by layer. In the same way, the spirits tear apart the shaman in the underworld in order to give him a more perfect and more powerful psyche. With the cessation of time, Levett's ego, too, ceased its life. It exploded and was atomized. What was left was "pure silence."

SELF-HEALING

Sarah Cartwright became ill at the age of twenty-three. She had already borne four children and was now an invalid. Her nervous system was weakened, and she was no longer in control of her feelings. The slightest provocation led to hysterical attacks. Doctors' efforts to help her proved futile. For five years she could walk only with great effort; she was unable to raise her feet over even the lowest threshold. After this suffering she described her sudden transformation and self-healing in the following terms:

> A new and strange element suddenly invaded my life at this period. One evening, while sitting quietly reading by a table, my right hand became slightly benumbed, a contraction of the muscles took place, and it was slowly moving toward a slate and a pencil lying on the table: my fingers grasped the pencil and I wrote, with no knowledge of what I was writing.
>
> The writing looked like mine, but the words conveyed but little meaning to me. It was a medical prescription, giving the botanical names of various plants. I felt very little surprise, but wondered in a passive way what the names meant, when my hand seized the pencil and began to draw rapidly and perfectly leaves, flowers, and roots of plants, affixing the common name to each, and adding the advice to take them. I now know that the prescription was the antidote calomel and a remedy for nervous debility.

One day Cartwright produced in automatic writing the instruction that she should go into a dark, quiet room:

> Out of curiosity I complied, and received almost immediately on entering the room an electric shock from my head to my feet, which vibrated through every nerve in my body, and then I made a discovery. I found I could go up and down the steps from the piazza without a sign of the weakness from which I had suffered so long.

She kept quiet about her strange self-healing and tried to dissociate herself from this "outer intelligence." But a "force" coerced her to heal other people against her will. Finally, driven by need, she concluded a regular "contract" with the force whereby she gave herself over to its service in exchange for the promise that it would protect her in all situations of life. Soon she developed clairvoyance, and her career as a healer began (Cartwright 1884).

The story of Sarah Cartwright's illness and spontaneous cure follows the familiar pattern of shamanic vocation: serious suffering over a period of years; no improvement or help from conventional medicine, but help from an indefinable nonhuman source; an astounding cure that no one expects; an attempt to free oneself from a superhuman or unconscious force in order to follow a particular lifestyle, followed by capitulation to an unyielding demand; acceptance of one's fate; the beginning of a new life along with a willingness to acknowledge latent extrasensory faculties and to use them for the sake of humanity; and finally the development of further paranormal faculties. In a tribal culture, Sarah Cartwright would have followed a shamanic vocation. In our culture, she became a spiritistic healer.

The threefold sequence of illness, self-healing, and the development of healing powers is a universal, transpersonal pattern that we are still far from understanding. Evidently illness can unleash fundamental forms of psychic knowledge that far surpass the normal expressions of intellect and feeling. Extrasensory perceptions and experiences take place that have aroused fascination since archaic times and provided the grounds for an understanding of the universe as filled by an active force beyond human grasp.

SPIRIT MEDICINE

A rare example of how a psychic healer can become a folk hero is the story of Arigo, or José Pedro de Freitas: To begin with, Arigo was a simple mine worker from a small mountain town in Brazil who had become politically involved. His development as a healer began with a series of hallucinations in which a spirit doctor from the other world forced himself on him. The spirit warned Arigo that if he did not accede to the spirit's demands, the spirit would leave him no peace.

One night in a dream Arigo saw an operating table around which a number of surgeons were standing and operating on someone. One of the doctors spoke with the same accent as the man whose voice had been plaguing Arigo for such a long time. The hallucination became full blown as the doctor with the familiar voice introduced himself as Dr. Adolpho Fritz, who had been killed in 1918 in World War I. He said that he had been observing Arigo for a long time and had chosen him to continue his work because of Arigo's good heart and kindness. If Arigo wanted any peace, from now on he would have to help sick people and while doing so simply hold a crucifix in his hand. It really seemed to Arigo as if he were standing face to face with this person, whose command seemed to offer him no choice. Overwhelmed, Arigo fled. Screaming, he jumped out of bed and ran naked into the street.

After this incident, Arigo underwent psychiatric treatment, but no indications of psychological disturbance could be found in him. An exorcism by a Catholic priest also failed to free him from his faints and apparitions. Soon he began to regard them as natural, since they were so overpowering that he had no chance of fending them off. Now he became interested in finding out what would happen if he acceded to Dr. Fritz's demands. He tried to cure someone: He tore the crutch from the grasp of a well-known cripple in the town and commanded the man to walk. Momentarily, the cripple regained the use of his legs. Amazed by his own success, Arigo now tried his luck with his friends. Although he gave commands without his own conscious participation, instant cures took place.

The Church finally called him to account and succeeded in

having him brought to various psychiatrists. In doing this the
Church was accommodating Arigo himself, who was now intensely
tormented by pains and hallucinatory images. He was also worried
about keeping up with his duties at the restaurant he managed, as
well as his political obligations.

It was not long before Arigo's resistance was broken. He began
spontaneously to heal sick people; his treatments resulted in immediate success. When he healed, his visions and headaches subsided.
Years later, in spite of a prison sentence and the ongoing hostility
of the Church, he established a regular practice with the support of
his fellow townspeople and the many thousands of patients whom
he had already helped. Treatments often lasted only a few seconds.
Half in a trance state, he operated with a rusty knife. During these
times his facial expression became rather arrogant; he spoke with
a German accent and claimed to be Dr. Fritz. It was not he, Arigo,
but the German doctor who performed the operations and scrib-
bled out prescriptions on pieces of paper almost like an automaton,
hardly looking. These prescriptions conformed to normal medical
usage and sometimes called for medicines that had been on the
market for only a short time. The medical terminology that Arigo
employed in his state of trance or possession was far beyond the
level of his knowledge in his normal state.

In his mediumistic surgical operations, the only instrument he
used was an old switchblade. He paid no heed to anesthesia or
antisepsis, yet under his hand the patients neither felt pain nor bled.
Often he operated without looking at what he was doing, amusing
himself by chatting with other patients, even while he was performing difficult procedures involving the head and eyes. Arigo practiced
for nearly twenty years and treated thousands of patients. Over
time he came to espouse spiritistic beliefs, against which, as a good
Catholic, he had long struggled. He truly came to believe that the
deceased Dr. Fritz worked through him, along with a host of other
otherworldly helpers, including a thirteenth-century monk.

Various American medical teams investigated Arigo and certified
the validity of his cures. They ruled out any kind of deception but
were unable to discover the mechanism of his healing process.
Arigo accepted neither money nor gifts for his services. He continued to hold his regular job as a night watchman, even while he

treated up to fifteen hundred patients from all over the world every week. Nevertheless, he never seemed to be exhausted. Arigo lost his life in 1971 in an auto accident that he had precisely predicted. Just at that time the then-president of Brazil, Kubitschek, a patient and personal friend of Arigo's, had established a national fund and a national committee for Arigo's support (Fuller 1974).

The Brazilian healer Arigo, like many shamans, initially dramatically rejected a connection with the spirit world. Eventually his resistance wore down, and he accepted his role as a will-less instrument of the beyond. He never claimed to possess personally the ability to heal or any other gifts. He remained a simple and humble man who felt obliged to alleviate the suffering of others. After his death, one of his brothers seemed to undergo the same symptoms that had burdened Arigo's beginnings as a healer. It was said that Dr. Fritz wanted to continue his work in the body of Arigo's brother.

HE DIED AND CAME BACK WITH TWO MINDS

When he fell from a ladder, the house painter Peter Hurkos (Browning 1970) suffered a severe brain injury in the region of the hypothalamus, the pineal body, and the brain stem. The result was a schizophrenic, disoriented condition. Hurkos lost his ability to concentrate and could no longer make decisions of any kind; his intelligence level was that of a ten-year-old. Nonetheless, after various tests, new abilities were ascribed to him: (1) He could, in a conscious and controlled manner, transmit telepathic thoughts; (2) he had knowledge of events in the lives of other people; and (3) he could make accurate statements about objects and people regardless of how far away from him they were.

Like Edgar Cayce, the famous American trance healer, Hurkos had been a withdrawn and introverted child who was absorbed in fantasies. Where Cayce was hit in the head by a baseball, Hurkos landed on his head when he fell. Later, both were able to speak foreign languages while in trance. Cayce was born with milk in his breasts; the circumstances of Hurkos's birth, too, lay outside the norm. He was born with a caul—a kind of membrane—over his head, which had to be opened and removed immediately so that the newborn baby could breathe. In Holland, Hurkos's homeland, this caul is called a *helm* or *fliess,* and in medical folklore it has many meanings. It is a symbol of something mysterious. In general, according to the Dutch folk tradition, a person born with a *helm* has the ability to see into the future. Hurkos almost died from this birth complication. Though he survived, he was blind for the first six months of his life, and consequently during his younger years he preferred mostly dim places or darkness. Although his unusual ability began to manifest itself clearly only after his accident, his parents and friends describe him as a peculiar child who was always alone and saw things that were invisible to others.

The doctors had been able to remove the membrane from the infant's head after a few hours, but the operation over the eyes was successful only after six months. Hurkos continued to have various vision problems throughout his life.

After the fall from the ladder, Hurkos lay unconscious in the hospital and later had no memory for many names, dates, and faces. He recognized the members of his family only by their voices. Even today he does not retain names and telephone numbers, not even his own phone number. He portrays his accident as follows:

> The moment I fell down I saw my whole life go by in one second and then boom-boom, everything was black. When I came out of the dark I wanted to go back where I was, when it was all beautiful. Beautiful flowers and beautiful music and everything changed. Even a tulip was different, more beautiful than a normal tulip. Yes, I saw flowers and mountains, beautiful mountains. (218)

His near-death experience contained typical features: the flashback over his life; the feeling of sudden darkness, which was clearly a tunnel experience; and the vision of a radiant landscape.

Hurkos heard unusual sounds and thought that he no longer possessed any consciousness of his own. He saw images and heard voices that in every way he tried to get rid of:

> If I touched an object like the water pitcher next to my bed, I would hear sounds. When I touched the wall I would hear sounds and see things. Sometimes I would put the pillow over my head to cover my ears and eyes, but these pictures and sounds always came to me. And

even when I slept, my mind would travel to places I had never seen before. (46)

Also involuntarily, he foresaw people's futures. This was particularly disturbing for him. He describes his life during this period as a ghastly nightmare and himself after the accident as someone with two brains, his own and an alien one. Those around him noticed his personality transformation.

> I remember the time I was falling and I didn't want to die. Then everything was black. And when I woke up I had no mind of my own. And then I got my gift. I was in somebody else's mind, and I was scared because I didn't know what was happening. My father and mother said it's not the same Peter anymore. They said he died and I came back with two minds. (13)

After his release from the hospital, his bizarre gift drove him out of the house. He wandered for whole days through the streets trying to flee from himself. At the insistence of an inner voice, during this period he began to paint:

> I cannot paint what I see. I paint only what was in my mind then, when I was unconscious. I paint right here on the floor, and I stare and I grab the paint. I don't even know the colors. I paint upside down— it doesn't matter. I sit on the floor and paint in the dark. I see it anyhow. (219)

He learned to play the piano the same way. The first time he saw an organ, the inner voice whispered to him again and told him to sit down at it and play. At that point he remembered the wonderful melodies he had heard at the time of his fall.

> I never have played the piano in my whole life. I have never had lessons. But I just feel it, and I was playing Ave Maria by Schubert and the Warsaw Concerto. . . . Listen, I don't know music, but the voice tells me the combination. You feel, you go, you mix it like the paint, and so I play. . . . What my eyes see in the mind, it makes my hands do. (219)

This inner voice was the source of all his paranormal powers:

I don't want to talk about it. People think I am crazy. . . . It is a deep
voice like this [he did an imitation] . . . the old man voice, somebody
else inside me. (219)

But in spite of his new insights, Hurkos did not understand himself,
for he says:

But what I am fighting to know, Is it my mind that travels at night in
places where we don't know, or is it that we were born before? Why
can I wake up in the night and paint pictures of places where I have
been? Is it my mind that travels while I am asleep? (219f.)

His consciousness left his body and traveled to unfamiliar, visionary places—very much like what shamans describe. But there is one
difference: At the beginning of his career as a sensitive, Hurkos had
to face these phenomena completely without help. Only when he
finally made contact with parapsychologists did he receive any
illumination concerning his unusual powers.

The story of Hurkos's life and sufferings is in every way exem-
plary of shamanic vocation. The presence of a sign at birth, the
childhood during which his singularity was conspicuous, and finally
the accident that unleashed the entire spectrum of extrasensory
phenomena follow the classic pattern of shamanic psychogenesis.
Then he passed through a phase of reorientation and self-discovery
in a world full of riddles, until finally he acknowledged his transformation and rebirth. The near-death experience of his accident revealed a dimension of existence of which he had never even
dreamed, and which is portrayed in his paintings. Hurkos displays
the full range of shamanic knowledge: clairvoyance, telepathy,
otherworldly travel, and contact with an inner voice—the voice of
his protective spirit. As we might expect, Hurkos did not become
a priest. In his society he had to remain a loner. He put his psychic
gifts at the disposal of the police, and he underwent a lengthy
odyssey through parapsychological laboratories as a guinea pig. The
parapsychologists were the only ones who provided him with any
kind of support. They also provided a system of orientation for his
ostensibly absurd abilities.

PART TWO
VISION OF KNOWLEDGE

Mostly it's that specific thoughts are impressed on my consciousness so clearly and so definitely that I have the unequivocal feeling that someone has said something to me. Sometimes I actually hear a voice communicating. It's none that you would hear, though, because I sense it with my inner ear only. And still other times I actually see a spirit form near the person with the problem, and get messages from this spirit man or woman which are relevant to the problem and beneficial in its treatment.

—OLGA WORRALL,
American healer (1965, 41)

— 6 —
THE TRANCE OF HEALING
AND THE LOGIC
OF TRANCE

It is as if heaven and earth become one.
Everything becomes radiantly bright.
It is like the experience of making love for the first time.
As though you were walking lost across a wide country road.

—The Indian SAORA ELWIN'S
descriptions of trance (1955, 476)

T rance means "having a *loa*," being possessed by a god. "Understanding that I must go when the *loa* enters means understanding that man and god cannot exist simultaneously," says Maya Deren (1975, 235), one of the few white people who learned through voodoo in Haiti how to become possessed. The first sign of trance for Deren is a "vulnerability" of the ego, a shaking of the foundations of the ego, which must dissolve and make room for other forces. Here is her experience of dancing:

The air seems heavy and wet, and, gasping, I feel that it brings no refreshment into my labouring lungs. My heart pounds in the pulse at my temple. My legs are heavy beyond belief, the muscles contracted into an enormous ache which digs deeper with every movement. My entire being focuses on one single thought: that I must endure.

I cannot say, now, why I did not stop; except that, beneath all this is always a sense of contract: whether, in the end, one be victor or victim, it is to be in the terms one has accepted. One cannot default. So focused was I, at that time, upon the effort to endure, that I did not even mark the moment when this ceased to be difficult and I cannot say whether it was sudden or gradual but only that my awareness of it was a sudden thing, as if the pace which had seemed unbearably demanding had slipped down a notch into a slow-motion, so that my mind had time, now, to wander, to observe at leisure, what a splendid thing it was, indeed, to hear the drums, to move like this, to be able to do all this so easily, to do even more, if it pleased one, to elaborate, to extend this movement of the arms towards greater elegance, or to counterpoint that rhythm of the heel, or even to make this movement to the side, this time.

As sometimes in my dreams, so here I can observe myself, can note with pleasure how the full hem of my white skirt plays with the rhythms, can watch, as if in a mirror, how the smile begins with a softening of the lips, spreads imperceptibly into a radiance which, surely, is lovelier than any I have ever seen. It is when I turn, as if to a neighbour to say, "Look! See how lovely that is!" and see that the others are removed to a distance, withdrawn to a circle which is already watching, that I realize, like a shaft of terror struck through me, that it is no longer myself whom I watch. Yet it *is* myself, for as that terror strikes, we two are made one again, joined by and upon the point of the left leg which is as if rooted to the earth. Now there is only terror. "This is it!" Resting upon that leg I feel a strange numbness enter it from the earth itself and mount, within the very marrow of the bone, as slowly and richly as sap might mount the trunk of a tree. I say numbness, but that is inaccurate. To be precise, I must say what, even to me, is pure recollection, but not otherwise conceivable: I must call it a white darkness, its whiteness a glory and its darkness, terror. It is the terror which has the greater force, and with a supreme effort I wrench the leg loose—I must keep moving! must keep moving!—and pick up the dancing rhythm of the drums as something to grasp at, something to keep my feet from resting upon the dangerous earth. No sooner do I settle into the succour of this support than my sense of self doubles again, as in a mirror, separates to both sides of an invisible threshold, except that now the vision of the one who watches flickers, the lids flutter, the gasp between moments of sight growing greater, wider. I see the dancing one here, and next in a different place, facing another direction, and whatever lay between these moments is lost, utterly lost. I feel that the gaps will spread and widen and that I will, myself, be altogether lost in that dead space and that dead time. With a great blow the drum unites us once more upon the point of the left leg. The white darkness starts to shoot up; I wrench my foot free but the effort catapults me across what seems a vast, vast distance, and I come to rest upon a firmness of arms and bodies which would hold me up. But these have voices—great, insistent, singing voices—whose sound would smother me. With every muscle I pull loose and again plunge across a vast space and once more am no sooner poised in balance than my leg roots. So it goes: the leg fixed, then wrenched loose, the long fall across space, the rooting of the leg again—for how long, how many times I cannot know. My skull is a drum; each great beat drives that leg, like the point of a stake, into the ground. The singing is at my very ear, inside my head. This sound will drown me! "Why don't they stop! Why don't they stop!" I cannot wrench the leg free. I am caught in this cylinder, this well of sound. There is nothing anywhere except this. There is no way out. The white darkness moves up the veins of my leg like a swift tide rising, rising; is a great force which I cannot sustain or contain, which, surely, will burst my skin. It is too much, too bright, too white for me; this is its darkness. "Mercy!" I scream within me. I hear it echoed by the voices, shrill and unearthly: *"Erzulie!"* The bright darkness floods up through my body, reaches my head, engulfs me. I am sucked down and exploded upward at once. That is all. (243ff.)

That is her trance experience: graphic, artistic, psychological. A landscape of feeling that arises from within extends before us. Maya Deren is a filmmaker and artist—maybe that is the reason.

Now, what aspects of her experience are characteristic of the process of trance? First there is the "vulnerability," the dissolution of the boundary between self and the world; then pain and suffering, which, however, disappear again as perception and concentration are increasingly narrowed by the rhythm of the drum and the movement of the body. This leads to a condition of spontaneity, of freedom, of unconstrained, unforced movement—Deren is not dancing, she is being danced. Now time leaps from image to image—in slow motion. The gaps between the moments of perception get bigger, but what is happening within the gaps? Emptiness, nothingness, non-ego, timeless space—fear, panic in the face of self-surrender, overwhelms her.

Then a doubling takes place. She sees herself from outside; there is a split between consciousness and body. This means that everything now happens as if by its own accord. There is no longer any deliberate, conscious dance step. There is neither effort nor exhaustion. The body has taken over. Depersonalization continues, but the "ego" is still there. Again there is fear, even terror, of letting go of the ego, and finally giving it up, abdicating. Terror is darkness. Joy is radiant white. A duality of fear and joy? But now the ambivalence is resolved. The decisive step toward self-surrender, toward the experience of the "white darkness," takes place. White is sublimity, and darkness is terror. They are unified at the climax of the trance. In this emptiness, there is oblivion; here the body moves in the most sublime fashion. It and the self want to be completely free from taboos and the tormenting deceptions of the ego world. Outer and inner are now one: "My skull is a drum." The real power latent in human beings breaks through: " 'Mercy,' I scream within me." The power takes over; the body is a mere instrument. This eruption of energy explodes her feeling of self. She explodes inside herself: this is the breakthrough to an altered state of consciousness, a rebirth.

Later, remembering her experience, she wrote:

> I see everything all at once, without the delays of succession, and each detail is equal and equally lucid, before the sense of relative importance imposes the emphasis of eyes, the obscurity of nostril, which is a face. Yet even as I look, as if to remember forever this pristine world, already the forms become modulated into meanings, cease to be forms. (246)

Characteristic of trance is the dissolution of the world of things. What are things but fragments of existence that have been artificially excised from the wholeness of being and captioned, laden by us with a relative sense of meaning; entities that do not really exist for us except in a conditioned way? Word, action, thought, sensation—these dissolve and come together again afresh, but this time without boundaries separating them. Once we leave behind the world of relative concepts, the radiant world with its radiant beings and radiant forms suddenly appears before us. Why it is that in the unconditioned state the world appears radiant, as everyone who has experienced altered states of consciousness reports in one form or another, I cannot say. Time and space and causality, in any case, pass away; sequence is extinguished. Deren perceives everything at once, independent of temporal sequence. Here she approaches, but only approaches, real enlightenment, *unio mystica.* This is trance as a preliminary form of enlightenment.

Larry Peters, an ethnologist, tried to learn trance from his Nepalese teacher Bhirendra. His master and the other students had already, through drumming, brought themselves to a state of spiritual ecstasy. Wild spasms ran through their bodies and, sitting cross-legged, they bounced into the air, sometimes as high as a half-meter. Peters describes how they performed the exercise over and over. He began to shake consciously and gradually let go, becoming "part of the beat itself." After a while, the shaking in his legs became more automatic. Next his whole body began to shake, and he bounced all over the room. His attention was focused on his movements and his eyes were closed. But as soon as he became aware of his surroundings, the shaking stopped being automatic, and he felt fatigued.

Looking back on the drumming that night, it seems we played as fast as possible, everyone playing the same rhythm, bam-bam-bam, bam-bam-bam, in threes until the beating became even faster. The trembling seemed to evolve from conscious to automatic at the moment Bhirendra inserted a loud extra beat between two of mine, changing the rhythm and causing it to quicken. I'm sure he did this purposely and always used this method with his disciples. He made two or three of these drumming maneuvers before my drumming and shaking became automatic. At one point, my shaking continued until I felt a fleeting fear that I was losing control and being overwhelmed, at which point I became aware of my body trembling. It was a disturbing feeling, not very traumatic but nonetheless jolting. Afterwards, my heart pounded and I reasoned that my resistances were strong against surrendering to the experience. I hadn't fully "let go." . . .

Bhirendra took complete charge of the ritual; setting the pace, his drumming echoed against the walls. I followed his beat. While my body was swaying, I lost myself in the music and began to shake. Bhirendra broke my pattern by inserting an extra beat or two in the rhythm, and my beating quickened. He repeated this three or four times and then I lost control of my movements. My heart pounded, I forgot about the shaking and drumming and felt my body rise up. There was a tremendous amount of energy. At first, the shaking seemed to emanate from my genitals. I felt the drum rise up into the air, and the nervous feeling went along with it. The area near my solar plexus began to tremble, and then my chest, shoulders, and finally my head. When I became conscious of these movements, fear swept through me. I felt a flash of heat throughout my body. Then my mind split off from my body. I watched my body shaking and jumping into the air as if my consciousness was separated from it. (Peters 1981a, 10–11, 13–14)

When Serge Bramly (1978) spoke with Brazilian Macumba priestess Maria-José, she gave him detailed information about behavior in trance. Her presentation provides us with a well-rounded picture of the trance process. Trance mediums offer the gods their bodies so that the gods can enter them and establish themselves there. The gods slip over their body the way a rider slips a bridle over a horse. The medium's own consciousness is disabled and serves the god in some fashion as a transmitting station. At the beginning of the trance the medium often has the feeling of being a child again. She disturbs the ceremony with her pranks and jostles the other dancers or the audience. Then she has to be made to behave. That is the childhood stage of the trance, as it were. After the trance, the medium is left with a pleasant feeling: her mind has been empty for a while and has been able to regenerate itself; the god has left its power behind. In other forms of trances, mediums become totally exhausted and are often sick and depressed for days afterward, feeling divested of all energy. If the medium's own energies are used for healing, a state of exhaustion results; the medium is then like a worn-down battery. By contrast, when a god or a spirit works through a person, no energy loss ensues. Apparently, there are various possible ways to work with energy—with one's own or an alien energy.

During the Macumba trance, the mediums smoke a great deal and drink several liters of brandy. Amazingly, they do not get drunk, though in a normal state they would be unable to tolerate such quantities of alcohol. Apparently some mechanism works here to neutralize the alcohol. Various other trance phenomena are also present, such as an increase in physical strength and a heightening of sensory functions. One hears, sees, and smells everything much better; the contents of the unconscious are more easily accessible; exertion brings about no decrease of energy; thought and feeling are intensified; and the capacity to learn is heightened. According to the followers of Macumba, it is the gods who drink the alcohol, not the mediums.

Maria-José's task is to guide the trances of the mediums and to calm down their gods, who often overestimate the mediums' strength; this can quickly harm the mediums. To avoid this, she intervenes and breaks off the trance. If a nonadept falls into a trance, she orders a change in the chanting or the drum rhythm in order to liberate the person from the god that has entered him or her.

Rhythm is a key element in bringing on a trance. Maria-José says:

Our gods react especially to rhythm. If the rhythm changes, the behavior of the gods changes too. The drums are our spokesmen to the gods. They are our most persuasive voices. Our instruments are no ordinary worldly drums. We consider them living beings. Drums are fed, they consume the offerings, and a woman having her period is not allowed to come in contact with them. It takes away their power, it distorts the voices of the drums. (Quoted in Bramly 1978, 46)

If the medium is able to go out of herself—that is, if the god rides her—then she becomes an "obedient mount." This is how a new medium is born. The gods seek her out and attack her during sleep or trance. Occasionally, a medium into whom a god has already entered takes hold of another person from among the spectators, carries him on her shoulders around the ceremonial hall, and offers him a ceremonial greeting. This is an expression that the god would like to embody himself in that person.

Once a medium senses that she has the gift of trance, she can begin to receive proper training. She moves into the *terreiro*, the cult house, where an attempt is made to discover the identity of the god who has entered her. Once it is known who the god is, the medium and the god make a pact, like the marriage to a spirit husband practiced in many tribes. During the initiation, the novice is strengthened by baths of blood since she has not yet mastered receiving the god into her properly. She lies motionless the whole night long until the blood has dried and the contact between her and the god has been firmly established. Before this, she must live entirely alone in a small room. She is to speak as little as possible within the *terreiro* and have no sexual relations. She takes regular spiced baths. Bathing, says Maria-José, the "mother of the gods," is a "death by installments." That is, the baths are sacred to the god who enters them, and the personality of the novice is washed away bit by bit until it is entirely extinguished. The novice arises from the bath reborn; she is purified, consecrated; she has been divested of her old personality and now becomes a *yao,* a consort of her god.

Soon the novice experiences her first trance. The god and his "child" unite. Prayers to the god are sung, and dressed all in white, the initiate receives her god-consort alone in the middle of the *terreiro.* Now she moves in a circle, and the god enters her. Fireworks are shot off, and there is applause. The "mother of the gods" runs a burning candle under the armpits of the initiate to test whether it is a true trance. If it is fake, the initiate is burned. Otherwise, the flames lick her skin without leaving burns. Then the girl returns to her everyday consciousness. During her training, she has not left the *terreiro.* Her family must buy her back—which amounts to paying the costs of the initiation. This money is distributed by the *terreiro* as an offering during large public feasts.

Bramly asked the "mother of the gods" if a foreigner could also be initiated. "I don't know," she said.

> It depends on the person him or herself. But why not really? I really am not sure. Foreigners often have a barrier in their heads, preconceptions that block them, which prevent them from really letting themselves go, offering themselves entirely, emptying their heads enough so that the god can establish himself there. . . . In general foreigners are too hampered by their education. Our dances and our sacrifices scare them. Also they are afraid of lowering themselves by accepting something that they really consider pure superstition. They

see the obvious with their own eyes but deny it with their heads. Their body says yes, but their intellect sets up a defense. They constantly hide behind the thought that there is no place for such things in the civilized world. (56f.)

Of course, altered consciousness conflicts with normal consciousness—they are mutually exclusive. Therefore Maria-José had to say:

Macumba doesn't explain anything. It can only be measured by its effects. It is not practiced with the head but with the body. What you feel is more important than what you think. If people would just learn to follow their intuition, they would be a lot happier. (60)

Here we come to the essence of the altered state of consciousness, of Macumba, of a world born out of an unconscious, high wisdom of the body and the mind: "Macumba is the central axis, the center around which human activity is harmoniously arranged" (60). Maria-José continues:

Everything can serve prophecy. You only have to pay attention. The universe is full of signs. When you learn to look at things the right way, you will understand what I'm trying to say. The shape of clouds, the way birds fly, the sounds of nature, an unexpected meeting—all these transmit a message that expresses the will of the gods. The universe is a whole that fits together logically and that maintains itself and develops in a meaningful way. (78)

Here, as everywhere in tribal societies, we find the idea of a universe in which everything can provide knowledge about everything else, and the whole of being is fundamentally an immense signal system. The trance is the first step toward deciphering this signal system. But deciphering it means doing away with our cultural program, our way of thinking and feeling, taking it off like an old glove.

The human being lives in a prefabricated universe, isn't that true? In an unreal universe that has been imposed on him by his culture and education. He lets himself be forced into this framework and imagines that it is the world of his own ideas. It is really necessary for him to be regularly referred back to his inmost nature. . . .
On the contrary, thought kills life, my son. It draws the power out

of things. Ask our followers. They don't explain what they do or experience. It is also not necessary to explain everything. Many thoughts go through my head. But I only believe what I have tested out. Our religion is practiced, not studied. For this reason, I don't understand your book. It is like a chant that one only knows the words to. And I tell you, it's the rhythms that are the most important thing. (127, 123)

Recent research shows that if a drum rhythm is synchronized with brain-wave frequencies, it is easier to achieve an altered state of consciousness. Hence the importance of drumming, rhythm, and chant in tribal cultures. To this, of course, must be added, as Larry Peters's example shows, the courage to let oneself go completely. It is our archaic fear of this that continually stands in our way. The history of humanity, it might be said, is a struggle between letting go of the self and keeping a tight rein of waking consciousness to establish security through reason. It might be interesting to rewrite history from this point of view.

A widespread technique for engendering trance is the inhalation of juniper smoke. This is still done in Hunza, a small kingdom in the Karakorum in northern Pakistan. In Hunza, when the trance reaches its apex, a transition is made to an out-of-body experience. The *bitan,* or shaman, Ibrahim of Altit acquired his shamanic powers at the age of fifteen on the mountain meadow of Chikiso Runanch. His mind left his body and traveled to the fairies, to the Great Mother, the mistress of nature—that is, of our inner nature. From her he received his shamanic power. He drank her in the form of blue milk from a blue glass. Here is the color blue, which so frequently crops up in connection with the acquisition of powers and extraordinary energies:

When I received my *bitan*ship, the Mir also heard that someone in Altit had become a shaman. At that point our king commanded: have the new *bitan* dance in Altit. I danced on that day in Altit, and when the fairies appeared before my eyes, I saw seven of them. Three days later, I danced in Berishal. Three days later, I was brought to the prince's court. From then on, I had no more conversations at all with people. . . . When it was new moon and the protecting fairies came, I could no longer hold myself back. My mind left my body and hurried away to the mountain. For five days, I stayed there with the fairies. They gave me a blue glass with blue milk. I drank the milk. After the fifth day, there was a great festival in Baltit, then another in Surias. I was not aware of any of that. But then the Great Mother gave me permission to go back. I arrived with all the fairies. One was Galzali, another Sabaramgul. They laid me under the walnut tree by the well in Altit. When my relatives and friends saw me, they were very happy. I was back; I wasn't lost anymore. I went home with them, but I couldn't eat anything. I was still with the fairies; my mind was still with them.

It's like this: Ordinary people can't see the fairies. But who sees them? First of all, the *bitan*; and after that, the *pashu*, the seer. Between people and the fairies, there is a veil. When we hold a festival, when we beat the drums and make the flutes speak, when we make smoke with juniper branches and *gulgul* canes, then the fairies come. Then afterward, when water is poured on our faces, they leave.

On the day of the festival, the *bitan* doesn't eat anything. He takes only unsweetened tea. The tea is from the *tilpushing* flower that grows in the mountain meadows. We inhale the smoke of the *tilpushing*, of juniper and *supandur*. We pour millet over it and worship the *peri*. We do *barayo* (calling and requesting). At this request, the fairies begin to gather during the night, from a distance of seven days' travel. Then together we approach the assembly place. And when our king gives the sign and says, "It is up to you—now dance," then we dance. That is the way it is, sahib. My name is Ibrahim of Altit. (Schaefer 1978, 157f.)

In March 1975, the Tham, the father of the crown prince Ghazan-far Ali, requested Ibrahim to dance for him and look into his future. For this prophesying many people came together. Ibrahim was received with music, applause, and drums. In Hunza, the *bitan*'s seance is a folk festival. He goes to the drum and listens to its sound. Four assistants watch over him during his "absence," his journey to the heavens. They arrive with a mountain goat and a pan full of herbs and juniper branches. The *bitan* drinks blood from the goat and deeply inhales the smoke from the branches. Then the drums chase him around the castle courtyard. After going around the courtyard seven times, which for him are seven steps, his movements slow down. Ibrahim loses consciousness. His assistants now carry "he who has gone home" to the king. But before he can give the king information about his journey, he sings a song in Shina, a Dardic language, which normally he is unable to speak. This time, he prophesies the death of the Tham; he will pass away a year hence, exactly on the first day of the dark of the moon after No Ruz. A year later, in March 1976, the Mir of Hunza died, just as prophesied (78, 162f.).

Essentially, there is no distinction between trance and deep hypnosis except a purely linguistic one. Whatever is suggested in the shaman's song or by cultural symbols is taken up by the psyche, which transforms it in the trance state into reality. Since there are no limits to suggestion, there is nothing of which shamans are not capable. They walk on hot coals, dip their arms in boiling water, and are proof against all kinds of pain. If an animal spirit takes possession of their consciousness, they take on the animal's movements and behavior. If the spirit is a pregnant woman, the shaman's belly swells up. If it is an omniscient god, the shaman becomes "omniscient." If it is a wrathful god, the shaman too becomes wrathful. If spirits from other tribes enter into him, he speaks other languages.

The range of the power of suggestion is without boundaries; it can relate to any area of life, all aspects of the mind and spirit, any kind of behavior. Trance thus heightens our inherent powers and faculties and brings out our latent potential. A lost memory can be retrieved, the ability to learn languages or to paint skillfully can be heightened; the hitting power of a boxer or the agility of a fencer can be enhanced. It is not, however, only a matter of realizing potential abilities. In trance we also gain access to a field of consciousness beyond three-dimensional space, access to hyperspace, to other realities and parallel universes.

Entirely on their own, many children hit on the idea of playfully trying out trance techniques. They spin until they get dizzy, they play hyperventilation games, they press the chest of a friend until he is completely out of breath. Babies are rhythmically rocked. Children generally keep such games a secret, but if you ask them what they experience, they answer: "It's like flying"; "It makes you dizzy and you feel good"; "It's like going crazy"; "It's like floating"; "I feel energy building up around my body"; "It's fun" (Weil 1977).

Eskimo children play "going into a trance." They hang themselves by their hoods until their throats are entirely constricted. No
more blood flows to their heads, their consciousness is darkened,
and their faces get purple and blue. Only at this point do their play
companions take them down. The children say that this state is a
very pleasant one; that is why they play this game again and again
(Freuchen 1961, 157f.).

In the same way, among the African !Kung, the Siberian Tungus,
and the Magar of Nepal, children play trance games and emulate
shamans, central figures in the tribal community, in all their actions. Particularly noteworthy are the trances of Balinese children,
who begin participating in the great trance dramas and public
theater performances at an early age. This confirms how inborn the
urge toward altered states of consciousness is and how natural the
tendency is to create for oneself a multidimensional universe of
consciousness in which the waking state plays only one role among
many.

Alternative states of consciousness are not to be regarded as
pathological. Every human being spends a great part of his or her
life in sleep and dream states. To these can be added daydream
states, faints, lapses, anesthesia, orgasm, stress, ecstasy, and of
course outbreaks of strong emotions such as hate, anger, envy,
antagonism, affection, romantic love, shock, and exhaustion. Then
there are the psychopathological states of psychosis, neurosis, and
so forth. In addition, there are the states evoked by psychedelic and
narcotic drugs. On the whole, it is absurd to say that people spend
most of their time in a normal state—quite to the contrary. There
is no basis for, or possibility of, distilling a single state out of all
these various emotions and mental conditions and calling it normal.
Human existence is open in all directions for experiences of consciousnesses of all kinds. We continually swing back and forth on
a consciousness continuum between subwakeful and hypercon-
scious states. Indeed, we live in a mercurial universe of consciousness. This leads to a conception of the psyche as a journey through
various zones of consciousness. I believe it is one of our tasks to
learn to distinguish these states clearly from one another in such a
way that we can become masters of our own "creations." As we
have seen, as children we already experiment in an entirely natural

way with these states. In shamans we may recognize the masters of consciousness transformation, the lords of the continuum of existence.

Among the Lapps, sorcerers have themselves brought out of their trances by their relatives at prearranged times. Nevertheless, there are many stories of Lapp sorcerers who have never returned—whose sons or wives forgot to wake them at the agreed time with the right expression or forgot how to utter this expression properly. The companion of one old sorcerer forgot to sing him awake. When the companion tried it later, the old man revived briefly and said, "You can't make a man out of a dead man if you haven't remembered him sooner!" Another sorcerer was forgotten for three years; only then did his companion remember the life-saving words, which were the description of the place where his soul was: "In the coil of the pike's intestine, in the third dark corner!" Hardly had these words been spoken when the sorcerer's legs began to shudder, and without cosmeticizing his plight, he yelled out: "A rotten man isn't worth a damn!" (Itkonen 1960, 26f.).

Today, unfortunately, there is a tendency either to mythologize altered states of consciousness or to discredit them. Both tendencies are equally harmful. Like the artificial separation of normal and altered consciousness, both tendencies hinder research, whether the research subject is an intensification of all forms of perception or a modification of inner physiological and biochemical processes. Such research is not at all mysterious; it is simply a question of physiology and psychological chemistry. As harmful as the rejection of altered states of consciousness is the appropriation of them by spiritual philosophies, churches, sects, and religious believers. Altered states of consciousness belong to the natural history of mankind; they should be seen in the framework of human sensory activity and have little to do with religion and faith. They are physical phenomena, a matter of biology. They are partially chemical and partially energetic processes. It matters little if they are cognized at the time they take place. In any case, appropriation of them by ideologies and systems of belief is very dangerous—for the faithful and quite simply for the clarity of the human mind. The words *religion* and *spirituality* should not appear in this context; when they do, it is an ideological abuse of a natural condition, although this is very difficult to avoid. If we want to investigate altered states of consciousness or consciousness altogether, at the outset we must set aside all the dogmas and traditions and ethical systems that have become bound up with the investigation of consciousness throughout history. The spiritual experiences that have been venerated, cultivated, and fostered by these traditions are nothing more than a metabolic process, electrical stimulation at the organic molecular or cellular level. Even out-of-body experiences and spiritual substances independent of the body are matters of biophysics, though on a higher level. The history of the mind and the history of nature coincide.

Recent research informs us that endorphins, the natural opiates of the brain, are responsible for alterations of consciousness. They suppress pain and produce euphoria (Prince 1982). That there is a connection between religious experience and the body's psycho-active substances has been largely proven. Stress and battle situations elevate the endorphin level; as a result, psychological euphoria overcomes psychological chaos, and calm ensues. Heightened stress, fear, panic, excessive effort, and physical overexertion stimulate endorphin production and trigger euphoric states. Recall that in the trance experience of Maya Deren, at the apex of physical exertion, which she described as a state of terror, a switchover suddenly took place that resulted in euphoria. At that point, everything flowed as if by itself. She experienced the slow-motion effect, depersonaliza-tion, and trance. But states of terror and euphoria go together: one does not displace the other—both continue to coexist in the form of "white darkness." Exertion carried to the limits of a person's capacity leads to a state of trance. States of physical exhaustion and extreme psychological concentration are the precursors of bliss, the gates to mental and spiritual greatness. On this point, Aldous Huxley tells us:

> But, in one way or another, *all* our experiences are chemically condi-tioned, and if we imagine that some of them are purely "spiritual," purely "intellectual," purely "aesthetic," it is merely because we have never troubled to investigate the internal chemical environment at the moment of their occurrence. (Huxley 1963, 155)

Huxley points out that in the Middle Ages, winter meant invol-untary fasting and vitamin deficiency. This was aggravated by the official fasting period of forty days before Easter. During these times, people's body chemistry turned ecstasies and visions into everyday occurrences. The whip of knotted leather thongs triggered the production of a good deal of histamine and adrenaline, and festering cuts released poisonous substances into the bloodstream. All of these physiological reactions broaden the reduction valve that is the brain, and strange and bizarre phenomena occur.

Overexertion resulting from uncomfortable positions, vitamin deficiency, reduction of blood sugar, reduced sleep, breathing exercises, and chanting—which increase the proportion of carbon dioxide in the lungs and blood—broaden the "cerebral reduction valve":

> To make biological survival possible, Mind at large has to be funneled through the reducing valve of the brain and nervous system. What comes out at the other end is a measly trickle of the kind of consciousness which will help us to stay alive on the surface of this particular planet. (Huxley 1963, 23)

We have seen that drumming is particularly important for the development of trance. Huxley says of this:

> No man, however highly civilized, can listen for very long to African drumming, or Indian chanting, or Welsh hymn-singing, and retain intact his critical and self-conscious personality. It would be interesting to take a group of the most eminent philosophers from the best universities, shut them up in a hot room with Moroccan dervishes or Haitian voodooists, and measure, with a stopwatch, the strength of their psychological resistance to the effects of rhythmic sound. Would the Logical Positivists be able to hold out longer than the Subjective Idealists? Would the Marxists prove tougher than the Thomists or Vedantists? What a fascinating, what a fruitful field for experiment! Meanwhile, all we can safely predict is that, if exposed long enough to the tom-toms and the singing, every one of our philosophers would end up capering and howling with the savages. (Huxley 1952, 322)

Rhythmic stimulation, resulting not only from sounds but from other factors, influences consciousness. We breathe with a particular rhythm, our hearts beat rhythmically, we walk and speak with specific rhythms, and so on. Throughout our lives, we are exposed to psychological, physical, biological, and cosmic rhythms that determine our existence in an essential fashion. Rhythm and consciousness are intimately bound up together. An alteration of our bodily rhythms creates a change in our consciousness.

Research into rhythm and sound will one day reveal an entirely new picture of human consciousness. The human being is essentially sound, vibration, and melody, and perhaps our consciousness frequencies can be arranged in scales. That would be the first step toward creating a fundamental representation of consciousness. Holophonic sounds bring about synesthetic experiences; that is, music is not only something we hear but something we feel with our bodies and see and smell (Zuccarelli 1983).

As the experiences we have described show, trance states can be meaningfully and creatively applied to many problems of our everyday lives. Indeed, if we were to make extensive use of trance procedures in therapeutic, pedagogical, and psychological applications, it could lead to a resurrection of the powers latent in our consciousness, a scientific renaissance in which broader forms of perception would advance our research, our knowledge, and our ability to solve problems by leaps and bounds. Indeed, the trance state is actually the real perception of mankind. It is just that it has been consigned to oblivion by a grand-scale cover-up strategy.

William James tells us this in his fashion:

> The human individual . . . lives usually far within his limits; he possesses powers of various sorts which he habitually fails to use. He energizes below his *maximum,* and he behaves below his *optimum.* In elementary faculty, in co-ordination, in power of *inhibition* and control, in every conceivable way, his life is contracted like the field of vision of an hysteric subject. (1962, 221).

Trance states are usually arrived at through extreme efforts of body and mind: through singing, dancing, and any activities that lead to fatigue and exhaustion. I would like to give an example of this from our own cultural sphere—peak sports performances. In their book *Psi in Sport,* Rhea A. White and Michael Murphy (1983) compiled comprehensive documentation for psychic states among high-performance athletes. The alterations of consciousness that take place during these activities resemble trance experiences in tribal cultures in many respects and are worthy of a brief overview.

A feeling of supreme well-being appears. Peak experiences and feelings of freedom, composure, and calm come over the athlete in the midst of competition. Such athletes experience a sense of letting go and freedom, a sensation of floating and flying, of weightlessness, ecstasy and power, total control over themselves; a feeling of being totally present in the here and now; of total dedication; of fusion with the action, accompanied by a sense of great awe toward the mystery of life; a feeling of union with everything living. During games and matches, their perception of the size of the playing field or the player often changes; time passes more slowly, allowing them to see, for example, the approaching ball better, or the opponent's punch in boxing. It can happen that the whole of the athlete's life suddenly passes before his or her inner eye, as if on film. They may experience flashbacks on their life, stoppages of time, all manner of extrasensory perceptions, out-of-body experiences. They may have a sensation of suddenly being projected into other players.

Through these altered states of consciousness, peak performances come about, extraordinary acts of strength, speed, balance, and—something that all the spectators can see—effortlessness of achievement. Other such experiences are found among wrestlers, boxers, and football players, when an absence of pain as a result of their concentration enables them to continue despite broken hands or ribs. They may experience alterations in their subjective images of their own body; a sensation of floating above their own body; a sense of being able to penetrate solid objects; access to the inner worlds of music and rhythm; synesthesia—in which sounds are seen as colors and vice versa; a perception of inner body structures on the cellular level; a sensation of being able to expand their body limitlessly and thus exercise influence over opposing players or over the ball or javelin, for example; manipulation of other players psychokinetically or by suggestion, either positively, in the form of stimulation and inspiration, or negatively, in the form of psychological disablement; the power of the evil eye; breaking the spell of a hostile crowd through sorcery, mass hypnosis, or a curse. Also reported are incredible feats in dodging opposing players; runners' sensations of floating or running on the tips of their toes; a feeling of moving through a sacred time in a sacred place; enormous uninterrupted attention and concentration strong enough to produce complete oblivion to the environment; and a quest for perfection, beauty, or divinity in movement or performance (White and Murphy 1983).

All these transpersonal states arise as a result of the restriction or concentration of perception that comes about naturally in the activity of sports. Our next example, however, illustrates an even stronger form of concentration of the psychological energies. These are altered states of consciousness in near-fatal circumstances, such as falling while mountain climbing (Heim 1892) or suicidal leaps (Rosen 1975; Noyes and Kletti 1976).

Death is preceded by a series of altered states of perception that may be understood as ego-death motifs. The death of the ego entails the stripping away of all learned limitations, of a restricted thought process, and of a physiology that seeks to maintain an even level of nervous stimulation. For Charles Garfield (1977), ego death means an expansion of consciousness, a heightened sensitivity to all modalities of the senses, a dissolution of the I/world boundary, a collapse of the cortically filtered system of judgment, a heightened receptivity to emotional stimuli, and a reduction of the stimulus threshold between conscious and unconscious processes. Ego death is destruction of the organization of the senses, a shifting of attention and alertness to a deeper level of the psyche. The concept of ego death can be misleading: the ego does not die; nor does it dissolve. Rather, it joins itself to the rest of the world, establishes relationships with the environment, and steps beyond the boundaries of a previously encapsulated existence.

In mountain-climbing falls, a peculiar sequence of perceptual alterations occurs. In situations of minor or negligible danger, many people are paralyzed by fear and become incapable of action. But in serious accidents with possible fatal consequences, no shock appears. Of course, the person involved is filled with great fear and does initially struggle desperately for survival; but as a result of the hopelessness of the situation, this behavior is soon abandoned and gives way to a profound sense of resignation.

Self-surrender, resignation, and a willingness to die seem to be the motivating forces that trigger all subsequent patterns of action. In the face of mortal danger—as when one's body is in free fall—and when all means of escape within human capacity are futile, consciousness abandons itself to its fate. The fear of ego dissolution vanishes, and one's identification with his or her own life story and existence falls apart.

Once people are liberated from the crazed fears of their ego, they can adopt a more objective, emotionless standpoint. At that point they are in possession of a clear consciousness, and the activity of their thoughts intensifies to a level resembling a filmstrip running at high speed. At the same time, their thoughts become a great deal more precise. They calculate the sequence of events of the accident and its outcome in advance with lightning speed, as though with a computer. They calculate their own chances of survival realistically, they run through possible preventive reactions, and in the midst of all this they remain capable of suitable spontaneous action. Instead of confusion, their minds are filled with clarity, objectivity, and an extraordinary inner calm and seriousness. Since they undertake no unsuitable or awkward survival efforts, their bodies remain completely relaxed. Calm, composure, and a feeling of peace prevail. They accommodate themselves to their fate and no longer attempt to brace themselves against the inevitable results of the fall through space. According to Kenneth Ring (1985), 60 percent of people who have been through a fall experience a feeling of peace but are afterward unable to express this in words—the wonderful experience has touched them too deeply.

In danger situations, many people react swiftly and decisively and, above all, the right way—spontaneously. This nonintellectual, spontaneous behavior can be explained in part by a heightening of their capacity for perception and thought, as a result of which they can process many signals in a short time, which leads to precise and immediate actions. In addition, some imponderable factor like "body wisdom" may be involved—that is, a hyperoptimalized functioning of sensory and motor capacities that appears as automatic, unplanned action.

During free fall, some people have a feeling that they are being influenced by outside forces, an unmistakable phenomenon of trance. They look at themselves and are astonished by the autonomous flow of their behavior. Without their conscious participation, spontaneously, as though guided by outside forces, their actions complete themselves. This sensation is also typical of "passive" states such as trance, peak, and enlightenment experiences. In these experiences, reasoned conscious supervision by the higher ego—the self or surface consciousness—is surrendered. We often labor under the misapprehension that the body will not work without the supervision of our waking "daytime consciousness." In point of fact, our psyche works better, more uninhibitedly, and more effectively in our "night consciousness" during sleep, in dreams, or in trance.

During a fall, one's perception of space is also altered. The size and distance of objects can no longer be estimated appropriately. The same applies to the sensation of time—a slow-motion effect occurs. The subjective moment is extended, and this is what makes precise and calm observation of the sequence of events during the fall possible. In my opinion, the sensation of the slowing down of time is an essential part of altered states of consciousness, trances, and parapsychological experiences generally. Existential experiences that take place in the nearness of death or during the collapse of the ego lead to a switchover from normal to trance consciousness.

Obviously, there is a relationship between the level of danger in a situation and the vividness of the altered state of consciousness and of all the accompanying characteristics of trance, such as the slowing of time, clarity, beauty, and speed in processing information. There is also a similarity between the heightening of perception in the slow-motion effect and the so-called flashing of one's life before one's eyes during a fall. How is it possible for one's whole life to pass before one's eyes in a few instants? I believe that this biographical flashback and the strengthening of the perceptions are conditioned by, among other things, the slowing of one's personal time. If time passes more slowly for us, we have more leisure to appreciate the stream of images rushing by. Many people say that this review of their life takes place in the twinkling of an eye. But this holds true only if one's personal perception of time has been slowed. Time plays a prominent role in the process of trance. And of course one's ability to gauge the situation during a fall and to consider possible preventive measures arises only through the slowing of time. This in turn occurs only as a result of the extreme directedness and restrictedness of a person's attention to the event taking place and the blocking out of all inessential stimuli. When unnecessary thoughts and feelings are turned away, we acquire, so to speak, more space in our minds to let in the here and now; we therefore experience the present more strongly, more vividly, more colorfully. Subjectively, we have more time to occupy ourselves with every single object of perception. The fewer the stimuli of which we are conscious, the more attention we can apply to each; as a result, they become clearer to us. This can peak in the vision, as described by Albert Heim, of supernatural beauty—but, note well, during a fall, just before death!

We encounter the same principle among people who have experiences of the beyond. That which they perceive is of a more than worldly beauty. They also experience the biographical flashback and the slow-motion effect. Many shamans traveling in the beyond for the first time think they have spent only a short time there. Time is often much denser in altered states of consciousness. The journey to the beyond, the trance, the climbing accident—all take place, as it were, in another dimension of time. This assertion can be proven very simply. All studies of meditation show that the focusing of mindfulness and attention on one point, one object, intensifies that object's color, form, and meaning to the level of sublime beauty. By contrast, the more chaotic the perception and the more objects there are in the field of view, the flatter and vaguer the impression. An accident quite naturally focuses one's attention to the utmost. All shamanic consciousness techniques are aimed at narrowing perception to one-pointed conscious being.

But this does not exhaust the noteworthy aspects of the psychology of the fall. The final point is the development of a split between consciousness and body. Thus, the well-known mountain climber Reinhold Messner writes in his book *Grenzbereich Todeszone* ("Border-Area Death Zone") that he himself had out-of-body experiences three times during climbing accidents. At the moment in which the hopelessness of all countermeasures is acknowledged, an ego split occurs:

> The so-called body sensation vanishes almost completely; we are outside our body. We feel unreal, free of all worldly ties. It is idle to argue about whether this state is possible in reality or if we are merely dealing with a phantasmic derealization effect. It is sufficient to note

that in greatest peril of death this experience of separation between body and soul can occur. (1978, 87)

A sense of unreality accompanies the beginning of the accident and manifests, as Noyes and Kletti (1976) call it, in a depersonalization, a separation between the participant and an observer. According to Kenneth Ring's typology of death experiences, thirty-eight percent of those involved had an experience of alienation from the body. This sense of remove from one's own experiences and from external events increases noticeably during a fall and reaches its apex in an out-of-body experience. Through the separation of consciousness from the body, emotion loses its basis. Feeling and thought, which are now located outside the body, logically need not identify themselves with the body in danger. The situation can now be coolly and soberly appraised. Thus, many people have reported floating calmly next to their falling bodies and, as it made impact, experiencing little sense of sympathy for their own situation of the moment. Later, they were able to describe the rescue operation, the people who appeared to help, and so on quite precisely, because they were literally "beside themselves." Many other fallers leave their bodies only at the moment of impact.

Trance and deep hypnosis are healing. They liberate us from the machinery of thought; they purify our consciousness of its compulsive, incessant inner dialogue, of its relentless, ongoing evaluating and judging. Interestingly, many researchers (for example, Shirokogoroff, particularly concerning Siberian shamans) report that shamans who have not undertaken a seance for a long period of time feel "heavy in heart and head," a feeling that they can get rid of only through the trance state, after which they have a light and pleasant feeling (1935a, 364ff.). Trance means healing through inner recuperation from the unending stream of external stimuli, from complex thinking, from complicated emotions. The trance, however, does not exclude all stimuli. On the contrary, it heightens perception and brings out the colorfulness and vividness and wonder of existence. But this occurs only after a phase of narrowing consciousness, which is what is defined as trance in the most restricted sense of the word.

7

THE GOD-MAN
FROM AGLIN

The desert dust had settled. Wind had blown the clouds away, and snow had appeared on the five and six-thousand meter peaks, a sign of oncoming winter. We climbed out of the Jeep. Before us lay the miserable camp of Tibetan refugees who had left Tibet in 1959 in the hopes of finding a better existence in exile than under Chinese rule. Human beings in a wasteland, in a stone-and-sand desert in one of the highest settled valleys of the world, in the "Land of Passes," Ladakh, west of Tibet.

Many people had assembled on this usually vacant village square, a rectangle enclosed by houses. Children dash about playing with hoops. Groups of Tibetans stand near us talking. We represent a small "event." The god-man himself is not at home; however, he has been sent for. He is in the meadow. Only his barking dog disturbs the peace. Finally, an old man arrives, dressed entirely in traditional clothing: Tibetan shoes with a long robe, earrings, long hair woven into a braid. He washes his face and hands and then comes to greet us. No need for further ado—the ceremony can begin at once.

Six of us take our places in this tiny shelter built by the Indian government for refugees. A window with broken panes provides only a minimum of light, but an additional beam of light from the open smoke hole falls on the floor, which is of beaten earth. Tin boxes piled one on top of another, as with so many oracles, constitutes the altar. On a broken-down bed in the corner, an infant lies with some under a tent of fly screening. As for the rest, nothing but the once-white walls. A few pictures of bodhisattvas and saints over the would-be altar make up the house shrine. The *lhapa*, the god-man, takes his shaman's pouch from the wall, and we hand him some incense sticks, half of which are lit at once.

The first thing the oracle-healer does is set up the altar. He puts a cloth over the tin boxes and strews a good kilo of rice over it. Then on top, one after the other, he puts a butter lamp, six little bowls filled with rice and water, and one little bowl with tsampa (roasted barley flour) that has been formed into a little cone. A round copper mirror is laid on top of the rice, and another is placed on its own special stand after both have been thoroughly wiped clean with a ceremonial white scarf, a *khatak.* The mirror, *melong,* opens the door into the trance world and is at the same time a symbol of the world of forms, which has to be transcended. The mirror's shine is the focal point of concentration.

Now he shakes out the entire contents of his pouch, and out comes a hopeless tangle of *khataks,* which, when examined, more closely reveals itself as his five-sectioned crown. Hundreds of these ceremonial scarves have been tied onto it in the course of his career by those who requested his services. In the meantime, his daughter, still with her child on her back, has brought a large plate of rice. The old god-man digs out from the heap of *khataks,* which over the years have turned gray and black, some further ritual objects. Finally he finds what he is looking for: the thunderbolt, the *dorje,* the palm-of-the-hand-sized double drum *(damaru),* and the bell *(drilbu).* As he does this, his daughter offers around roasted barley and, of course, tea for the unusual guests—for us.

We now learn that, in addition to healing, he can allow us only three questions in a session. Now he begins to sing softly. Presently he adds drum and bell as accompaniment and looks into his copper mirror. Gradually, he gets into the swing of it. The drum turns faster, the chant becomes more penetrating, the bell strikes harder and harder. Only when he is sufficiently into the trance—or, as the Tibetans say, when the god is completely ready to enter into him—does he put on his apron, drop the lotus-shaped shoulder drape over his head, tie a red cloth around his forehead. Then, finally, he puts the crown of painted cardboard on over that.

Now the trance deepens. A soft, almost melodic whistling is heard. The old man, who is now possessed, trembles slightly. He kneels, still facing the altar, and sings indefatigably as he sprinkles water from the little bowls with a spoon and then tosses rice over us and into the air as a blessing. It takes a good while for the trance to become firmly established. From time to time the chanting swells. The god-man, who not long earlier was joking with me and mischievously suggesting that I have my ailments treated by a doctor, has now completely gone beyond. The drumbeats come ever faster, and the muttered chanting becomes more articulate. His body sways to and fro, back and forth, and wild glances from the corners of his eyes fall upon us. We are told that with these looks he sees the gods and spirits approaching.

While this is going on, his daughter continually works to keep him free of the tangle of *khataks.* And as the drumming and ringing mount to a deafening crescendo, the god—for it is he who now governs the body of the *lhapa*—jumps to his feet. The trembling of the body has now subsided. The *lhapa* now dances to and fro in the little room, leaping, casting his legs out to the sides, and spinning. In the meantime, we have purified our *khataks* in the incense smoke and are waiting to ask our questions.

Now what one hopes for from a great seance has taken place: a person has wound himself so deeply in concentration that he has even drawn the onlookers into this vortex of self-oblivion. The tiny room is fairly bursting with tension and expectation. Life has been captured within these four rude walls. I have long since given up my aim of observing carefully. I am too deeply moved by the selfless abandon of this man, the facility with which he follows the ebb and flow of the drum rhythm, entirely loses himself in the waves of sound. This shaman has drawn me to the utmost point into his state of mind; his rocking motions have become for me the flow of being. In this process, the development of trance—which our Western science has been unable to explain, no matter how hard it has tried—has revealed itself in the simplest way.

We ask our questions. But before he answers, there is more dancing and drumming. Then come the answers, poignant and prophetic—and right on the mark. Then finally the healing. Before that, once again, dancing. Another god is entering the oracle, as indicated by a change in the drumming, a different chant, and renewed whistling. Whistling always indicates the departure or arrival of a *lha,* another being. A cloth is laid over the painful spot, and the drum, held upright, is pressed onto it. Now the *lhapa* sucks the sickness out through the drum with his mouth. Then slowly, visibly for everyone, he spits out a black fluid. Next he rinses his mouth out with water. It is healing by sucking, the most archaic approach to healing sickness.

The seance now approaches its end. The *lhapa* kneels down, drums vigorously, and once again the chant reaches a climax. Then he pulls the crown from his head, and abruptly quiet returns. Only the soft whistling of the receding *lha* is still to be heard. Now there is utter silence. Suddenly a belch is heard in the room. The god has left us for good, and the man is there once more. Mischievously he glances at the round of exhausted, empathizing faces; we can still hear the drumming in our ears. (Toward the end of another seance, his daughter had to quickly lean against his back to keep him from falling over when the god left him.) He muttered audibly, stretched, and leaned against the wall, by way of conclusion tossed another handful of rice into the air, and finally came to himself again completely. At once everything was gathered up and stowed back in the shaman's pouch. We began to make small talk.

To get into a trance, this *lhapa* did not use hyperventilation—he breathed completely normally—nor were any particularly violent body movements to be seen, only a slight trembling of the legs. He was old, and perhaps because of long practice, he had less need of drastic triggering techniques than younger shamans. He seemed to have developed his own style and to be completely tuned in to it. Nothing could have perturbed him. His whole consciousness attended to the eternally identical drum rhythm. His nerves had already been trained by many trances, and in the course of time his trance ritual had grown ever shorter. His ceremony made a greater impression on me than that of any other oracle. His chant, now tender, now erupting with great force in concert with his dancing, which lasted well over an hour, put me into the state of mind that all rhythmic repetition brings, the feeling of being on the threshold of trance.

Afterward, with buttered tea and tsampa, the *lhapa* recounted to me the story of his life and vocation:

When I was twenty-four years old, the *lha* came to me for the first time. Now I am seventy. My father came from a certain part of Tibet called Rawang. My *lha* is also from Tibet.

Something has to link you with the *lha*. The *lha* only comes when there is an intimate relationship between the person and the *lha*. Only a *lha* that the person is already familiar with will come.

When I concentrate on my three *lha*, I soon lose control of my consciousness. I get crazy, and the *lha* comes down into me. At that time I have the feeling of looking into a deep empty heaven. Only there is nothing to see there.

How do I know that the god is going to come down to me? The mirror that is on my altar becomes bigger and bigger. Then comes the emptiness, and my consciousness no longer knows what's happening. When I am this state, people approach me with questions, and the *lha* in me answers them. If your father was already a *lhapa*, and if as a child you always kept yourself clean, spiritually as well as physically, then the *lha* will also come to you. You only have to invoke the *lha* then, for he won't come to you on his own. Also, he will only come to a family that already has contact with a *lha*.

One *lha* does the sucking out, another one takes care of the prophesying. With each new generation, you have to invoke the *lha* again. Only then does the family *lha* come down—always the same one, never another. Every *lhapa* has his own *lha*. One *lha* is called Thebring; he is a good *lha*. You can tell him by the fact that, as soon as you've lost consciousness, his message become legible on your thumbnail. One *lha* I took over from my father. He is called Gang Rinpoche. He is connected with Palden Lhamo or Gangri Lapzen. After my death, the *lha* will pass to my son, who is now doing military duty. My father was good at prophesying, and most of the time his predictions came true. On top of that, he could heal almost all animals. In order to lose consciousness, you only have to concentrate powerfully enough on something, and then the *lha* comes. If somebody then asks for a prediction, I just look in my mirror, which then becomes bigger and bigger. In it, I suddenly see the answer. In short, I become crazy, and then people can ask me anything at all, and my *lha* will give advice, solve all kinds of problems, and heal. When I'm empty, I understand everything my *lha* says. You, however, couldn't understand any of it.

My *lha* has already been appearing for three or four generations. He can keep showing up for as many as nine generations, but that is of course different from family to family. People speak of a *lha gyud*, the inheritance of a *lha* within a family. When the *lha* comes down, I become empty. I am then not myself anymore, and afterward I can't remember anything. Everything that happens is the action of the *lha.* The only thing that is left of me is my body, which you saw moving; but everything it does and says is the action of the *lha.* If a sick person comes, the *lha* heals. If someone comes needing advice, the *lha* recommends to him a particular prayer or ceremony to be performed by a lama.

I don't feel sick when the *lha* descends; I just lose myself. At the beginning my father called the *lha* for me, and since then, he enters into me. When the emptiness comes, then I am able to distinguish between the individual *lha,* and I also know what is right and what is wrong. For the most part, my parents' *lha* comes first, and he knows right away who the individual *lha* are and which *lha* should undertake which task [a kind of supervisor spirit!]. As soon as I invoke the *lha,* which we call *lha bab,* then he has plenty of *wang,* power, to explain and predict things, to give advice, to help all people. The *lha* appears as soon as my mind disappears. At that point the butter lamp gets smaller and smaller and I float higher and higher up, until I have left behind and forgotten everything here. Since our family *lha* has already been coming to us for generations, I know exactly how to deal with him, how to address him. If you tell him something, he understands it. But as for his answers, only I understand them, through the power of my father's *lha.*

When the *lha* comes down, my consciousness is empty and I am high up in the heavens. If I don't feel good, I make offerings to the deities, and then the *lha* appears to me and I feel better right away. No sooner has the *lha* gone out of me again, I feel full of courage and power.

I'm crazy when the *lha* comes down. And out of this craziness, without quite knowing what I'm doing, I look in the mirror and the answers come by themselves, and I can answer all kinds of questions. The *lha* only makes his appearance when I summon him with prayers. That is the way my father used to do it, and until today nothing has changed in this ritual.

I made a pilgrimage to Thokang Rinpoche and two or three other holy places. Later I visited Otar Rinpoche so that he could open the pulse for the *lha* to come [there is the notion of a divine vein through which the *lha* circulates in the body]. This Rinpoche tested me also.

He sat next to a curtain, and when the Rinpoche pulled it back, I saw a mirror and a person behind it. But the second time he pulled back the curtain, I didn't see anything. . . . Then the Rinpoche asked me to write on a piece of paper what *lha* came to me. And precisely at that moment, he commanded the *lha* to appear. In a further test, the Rinpoche held a piece of paper in each hand. On one of them was the initial letter of the *lha's* name, and on the other was the initial letter of the name of the *dre,* the evil spirit. I was supposed to choose and blindly chose the *lha,* the good god. The *dre,* though, was caught and imprisoned by Rinpoche, so that it could do no more harm.

Only those *lha* are good that serve all of humanity and all beasts. For example, there is the *lha* Tse Tsempo. He is one of the holiest and he helps all people. Nowadays, however, there are lots of lower *lha* that help one person at the most. Then there is the *lha* of Palden Lhamo. He has a red horse's head and three tongues. Compared with the others, he is extremely powerful. For that reason he does not come down into every person. He rules over all of humanity and over all generations. Lha Chen, that is another great *lha.* He is the lord of all the lesser *lha* and knows all their names. There are three hundred and sixty *lha,* all endowed with different powers. But normal *lha* (not counting the spirits of the dead) have no powers at all.

THE SEANCE ATMOSPHERE

Almost all accounts of oracular seances fail to describe the general state of mind, the onlookers' sense of experiential participation. The whole suggestive-hypnotic framework in which the patients are placed or into which they are drawn is an artfully arranged setup that is perhaps equal in effect to the subtle process of the trance.

A session with an oracle is like a short psychotherapeutic treatment, although modern psychology comes nowhere near its power of psychological and emotional impact on the individual. Here, centuries, even millennia, of trial and error in generation after generation have accumulated a clear knowledge of how body and mind, feeling, thought, and action may be consciously altered and influenced.

The hellish din, the wild, unbridled movements of the oracle, the living presence of a god, the unexpressed expectations of the spectators—all this brings about a loss of ego that is further intensified by the general excitement and the tumultuous disorder in one's normal thought flow. In this atmosphere, we find ourselves in another world, which purifies us of our everyday mental pettiness. The tumult of the seance aims at a first level of catharsis. The patients, impressed by the supernatural events, direct their attention entirely toward the arriving god; awe overcomes them.

To begin with, we are dealing with a deluge of stimuli, which then turns in a natural way into stimulus deprivation, a narrowing or focusing of consciousness that is the goal and purpose of the entire drama. Now we are sufficiently prepared to follow the oracle's words with rapt and reverent attention and receive his message in an appropriate manner, for we are inwardly empty.

Helplessly our gaze roves about the extravagant, colorful scene of the drama, always seeming to lag moments behind the action. Everything goes much too fast. Thus compelled by our ineptitude to register everything purely, we are carried away on the current of events. An auditive and visual vortex develops around us that we are incapable of pulling ourselves out of. The high voice of the oracle and the sound of the bell vibrate in our ears. We actually experience the sound waves and feel our own "drumskin" vibrating in sympathy. The collaboration of the drum and bell seem to me to be no accident. The drum in the right hand and the bell in the left complement each other. The low dull sound of the drum and the high-pitched sound of the bell come together. If we really listen and let ourselves be carried along by the rhythm, then we truly enter into the action of the seance, which, if looked at purely in the light of reason, seems to be no more than a jumble of cheap effects. Anyone who does not deliberately fight against the spectacle can for at least a time let himself be drawn into the vortex of this wild symphony. I myself was always carried away again by the breathtaking spectacle, though I would rather have remained a detached observer.

The inner participation of the audience is of great importance, as the oracles also never tire of stressing. Once the ceremony took place under inauspicious circumstances. I had brought a number of other Europeans along, who regarded the goings-on as an insult to their rationality. This not only led to a very short seance, but also provoked the god to unfavorable comments about us. We did not believe in him, and therefore he produced no healing effect for us. The atmosphere was simply no good. As the oracle was constantly interrupted and struck at by the disparaging glances of the European participants, no real trust or mutual attunement could develop. Critical and fault-finding attitudes, lack of understanding and narrow-mindedness had blocked the free impulse to let go of ego.

By contrast, in good seances, I often forgot to keep the watcher in myself alert; I finally gave up my running commentary on events, stopped classifying. And then something developed that I would like to describe as a symphony. I could identify with the dancing shaman, the chanting oracle, and at least from time to time enter into his state of mind, experience in sympathy with him the fragmentation of the ego structure and the external world. I became myself a little bit of a shaman. The urge arose to emulate him. I wanted to jump up and join in his work. His ritual had a contagious effect. As the drama began to draw to a close, I felt a bit crestfallen, disappointed that it was already over. Finally it had been possible to abide in this whirlwind of ego-abandonment, just as a child spins in a circle in order to experience that feeling of giddiness that stands outside our normal ego-defined experience.

Already in the child's game we experience the longing of our kind toward decentralization. Everywhere in the world children have discovered this game, and here lie the true origins of shamanism—in this longing for the happy feeling of ego loss. All of humanity seeks it in its clinging to love, in singing, dancing, dreaming, or spinning in the intoxication of alcohol or drugs. All of these, though diluted, are trance-fostering states or states tending toward trance. Trance is no special or exceptional state. The whole of our emotional life strives toward one point, to attain a pinnacle, the experience of flowing, in which compulsive and rational moments, which always dam the flow, are disabled. Our overall human quest for good humor, for feeling good, present here only as a hint, reaches the point of intense feeling in trance. And the whole atmosphere of the seance is itself in some way only a reduced, diluted reflection of the trance itself, of that state of sympathetic flow, dissolution, emptying out, pure being.

8

THE VISION QUEST

The real vision has to come out of your own juices. It is not a dream; it is very real. It hits you sharp and clear like an electric shock. You are wide awake and, suddenly, there is a person standing next to you who you know can't be there at all. Or somebody is sitting close by, and all at once you see him also up on a hill half a mile away. Yet you are not dreaming; your eyes are open. You have to work for this, empty your mind for it.

—LAME DEER
and ERDOES
(1972, 53–54)

Fay Clark was adopted for two years by Chief Michael Red Cloud, a Winnebago from Wisconsin, and was sent on a vision quest. He recounted his experiences to writer Brad Steiger. At the age of around thirteen, he and others were tutored for several weeks on what to expect and then were asked to go and pick a spot in the woods near a stream. They were not to bring food or look for any kind of wild food, nor were they to seek shelter, but instead had to be exposed to the elements. They were to weaken their bodies and pray at least three times a day for their guide. The main idea was to exhaust the body as quickly as possible, occupying the mind with a monotonous physical activity while the subconscious mind focused on finding the guide.

After a while, one would begin to see wildlife that would seemingly become friendlier. After a time, some creature would approach, as if to offer itself as a totem, or guide. It could be bird, a chipmunk, a gopher, a badger. If the boy were very hungry, and if he were afraid of staying out in the wilderness alone, he could accept the first creature that approached and say that he had found his guide. But we were taught that if we could endure, Manitou, or one of his representatives in human form, would appear and talk to us.

I spent twelve days fasting and awaiting my guide. I had many creatures, including a beautiful deer, come up to me and allow me to pet them. The deer, especially, wanted to stay. But I had been told that if I did not want to accept a form of life that offered itself to me, I should thank it for coming, tell it of its beauty, its strength, its intelligence, but tell it also that I was seeking one greater.

On the twelfth day, an illuminated form appeared before me. Although it seemed composed primarily of light, it did have features and was clothed in a long robe.

"You I have waited for," I said. And it replied, "You have sought me, and you I have sought."

Then it faded away. But it had appeared before me just as real as you are. (Quoted in Steiger 1974, 144)

It is difficult for us outsiders to relate to the meaning and significance of the vision and power quest as it is carried out by members of Native American tribes. Such spiritual exercises are unfamiliar to Western psychology. The conflict with the scientific worldview and their religious origin make them doubly suspicious. They strike us as primitive, savage, even unnatural. The suffering and exhaustion that accompany a vision quest do not correspond to the mild and gentle style of modern psychotherapy. Westerners do not want to have to exert themselves to solve their problems. Our milder way is the way of a materially sated existence that, within the protective sphere of economic well-being, is content with little spiritual profundity and vitality. But the radical spiritual cure entails injury, pain, and inhumanity. No civilized person believes in finding salvation through pain. Rendered secure by the existence of hospitals and the medical establishment, Westerners banishes all suffering from their perspective. Since it has required all our effort and intelligence to keep suffering out of our world, why should we bring it back in again? Is it not the real achievement of the West to have liberated humankind from a raw and rugged struggle for survival and physical pain by extricating people from their natural conditions?

In the outlook of Westerners today, dependence on nature seems reprehensible, even archaic, and every contact with the natural world seems to us like a descent into primitivity. Anthropology has developed completely within this mindset. Its theories and research strategies are pervaded by it, and if one were to try to divest anthropology of its theory of the separation between humanity and environment, its entire structure would be in peril of crumbling. It is inextricably bound up with an attitude of praise for the comfortable life, a state without suffering, as well as with the idea that culture is the antagonist of nature. Thus, anthropology has no choice but to classify everything that strikes it as uncivilized under the pejorative heading of "primitivity," which it conceives of as hostile. As a result, it regards all ecstasies and trances as the products of undeveloped minds; it regards every spiritual gesture and mystical perception as an act of unreason and alienation from civilization. For Westerners, the inmost essence of culture is remoteness from nature; artificial—that is, nature-rejecting—culture has become our second, and supposedly better, nature.

Against this background, the views that ethnologists carry into the field become easier to understand. In our technologized culture, they too have lost touch not only with the outer world of nature but with their own inner nature. At most in our society, one may still find relics of our primordial nature in psychiatric institutions; but even there the psychology industry has found ways and means to still the primordial nature in people. As our institution of sociotechnical pacification, it distorts the last vestiges of the "savage" psyche and renders them meaningless and harmless. The manifold "archaic" drives of our psyche are enveloped in a thick layer of Freudian and behavioristic theoretical artifacts that restrain the richness and the developmental potential of the real psyche.

If civilization has taken a path of refined and indirect knowledge, tribal culture has taken a path of immediate knowledge. It is a hard path, fraught with privations. What is more immediate than to seek out solitude untouched by humanity, to withhold from oneself the biological needs of one's body, to fast, to be silent, alone, without family or group relations, to be exposed to the rigors of the elements, a naked child under the stars? It is no accident that in vision quests, everything that recalls culture, such as clothes and material objects, is taken away, and only sacred objects are kept. Also, ordinary activities are excluded. Without the protection of the family and the tribe, the initiate, continually vulnerable to the dangers of storms, lightning, and wild animals, is thrown entirely back on his or her own resources. When they are liberated from their daily concerns, the real, latent powers of the psyche, unobstructed by the trappings of civilization, fill the consciousness.

Vision. Even the sound of this word evokes for most people in industrial culture a sense of antediluvian, barbaric archaism. But the principle of the vision quest is not simply to return to "naked existence"; rather, the initiate is to take in the forces surrounding us entirely without the various intellectual filtering systems and cultural prisms to which we are accustomed. Our organism then begins to work, and a kind of unconscious self-regulation sets in. This is the free play of the unconstrained nature of our own mind. It is hardly surprising that people in tribal cultures, who live closer to the heart of nature and thus to the center of their own consciousness have found the way to this "psychotherapy." The biochemical processes are set in motion; fasting takes its effect; consciousness spins its own threads; and firmly rooted cultural categories loosen up and fall away. As we experience hunger and thirst and pain and intensely wish for genuine contact with a spiritual power that transcends our own existence, the last physiological and sensory stabilizing mechanisms that hold our perception and emotions in balance fall apart. Then a new world unfolds—a vision is born.

The visionary experience is not limited to people in traditional societies; others who follow the same methods have similar experiences. Vinson Brown, a writer on Native American subjects, describes his four visions on the sacred mountain Bear Butte, which he experienced under the guidance of Fools Crow, the ceremonial chief of the Oglala Sioux. Here is one of his visions:

> So I concentrated on singing my prayers outward as hard as I could as if my spirit were rushing out in all directions, and gradually the

initial overwhelming tendency to shiver stopped. . . . So I lay down on my rocky bed and tried to sleep, though it was nearly impossible because of the rocks stabbing into my back no matter what way I turned. But somehow, four times I managed to find a snatch of sleep that night and in each of those four brief moments of slumber I had a vision.

The first one was perhaps the most strange and weird, yet somehow not frightening. I sensed that a huge man was standing beside me in the darkness, a man of immense power. He soon reached down and placed his arms under my body and lifted me as if I were as light as a fluff of down. Then he carried me about a hundred yards down the mountainside till we came to the opening of a cave. Into this cave he carried me about fifty feet, it seemed, until we came to a room that was filled with a suffused light. The room was carpeted deeply with sweet-smelling sagebrush, sacred to the Sioux, and on this he placed me. As I felt myself sinking into that softness, for this sagebrush bed was far deeper and softer than my primitive bed of sagebrush on the mountain top, I felt surrounded by warmth, comfort and protection, a most happy contented feeling after the cold wind and the sharp rocks above. As I lay there he spoke to me six words: "Here you will be all right!" (Brown 1974, 170ff.)

Fools Crow told him later that his vision was *washtai! washtai!*— very good, very good. The first vision was explained by Fools Crow as meaning that the Mountain Spirit, as representative of the Great Spirit, had acknowledged Brown's purified spirit.

Another example is that of the first Guardian of the Feathered Pipe of the Gros Ventre, Whistling Man, to whom the Pipe said that every guardian could hold it for four years, and then it would tell him who should receive it next. It happened this way with five guardians, all of whom were endowed with the highest supernatural powers. After the first five, another sixteen were to follow, of which the first fifteen would possess various powers and the sixteenth, omnipotent supernatural powers. This cycle of sixteen pipe holders would then be thrice repeated, until finally a total of four guardians with extraordinary powers had watched over the pipe.

The last pipe holder with power was the sixteenth man of the fourth cycle, Bull Lodge, who died in 1880. After that, the guardians had only slight powers or were without supranormal powers.

Before Bull Lodge died, he called his people together and said: "My heart is sad; I grieve for my son, the Feathered Pipe. It will not be long before its powers vanish. There will be three more guardians after me, and then its task will be complete." Before Bull Lodge died, he had a vision, which Fred Gone recounted to the ethnologist Verne Dusenberry. A voice said to him one night:

"You have eight more days to live. There are seven who watch you. Four of these have been wanting to take you from the Earth, but three have not been in agreement that you should come. Now, these three have had the influence to check your coming, but they have given up and have consented that you be taken. So, your time is coming. You have eight more days to live. Now, prepare yourself. Just watch and wait."

Bull Lodge said nothing to his family. Each day he sat in his tipi and marked the time with a piece of charcoal. When he put six or seven marks on the tipi, he had a vision. Off to the East where the sun comes he saw a man standing on a ridge. The sky was getting golden, and the man stood there silhouetted against the rays. Just as the sun came up, a man approached. Bull Lodge saw that he was carrying a staff that was painted red and that he was dressed as a Pipe Keeper.

"I will give you this stick," said the man when he had neared Bull Lodge. "In your life time, things have been given you when you appealed for what you wanted. You have practiced things as you should have done. You have used your powers correctly. Nothing has been denied you. Now, I'm the last one to come to you—the final one. I am going to give you a crowning glory—something that is going to be a Supreme Power for man on this earth. That Power will be the resurrection.

"From your marks on the tipi, you know that you have just one more day. Your time is coming near. Assemble your family and pass along to them the information that I am going to tell you. Listen carefully to me, for these are the directions you must tell your family.

" 'I must die,' you must say. 'When I die, and if you want me back again, you must do these things.

" 'First, you must make four sweat tents and place them in a line that runs east and west. The one farthest east you must make with twenty willows; the next one, use eighteen; the next one, sixteen willows, and the last one—the one to the west—you must use four-teen willows. These four sweat lodges must be covered with four buffalo hides each. Then over each of these lodges must be placed a tipi, and each of these tipis must be made from buffalo hides. The robes on the sweat lodges must be placed according to the cardinal directions.'

"After the lodges are made, and the tipis placed over them, [tell your family that they must] have someone raise the robes on the sweat lodges so that there are openings to both the east and the west. So, likewise, must the tipis be opened. Now when all this is done, four men must take your body and carry it to this row of tipis. When the men carry your body in, two of them must be at your head and two at your feet. They must take you into the first lodge through the east entrance and place you on a bed of incense that they have prepared for you. They will lay your body on that bed and light other incense that has been prepared. Then, the two men at your head will go out through the west opening and the two at your feet will back out through the east opening, closing the openings after them.

"When the men have sung four songs, [you must tell your family,] they are to open the flaps and in exactly the same manner go to the second lodge within the second tipi and repeat exactly the same performance. When all has been completed there, the men will carry your body in exactly the same manner into the third lodge. Again, the same procedure is to be followed. While the men are singing the third song there, however, they will hear a movement in the lodge. They are not to become frightened but will sing the fourth song, and then again, in exactly the same way, the men are to carry you into the fourth lodge, light the incense, close the flaps, and while the men are singing, I will call you.

" 'Rides Tight, come forth,' I'll say. I shall repeat that call every time the men sing their song. On the fourth and last time when I make that call, you will come out the west side of the sweat lodge. Then, you will come back to life again if the people want you to do it and will follow these instructions. These are the instructions you shall give to your family. That is the Power that I will bestow upon you as the last one—the last great Keeper of the Feathered Pipe."

That day, Bull Lodge called his family together and told them of his vision and gave them the instructions that he had received. That night his family was with him. About midnight, he told his family to go to bed—all except his eldest son and his wife. Suddenly, Bull Lodge made a noise like a bear and trembled. When he quit trembling, his son and wife looked at him and realized he was dead.

The family called the people in the camp together and told them of the prophecy. A great conclave was held to decide whether they should follow the instructions given to them. In the end they decided that it was impossible to follow his instructions. The buffalo lodges and robes were gone. The Gros Ventre way of life was ending. Soon the Feathered Pipe would lose its Powers, too. But, it had tried to give one man, Bull Lodge, the greatest Power bestowed upon any man—resurrection. (Dusenberry 1961, 23ff.)

Native American children are prepared for fasting as early as their sixth year. Endurance of pain, contact with supernatural mysteries, solitude, and fear of the forces of nature bring them in touch with a spiritual protector who will guide them through life with a sure hand. Physical and psychological withdrawal phenomena bring to life an unconscious depth in us; they cause the individual's life situation and secret wishes to appear in the form of metaphorical visions. The suppression of sense perceptions and of normal body processes is the most effective way to attune body and mind to the transpersonal dimension. This way, the inner wisdom of body and psyche are activated.

A person wishing contact with the inner self must first disable all the mechanisms that maintain a stable ego fixed on the events of the external world. From time immemorial, the means of achieving this disabling have been solitude, monotony, and narrowly focusing the concentration by means of prayer and chant. Through these means, everyday reality becomes vague and dissolves, replaced by a visionary, paralogical, inner reality. We, however, tend too quickly to regard this visionary experience as a purely inner phenomenon. For visionaries, there is no inside and no outside; both meet in a single point—in consciousness; and consciousness becomes for them a factor that binds mind and matter and the outer and inner world with each other. What is within is also without and vice versa. The opposites that characterize our normal reality are resolved at this point. For the visionary, it is not inner experiences alone that exist; beings from the other world also leave behind traces and signs in our material world. Animals approach the adept, touch his body, and speak to him. The visionary is in harmony with the world around him; the result is that the separation between different kinds of living beings becomes extraneous and communication between different species becomes possible.

During his pipe fast, Arthur Amiotte, a contemporary Sioux artist and a student of the Lakota medicine man Pete Catches, saw eagles circling above him repeatedly, giving him the feeling that it was they who were leading the fasting ceremony. He refers frequently to the connection between all the elements of nature and all animals. The behavior of nature toward the seeker is a mirror image of his own state. Amiotte, who during his first fast had several experiences of this nature with clouds, cows, and hawks, tells us how he developed an inner relationship to a bird:

A little brown bird flew close and sat in a pine tree about ten feet from the square. I addressed it as I had the butterfly; there were other birds in the trees to the north, east and south, and they circled as though in response. A feeling of communication and of being a natural part of that place made me feel that I wanted to stay there forever. One of the birds, a blue one, remained long after the others flew away, and returned daily for the next two days, always coming by itself to the same tree where it sat for hours regarding me. I offered it the pipe each time. I did not know then that it would return for the next three years to sit in a tree to the east of me and, in the third year, sing me a song of encouragement, the words of which I would understand on my third pipe fast and sing on my fourth. (Amiotte 1976, 35)

Former physicist Gerhard Kunze, who for a long time lived with the Mexican Huichol, had similar experiences after the shaman Pedro de Haro had said to him: "For five days you may neither eat nor drink. And then on the fifth day, when you drink, the old woman (Great-Grandmother Earth) will appear." "Five days?" asked Kunze, horrified. "But nobody could survive that!" Pedro replied with emphasis: "It is possible to survive that!" (Kunze 1982, 86). Kunze is one of the few Europeans who has had the courage to undertake shamanic techniques of consciousness. He set out to get through the first practice of *mara'akame:* fasting, solitude, prayer. Even on the first day, as he wandered through the valley of the Rio Verde, he saw "signs" and had strange encounters with animals. A heron accompanied him for an entire day, always flying a hundred meters in front of him in a particular direction. Occasionally, it would land and wait for Kunze. Later, an eagle accompanied him and showed him the easiest way through the bush until Kunze could do without its advice. Then it flew away. He also received another kind of sign: every time he needed help, he opened the Bible, the only book he had brought with him, at random to a passage. As if it were a book of oracles, the passage he opened the Bible to each time gave him an astonishingly appropriate response.

Later, toward the end of the fasting period, out of extreme thirst Kunze wanted to take just a taste from a spring. But a big Mexican hornet stung him in the leg, which quickly swelled up. Would he now be unable to make his way back through the valley to civilization? He was overcome by mortal fear. He knelt and prayed. After two minutes, the pain subsided, and after a few more minutes the swelling and the sting wound vanished completely. Had the hornet protected him from prematurely breaking off his experiment?

It is always astounding that through the simplest alterations of consciousness, we can enter a world of living interaction and unity. Objects acquire meaning, animals relate to us, even enter into an inseparable unity with our situation, and randomly opened books reveal our mental state. A world of synchronicity, of signs and meanings, arises, a universe of the *unio mystica* in which we need not feel ourselves lost.

Although the vision is a transpersonal expression whose images and symbology are universal, it is nonetheless definitely tied to culture. By contrast, the essence of the transpersonal and the mystical is without symbology and without form—its nature is absolute purity. That is, at least, the way it is understood in Eastern philosophy. The yogi strives for complete formlessness, complete emptiness; Zen Buddhism seeks formless enlightenment. In tribal cultures, on the other hand, transpersonal experiences remain for the most part attached to the realm of forms and images. This does not, however, mean that the mystical experiences, of shamans are unlike those of Eastern saints and yogis. It seems to me, rather, that tribal cultures represent formless enlightenment in an outward fashion, symbolically, since they have to survive in a world that requires that they maintain more concrete relationships to the environment than the world of monasteries and meditation caves.

In states of intoxication induced by alcohol or drugs, as well as in fatigue and exhaustion, we readily see images in natural formations like clouds, mountains, and other geographical features. We also see patterns and phantoms, even whole films dancing before our eyes—we hallucinate. When the brain is isolated from external data, it can produce its own worlds on the basis of stored excitation patterns. But we can go still further, beyond the level of phantasmagoria. We then land in a spiritual sphere, the reaching of which is the goal of all esoteric and occult philosophies. Here we touch upon a sphere of consciousness in which we are able to communicate with the dead, spirits, animal entities, and amorphous beings, or with the creative principle, the superself. After a still further step and still further effort, we may enter into a "psychic emptiness," a space that is without the frame of reference of human existence— the absolute. The visionary experience is for the most part imaginal and metaphorical. It therefore corresponds not to the apex of mystical introspection but to a deeper psychic depth or the transpersonal sphere.

The physiological and biochemical analysis of visionary experience remains incomplete, but it is what is necessary to provide a truly scientific access to these phenomena. I have already referred to Aldous Huxley's view (1963, 150–54) that in the European Middle Ages visions were significantly more frequent, because for many people, during the winter and the six-week period of fasting, as a result of malnutrition and vitamin deficiency, fundamental psychological and biochemical changes took place that were conducive to visionary experience. Today, as a result of improved living conditions alone, visions account for a very small proportion of psychological phenomena. Self-mortification, too, has largely died out, but it heightens the possibility of visions, for through it large quantities of adrenaline and histamine are released, which influence consciousness. The canonized nineteenth-century Catholic mystic Jean Vianney remarked on this point, after his bishop forbade him to torment himself: "When I could do with my body what I wanted, God refused me nothing."

When a visionary encounters holiness, his life changes abruptly. Now that he has drunk from life's profound wellsprings, has been bathed in life force, and felt something of the essence of primordial existence, he is suddenly endowed with extrasensory perception, precognition, the ability to leave his body, to see spirits, and the like. He has received attributes of sacred existence and has himself become a messenger, an epiphany of holiness. Through his supramundane powers, he manifests a higher world.

Such transpersonal experiences are unfamiliar to today's psychotherapy. Nonetheless, they could be meaningfully applied to psychological healing and integration. The states induced by breaking physical and psychological habits could complement Western healing procedures. We have before us a mysterious realm of the psyche. When we begin to give our attention to it, we will have much to learn from shamans.

Since most anthropologists and psychologists do not try out on themselves such techniques as fasting and going without liquids, staying for a long time in a natural environment praying and alone, visions tend to seem to them to be pathological manifestations of the brain, hallucinations, or mental confusion. These researchers not only refuse to try these techniques, they also refuse thereby to test the research results of the modern psychology of consciousness. The denial of the existence of a more all-embracing spiritual reality is as old as psychology itself. In psychology, a new discovery can prevail against established opinion only with tremendous effort. When we compare the history of resistance to dream interpretation, the unconscious, and research into sexuality with present-day resistance to the transpersonal and the unconscious, we see that nothing has changed in people's fear of the riches of the psyche.

9

INNER EYES, DOUBLE VISION

From where I am lying here on the sand I can look right to Seventh Heaven and envision everything that is transpiring in the four planes of the spirit world and the three planes of heaven. I wish the veils that separate the supernatural from human vision could be torn from your eyes for even a minute so that you too could envision what I see. But you are yet too earthly-minded and bogged down with the trivial trials and tribulations of mundane living.　—TA RUAHINE,
an old Hawaiian fisherwoman (in Melville 1969)

Joemin, a medicine man of the Australian Kakadu who subsequently became a mythical hero, once noticed his own shadow as he was bending over the edge of a watering hole. He stuck his head under the water and opened his eyes in the process called *karareyu poro*, "washing the eyes." Through this technique a person becomes clairvoyant and learns to see into the distance or through trees and people (Petri 1952, 205).

Similarly, the Tierra del Fuegans speak of spiritual seeing, or *asikaku*, and the Hawaiians of *papalua*, double vision or double knowledge. The Australian *rai* speak of the inner eye with which they perceive the invisible, and the Senegalese Badyaranke of the "eyes of the night," which are between the normal eyes or beside them.

From time immemorial fantastic abilities have been attributed to shamans, and they themselves have not hesitated to boast of the most venturesome spiritual experiences. All tribal traditions re-count bizarre tales of mysterious powers. Academia has taken pleasure in this colorful collection of the unreal, so long as it could view its components as fairy tales, myths, or productions of the primitive mind. But the moment researchers claimed to seriously investigate these powers, they brought down the wrath of the academic community upon themselves. My own approach takes a pragmatic-realistic stance—that is, it infers behind the magical world a genuine spiritual and transpersonal experience. With this, we very quickly reach the limits of our ability to explain by means of present-day science the powers that arise from intensive psycho-logical transformation. The only field of research that provides us with any help is parapsychology, but so far the effective biological and psychological factors of transpsychic communication have re-mained hidden even from that discipline. Any way you look at it, the research methods of the academic disciplines appear limited. Fear of the unknown closes researchers' minds; an overblown self-evaluation misdirects their attention. For this reason, the psy-chology of primitive peoples cannot open for us the gates to their secret knowledge, for the mystery that we have failed to unlock until now is our own—the mystery of our own investigative self-limitation.

Even the great ethnologist Robert Lowie (1979) characterized North American Pawnee medicine men as "masters of sleight-of-hand" and their abilities as tricks. But in the ethnological literature there are scarcely any serious suggestions—let alone investiga-tions—of how these "tricks" are executed. Would-be exposés are generally limited to imaginative speculations. Even such straight-forward phenomena as walking in fire and the concomitant con-scious elimination of pain were believed to be cheap tricks. Today, however, these phenomena can be explained as psychophysiological self-control. Let us now take a look at the wide range of shamans' heroic feats and powers.

Martin Gusinde (1931, vol. 1, 775ff.) tells us that Adam, a Selk'nam tribesman of Tierra del Fuego, stuck three arrows into his body behind the collarbone, and they came out on the side of his body between the ribs. Gusinde explicitly states that this ability could have nothing to do with a hypnotic deception or any kind of charlatanism; it had to be based on real mastery over the body. Not only did the *xon*, the shamans, stick arrows through their arms and legs, they drove sharp objects into other people's shoulders without those involved either bleeding or feeling pain.

Gusinde observed a *xon* who had been beaten in wrestling and, ashamed of his defeat, wanted to make a show of his magic. He caused pus to flow from his collarbone area without any visible wound. Other *xon* brought about bleeding through concentration and ended it again at will. Still others made women infertile by a single stroke of their bellies.

Many recognized ethnographers have recorded observations that leave no doubt that they had witnessed psychophysical feats beyond the possibilities accepted by conventional medicine. Let us look at a few short descriptions of turning off pain, raising inner body temperature, and making the body fireproof. Franz Boas describes the following experience among the Eskimo:

> An angakoq began his incantations in a hut after the lamps were lowered. Suddenly he jumped up and rushed out of the hut to where a mounted harpoon was standing. He threw himself upon the harpoon, which penetrated his breast and came out at the back. Three men followed him and holding the harpoon line led the angakoq, bleeding profusely, to all the huts of the village. When they arrived again at the first hut he pulled out the harpoon, lay down on the bed, and was put to sleep by the songs of another angakoq. When he awoke after a while he showed to the people that he was not hurt, although his clothing was torn and they had seen him bleeding. (Boas 1964, 260)

Teb-Tengri, the magician who conferred the title Genghis Khan on the great Mongol emperor and went down in history with him, is supposed to have possessed control over magical flight and fire. He asserted of himself: "God speaks to me and I travel up to the heavens." In frigid cold, Teb-Tengri ran naked through the desert, and in the wintertime he sat down on the ice of frozen river. With the heat of his body, he melted the ice and steam rose from his body. A similar power is attributed to Qutula, the great-uncle of Genghis Khan. When he slept by a fire and the coals from a collapsing tree trunk fell on his skin, the most he did was scratch himself as though he had been bitten by an insect (Boyle 1972, 181f.).

The Alagiri Buryats recount of their shaman Machunaj that he possessed the ability to move on a sled without horses. When the Irkutsk government was about to forbid shamanism, all the shamans were required to assemble to demonstrate their powers. Machunaj had seventy loads of hay brought, sat down in the middle of them with his sorcerer's drum, and had them set on fire. The hay burned till none was left; then Machunaj climbed, unharmed, out of the ashes. With this, the government permitted the shamans to continue their activities (Nioradze 1925, 102).

Among the Luiseño, medicine people could put whole feather headdresses in the fire without their burning. One shaman, Turiyo, threw his feather headdress into the fire. Everyone smelled the scorched feathers and saw them burning. Turiyo circled the fire, looked around, and picked up his feather headdress lying not far away on the ground. The Luiseño also built huge fires, as big as a house, and the old men would jump into them and stay in the flames for several minutes. There would be an odor of scorched feathers, but they themselves would be unharmed (DuBois 1908).

Also in North America, the shamans of the Penobscot killed and wounded animals simply by pointing their fingers at them. If they were fleeing from enemies, they could make themselves invisible. They could leave footprints in solid rock, easily lift thick pieces of ice, walk through solid obstacles like doors, roll away heavy rocks, remain for a long time under water, recognize animals as disguised people, and cause their bodies to shrink or grow. Of course, they also possessed the powers of levitation, precognition, telepathy, and clairvoyance (Speck 1919).

Eskimo shamans can walk under water, stick quills into rock, walk through solid rock, drive fish out of the sea onto land to catch them more easily, talk to animals, move masses of snow that are blocking the way either on land or water, or change pack ice into smooth ice. The Eskimo believe that their shades, or souls, can disengage themselves from the shamans and move about quite independently of them. When this happens, it is thought, the shamans become transparent so that even normal people can see through them. In general, it is believed that shamans are capable of looking into other people as deep as their skeletons and thus seeing their nature. The shaman's "X-ray vision" is particularly highly emphasized in Eskimo cultures. Eskimo shamans are also said to possess the ability to grow a beard in seconds and to squeeze blood out of snow; having been tied up, to free themselves immediately; and to make a severed cord whole again by putting it in their mouths. Shamans also wound themselves just to show how they can heal themselves afterward. For this purpose, as already described, they stab themselves with their harpoons, shoot or burn themselves, or cut a finger off. Among the Copper Eskimo, shamans enter into contact with the spirits and thus can see in the dark and predict things that are about to happen, as well as smell the vapor that emanates from menstruating or pregnant women. Shamans read the future and perceive other people's secrets, sins, and the character of their thoughts. They see the souls of the dead and hear their conversations. They know the hiding places of game animals. In fact, they see, hear, and know everything (Blodgett 1978).

Dapic, a Crow shaman, was famous for his supernatural powers. He caused beets and berries to grow in winter, changed tree bark into dried meat, and healed his shot wounds (Lowie 1951, 30ff.).

The shamans of the Mossi of the Sudan enter ecstasies by dancing, then perform all kinds of feats. They emit monkeys and dogs from their mouths. They sow seeds that immediately sprout, bear fruit, then wither. They spew so much water from their mouths that they can stand up to their necks in it. They cut other people's throats, then immediately heal them. On their outstretched arms they make swallows appear out of nowhere, or make horns grow out of their heads and change themselves into wild animals—lions, wild pigs, and leopards (Friedrich 1939, 306).

The shamans of the North American Papago accompanied their war parties. They spoke with the spirits of Papago warriors who had fallen in enemy territory and then acted as spies, informing the shamans about the movements of hostile Apache troops.

The Hopi believe that seers can bear any pain. They possess the ability to project themselves into a person hitting them and make that person feel the pain of the blows (Simmons 1976, 74ff.).

The Siberian shaman Katshikat-Ojun of the Nasleg of Katshikat, about whom many stories are told, invited his colleague, the shaman Solkolooch, to accompany him on a journey. As they were trying to reach various towns, at one point they were obliged to cross the Lena. Katshikat-Ojun bound a willow twig ornamented with carvings on his feet and ran across the river, while Solkolooch attracted a boat from the other bank by making clicking noises and crossed the water in that (Ksenofontov, in Friedrich and Buddruss 1955, 188).

The shaman Küstach-Ojun of the second Nasleg of Maldshegar was once on a journey with two companions. On the left bank of the Lena, they were overtaken by night and lost their way in the dark. One of Küstach-Ojun's companions asked him if he wouldn't make use of his powers before they perished of the cold. Küstach-Ojun then asked the younger of his two companions to break a branch from a willow and carve a pattern on it. After he had struck the snow with the branch, a blue fire kindled itself out of nowhere. The fire then showed them the way to the settlement, where it finally disappeared without a trace (ibid., 185f.).

The *yékamus* of the Yamana of Tierra del Fuego were capable of expanding their (psychic) bodies until they covered more than ten meters. Within this zone of influence, the medicine man perceived everything as if it were part of his body (Gusinde 1931, vol. 2, 1390). And as various ethnographers assure us, the weather could be calmed as soon as a *yékamus* deigned to make use of his influence. In the *loimayekamus,* the Yamana school for medicine men, several medicine men always banded together to keep the weather favorable. When the Tierra del Fuegans' food supplies were menaced by storms, only the *yékamus* were able to avert the danger. For luck in hunting, the *yékamus* intoned his *cowanni* chant: he looked into the distance, stretched out his arms, drew back his closed hands, and pressed their invisible contents against his body. These movements attracted the *kespixes,* the souls of the animals. In a trance state, he called the *cowanni* spirits, who at once drove whole schools of herring and other fish onto the shore where the people suffering the shortage were living. The *cowanni* spirits also caused many round crabs to run up on the beach, birds to land on nearby stones, and whole families of whales to be stranded on the beach. After they had accomplished their work, the *yékamus* released the spirits again to the high seas.

Foreknowledge of all kinds made life under raw natural conditions easier. Gusinde reports that a *yékamus* said: "I see out there a long canoe with *touwisiwa* [a kind of bird] approaching!" The following day swarms of these birds did in fact appear. The devastating epidemics that plagued the Tierra del Fuegans were also foretold well in advance in prophecies (Gusinde 1931, vol. 2).

Helmut Petri recounts how, as a member of the Frobenius expedition of 1938, he stayed for a time at the indigenous settlement of Munja on Walcott Inlet in the northern Kimberley Division of Australia. There he had an inexplicable experience. A colleague of his rode to Brockman Creek in the northern part of the settlement and did not return until after dusk. When they talked in the evening, it came out that both Petri and his colleague had had a conversation at the same time with Yáobida, a native, and both conversations had been on the same subject, the kinship relations in the tribe. They were completely bewildered. How could Yáobida have been in two different places simultaneously and had two conversations on the same subject (Petri 1984)?

Many paranormal powers were ascribed to Old Wabik, a shaman of the North American Micmac. He could stop rifle bullets and cannon shot with his chest, and he possessed astonishing control over the elements. He could also produce devastating storms. Another shaman, Sapiel Syamau, was in the habit of smoking a clay pipe; when he was not smoking it, he wound it around his hat like a hatband without breaking it. With his bare hands he bent or dented church bells, especially when they disturbed his storytelling. Once he stopped a windmill because the miller had refused an old Micmac woman flour. For similar reasons, the Micmac shaman Morris caused a farmer's cow to stop giving milk for twenty-four hours. Gabriel, another Micmac shaman, played a prank on a priest: he made his boat sail backward so that the cleric was unable to reach his destination.

Shamans also, of course, use their powers for their own purposes, as in gambling, when they make the dice fall the right way. In general, shamans often support one side in a public sports event and try to manipulate the game for their side. Psychokinetic and clairvoyant influences play a prominent role in this (Johnson 1943, 77f.).

Hundreds of anecdotes about shamans influencing the weather are scattered in books, magazines, and travel accounts. Today, no thorough presentation, however, that is more than a collection of unprovable personal experiences is available yet. Though the various accounts repeatedly express surprise over an abrupt change in weather following a pertinent ritual, a causal connection has not hitherto been proven. Future research can no longer content itself with marginal remarks and subjective commentaries. Ethnology, to the extent that it wishes to treat shamanism adequately, must adopt the standards of the experimental sciences and make properly controlled investigations. When researchers and travelers are confronted with psychic manipulations of the weather, their initial reaction is bewilderment, then acknowledgment that a connection does exist between the ritual and the weather change. Yet after a few reflections we always find the same remark: "Though there are things that we cannot explain, really it cannot be true!" And here, so far, ethnology has let the matter rest.

The Paviotso shaman Jack Wilson made rain when he visited Sweetwater, Nevada. He began his ritual by taking a crow feather from his hat and fanning it about in front of his face. Immediately clouds formed, and soon it began to rain. When he stopped waving the feather, the rain stopped (Park 1934, 108).

The Lakota medicine man Lame Deer tells us:

> When I was a little boy I had a party where we played games. It was drizzling and I was mad. We wanted to play and the weather wouldn't let us. My grandma said, "Why don't you make the picture of a turtle?" Before we were through making it, the rain stopped. I could dry the country up, or make a special upside-down turtle and flood everything. You have to know the right prayer with it, the right words. I won't tell you what they are. That's too dangerous. You don't fool around with it. I see that white man's look on your face. You don't believe this. (Lame Deer and Erdoes 1972, 125)

Pete Catches, another Lakota medicine man, was able to keep a threatening storm away from a sun dance:

> A lot of people wanted to get away, to go home before the storm broke. And it was nearing, coming on fast. So, during the course of the dance, they handed me my pipe, the pipe that I always use. I call it my chief pipe. So I took that and asked the Great Spirit to part that

thunder, part it in half, so we can finish our ceremony. Before all the people that great storm parted, right before their eyes. The one part went to the north, wrought havoc in the White River country, clear on in, tore off the roofs, destroyed the gardens and acted like that. The part of the storm which went south, toward Pine Ridge, covered everything with hail, but on the dance ground the sun kept shining. (Ibid., 126)

The direction and steadiness of the wind also is within the control of the shaman. Among the Paviotso, when the river was still frozen in spring but the people needed fish to eat, they turned to a shaman from Pyramid Lake who possessed the ability to produce a warm wind that would melt the ice. The shaman sang, and indeed the ice drifted away. The people caught many fish and gave the shaman some of their catch. He could accept payment only in the form of fish; otherwise he would have lost his power (Park 1938, 60f.).

Franc Johnson Newcomb, the famous Navajo medicine man Hosteen Klah, and some others were on their way from Albuquerque to the Navajo reservation when they encountered a tornado that was about to cross the road about a half-mile in front of them. They stopped their car. Klah got out of the car and ran fearlessly toward the whirlwind. Newcomb writes:

We were already beginning to feel the side winds sucking in toward the center, when, to our horror, it turned directly toward us. We had all been standing in front of the car watching the progress of the funnel; now I told the girls to hurry and rushed to climb into the car. But not Klah. He started walking slowly toward the whirling mass, which was approaching with the sound of a thousand swarms of bees. Stooping now and then to pick up a pinch of earth or part of a desert plant, he put the accumulation into his mouth even while he was chanting. We could not very well turn around and go away, leaving him to face the tornado alone, and anyway, it was now much too late to make our escape, so we simply sat there—four of the most frightened humans anyone ever knew. Klah continued to walk slowly into the eddying wind, then suddenly held up both hands and spewed the mixture in his mouth directly at the approaching column and raised his voice to a loud chant. The columns stood still for a moment and then divided in the center of the hourglass, the upper part rising to be obscured by the low hanging clouds and the lower half spinning away at right angles to its former course like a great upside-down top. (Newcomb 1964, 198f.)

The ethnologist Paul Radin recorded a few stories about the Winnebago medicine man Midjistega. Like many other medicine persons, Midjislega had mastered the art of transforming things and producing them out of nothing. Once, when the men in the cabin began their chanting, Midjistega went around them on all fours four times, took some charcoal from the fire, and shook it about in his hand. Suddenly his teeth began to protrude like those of a grizzly bear, and he roared like a real bear. He put the charcoal into a bowl and as he once more went around the fire four times, it was transformed into gunpowder. He threw a handful of it into the fire, where it exploded. Later, in a similar fashion, he produced tobacco, colorful paint, and even axes, pickaxes, and awls. Then he declared, "As I have made almost everything, I will now try and make some whisky. If I fail, there will be no harm done anyhow."

Once Midjistega went to the trading post to trade his skins for corn meal. He said to the trader, "Say, trader, the boys have been out of paint for some time and you ought to give them some."

"No, Midjistega, I can't do that."

"Well," said Midjistega, "the paint boxes are small and not too much value anyhow, and you ought to make them a present of some. However, I knew you were very stingy."

The trader replied, "My business is to trade my wares for your furs, and I will not give you any paint for nothing."

"If I had some flour," said Midjistega, "I could make some paint myself. However, I am short of flour too."

One answer led to another, until finally the trader proposed a bet. If Midjistega was able to make paint by himself, he would get the trader's entire store; if, however, he failed to do this, the trader would get all of Midjistega's skins and pelts.

They agreed upon the bet. A shelter was built, and Midjistega's drum and flute were put into it. The trader provided some flour, thoroughly inspected the bowl in which it was to be put, since he was suspicious of tricks, and sat down with his employee at the entrance so as to observe the ceremony carefully. Midjistega danced four times with the flour around in a circle. First the flour turned yellow and then red. He said to the trader: "Now, then, trader, I have won your store."

"You won my store. I didn't think an Indian would be capable of that," said the trader. Afterward, Midjistega made some sugar out of the flour and gave it to the trader (Radin 1945).

A similar performance was given by the Selk'nam shaman Tenenesk for Martin Gusinde. He put a few pebbles in the palm of his hand, concentrated on them, panted a bit, and suddenly the pebbles vanished. Even when the performance was repeated a number of times, Gusinde was unable to discover any tricks (Gusinde 1931, vol. 1, 775ff.).

The shamanic ability to leave footprints in solid rock, or to disappear into the earth up to the waist or even entirely, is widespread. Frank Speck recounts a number of incidents of this sort. The shamans of the Micmac used to dance in a circle until their feet sank into the hard ground. Sometimes they went so deep that only their heads stuck out. Footprints and holes made by a shaman remained visible for a long time. One Micmac shaman stamped so hard when he got angry that his footprints remained in the stone.

A story is told of a Passamaquoddy shaman who made a bet with a white man about his ability to leave footprints. First the shaman emitted a bone-rattling cry that paralyzed everyone present and made them unable to talk; then he took seven steps on hard ground as if he were sliding through powdered snow, and his feet sank into the ground. Speck cites a whole series of eyewitness reports of people who saw footprints left in stone or who watched shamans perform this feat (Speck 1919, 263).

Frank Spencer, one of the founders of the messianic Ghost Dance movement of 1870 among the Plains tribes of North America, was known for his invulnerability to bullets. Once he tried to cure a young girl, but she did not recover. Another shaman was brought in on the case and accused him of black magic. The girl's vengeance-crazed father crept into Spencer's tepee in the night and fired three bullets at him. But Spencer stood up as though nothing had happened. The father shot him once again. Again, nothing happened. Spencer, in a friendly way, invited him in and explained that bullets and knives couldn't harm him and that the other doctor had deceived him.

Another time, in Lovelock, Nevada, Spencer got sick. He marked a bullet with his teeth and gave it to a man, whom he told to shoot him with it in the circle that he had painted on his chest. Many people came to watch. The shot did not sound quite as loud as a normal shot. After a few minutes, Spencer coughed and spat up the bullet in his hand. It was the same bullet. Then he began to feel well again (Park 1934, 109).

A similar performance was observed by J. Owen Dorsey (1889, 417) in 1871 among the Ponca. The shaman Cramped Hand had a pistol shot at him in the presence of two hundred spectators. When the shot was fired, he instantly fell to the ground dead. After a time, however, he got up again and coughed up the bullet.

The Tungus of Siberia say that when someone wants to communicate with another person over a distance, they must first have an intense wish to see the other person; they must think, "Please come here," and continue concentrating until they sense that the other has received the call. The better the people involved know each other, the better they can communicate telepathically. Shamans generally use this method. Often they go somewhere without knowing why—they just feel that they have to go. Then they discover that someone has called them.

The most favorable conditions for telepathy are calm weather at night. (Modern Russian telepathy experiments show that thoughts are transmitted most effectively in clear weather, without clouds.) Telepathic communication, according to Siberian researcher Shirokogoroff (1935a, 118, 364ff.), was a matter of course among the Tungus when they were unable to send a messenger. He himself made a telepathic attempt in 1921. He was one of the few ethnologists who was convinced of additional capacities of the brain. Shirokogoroff took sides against the Russian authorities, supporting the shamans in their activities and helping a female shaman to continue her training. This was at a time when the Tungus religion was being widely suppressed by the Moscow government.

The Hawaiians call people who know what is going to happen *ike papalua.* So we have seen, *papalua* means "double vision," a kind of second sight. People who possess it know what is happening in faraway places. They have an inborn gift—*mana,* or supernatural power—that comes from the gods. But *mana* is *e'epa* to them, strange and inexplicable.

The Eskimo of St. Lawrence Island call people who exhibit telepathic abilities and can find lost objects, "thin." Not every "thin man" is a shaman, but every shaman is a "thin man" (Murphy 1964, 58).

Many paranormal abilities are associated with the conscious splitting of mind from body—that is, with out-of-body experiences. In Dampier Land in northern Australia, the medicine man D'àlnge already possessed the alter ego or vital force as a *rai,* a preexisting spirit child, before he was born. This force attaches itself to the placenta and is responsible for human vital rhythms, for illnesses, and ultimately for death. For death is actually nothing but the separation of the alter ego from the body (Petri 1952, 58).

The Australian blackfellow doctors or *bàn* men possess the ability to send their souls, or *yá-yari,* on "walkabouts" to faraway places or into the depths of the earth or water in order to request new quartz crystals from Ungud, the rainbow serpent and the creative principle. By emanating their souls, the doctors can get hold of information that is inaccessible to them in their normal state. They can see in advance which visitors are coming from near and far, diagnose illnesses, and produce rain. Their souls' dream journeys are later put on as plays. One *bàn* man's *yá-yari,* for example, traveled two thousand kilometers to Perth, where he observed the life of the white people in the city. When he presented his experiences as a play, the players' faces were painted white, and they had to wear hats and walk behind or next to each other to show the way white people move about in the city. This medicine man had never left his own region (Petri 1952, 175).

PART THREE

SACRED JOURNEYS THROUGH SPACE AND TIME

I'm there again, there again, there again!
I came down from heaven on the sled of a constellation.
I swam on the sea like a floating pelt.
I came up from the interior of the earth like the horn of a devil stag when
he digs himself a passage in the steep banks of a river.
There I am again . . .

> —Nuwat,
> a shaman of the north Siberian Chukchee,
> after an out-of-body experience
> (quoted in Bogoras 1956, 15f.)

---------- 10 ----------

THE MOUTH OF THE DEAD

W hen Knud Rasmussen, the great Greenland explorer, asked
the Eskimo shaman Aua where people go when they die,
the shaman provided him with a powerful description of a spirit-
conjuring with all its dramatic moments, its suggestive mood, and
the collective awe at its unfolding mystery. The picture was set in
the endless solitude and stoic majesty of the storm-lashed Arctic
landscape.

The great spirit-conjurers often go up on a visit to the People of the
Day. When one of them wants to undertake such a spirit journey, he
sits down at the rear of the sleeping bench. A curtain of reindeer hide
conceals him from the people who gather in the house. His hands are
tied behind his back, and his head is lashed to his knees. As soon as
all the preparations are completed, fire is taken from the train-oil lamp
on the point of a knife and passed over his head, drawing rings in the
air. Everyone who is present for this journey through the air now says
in a loud chorus: "Let him who is going on a visit now be carried
away!" Then all the lamps are extinguished, and all in the house close
their eyes. So they sit for a long time in deep silence.

But after an hour strange sounds begin to be heard about the place.
A hissing comes from high up in the air, and whirring and whistling
tones. Suddenly the spirit-conjurer breaks in, shouting with all his
might: *"Halala, halalalê, halala, halalalê!"* And immediately all in the
house must shout: *"Alé, alé, alé!"*

Then a rushing sound goes through the snow hut, and all know that
an opening for the soul of the spirit-conjurer has been formed. It is

round and narrow, like the blowhole of a seal. Through this, the soul of the spirit-conjurer flies up to heaven, aided by all the stars that once were men. They travel up and down the soul passage to keep it open for the soul of the spirit-conjurer. Some travel upward, others down, and the whole air echoes with whistling sounds: *pfft, pfft, pfft!*

These are the stars, who are whistling for the soul of the spirit-conjurer. Now it is time for the people in the house to try to guess the stars' human names, which they had when they lived on the earth. If that succeeds, two short whistles are heard—*pfft, pfft*—and after that, a thin, shrill note that loses itself in celestial space. That is the answer of the stars and their thanks for still being remembered on earth.

There is always great rejoicing in the Land of Day when a spirit-conjurer comes on a visit; immediately, all the souls of the dead come rushing out of their houses. But they have no doors for going in and out, and therefore the souls come out anywhere they please—through the wall, through the roof. They pass swiftly through the walls of houses, and although one can see them, they are nothing; they are immaterial and thus do not need any hole through which to go in and out. They hurry toward the newcomer, glad to pay their respects, happy to make him welcome; for they believe that he is, like themselves, the soul of a dead man. Only when he says, "I am still made of flesh and blood," do they turn away in disappointment. When the spirit-conjurer has enjoyed himself for a while with the happy departed, he returns to his companions in his home place, tired and out of breath. Then he recounts everything he has experienced.

Everyone who has died a natural death from illness in house or tent passes to the Narrow Ridge Land. This is a big country that lies in the open sea, and a lot of hunting for all kinds of sea creatures goes on there. The spirit-conjurer can also journey to this place, but such journeys are just pleasure trips. A journey that has a definite purpose takes him down to the great Mistress of the Sea. She jealously watches over her seals, causing human to suffer want. The preparations for the spirit-conjurer to take such a nether journey are approximately the same as those for a journey up to the Land of Day. All the lamps in the house are extinguished, and the moaning and sighing of long-dead people is heard. This sighing sound gives the impression that the spirits are living like sea beasts under the water. One also hears the splashing and puffing of animals coming up for breath. Everyone in the house now sings a song of power that is repeated again and again:

We stretch forth our hands
To help thee up.
We are without food
And without game!
We stretch forth our hands . . .

Before the great spirit-conjurer, a passage opens up that runs down through the earth to the bottom of the sea, almost like a pipe. In this way he reaches the house of the Mistress of the Sea. It looks like an ordinary house for humans, but it has no roof and everything is open on top so that the Mistress of the Sea can keep an eye on the dwellings of men from her place by the lamp. All possible game creatures—ordinary and bearded seals, walruses, and whales—are assembled to the right of her lamp, lying there and breathing.

Before the narrow entrance of the house lies a vicious dog that has to be driven off before the spirit-conjurer can enter. When he finally gets in, as a sign of her anger, the Mistress of the Sea may be sitting with her back to the lamp and to all the game animals, which she would otherwise send up to human beings. Her hair is disheveled and out of order, and she is awesome to look at.

The spirit-conjurer must immediately take her by the shoulder and turn her face to the lamp and the animals. Then he must stroke her hair and smooth it down in a kindly way, saying: "Those above can no longer hunt seals." Thereupon the Mistress of the Sea answers: "It is your own trespasses that are barring them the way." The spirit-conjurer must use all his arts to appease her wrath. When she is once again positively disposed, she takes the animals one by one and drops them on the floor. Then it is as if a whirlpool were aroused at the entrance to the house—the animals disappear into the sea. That is a sign of fruitful hunting and plenty for human beings.

Now it is time for the spirit-conjurer to return to his companions waiting for him above in his home place. They can already hear him coming from a distance. They hear the rushing sound of his movement up the passage that the spirits have opened for him. With a mighty *"plu-a-he-he!"* he pops up in his place behind the curtain: *"Plu, plu,"* like a sea beast shooting out of the deep, driven by the mighty pressure in his lungs.

For a moment the house is completely silent. No one dares to disturb the silence before the spirit-conjurer speaks: "I have something to say." All in the house answer: "Let us hear, let us hear!" And the spirit-conjurer continues in the ceremonial language of the spirits: "Word wants to come up!" This is a sign for everybody in the house to confess taboo violations that they have committed, which have aroused the wrath of the Mistress of the Sea. "Perhaps it is my fault! It is my fault!" people call out in disorder. Women and men shout this out for fear of hunger and bad hunting. The names of everyone in the house are named. Each one must confess his guilt. In this way, everyone gets to know a great deal about things of which they had had no idea, about other people's secrets. But in spite of everything that is heard, the spirit-conjurer may still not be satisfied. He refers to himself as an unfortunate who has not yet learned the whole truth and repeatedly breaks out into laments.

It might suddenly happen that someone comes forward with a secret sin that they had meant to keep hidden. Then great relief comes over the spirit-conjurer, and he shouts out: "That was it! That was it!" Frequently quite young girls are guilty of the misfortune that has struck the home place. But if the women are are young and willing to do penance, this is always a sign that they are good women. As soon as they have confessed their guilt, they are immediately granted forgiveness by the Mistress of the Sea. Great joy that a misfortune has been averted now fills everyone, and all firmly believe that the next day there will be an abundance of game. (Translated from Rasmussen 1946, 39ff)

To get an impression of the suspenseful atmosphere of a spirit-conjuring, we must try to form an idea of the general mood of the assembly. There are no nonparticipating spectators; everyone takes part. Through their chanting, their questioning of the spirits, through their expectations, fears, and hopes over whether their deceased relatives might soon be standing next to them in spirit form, they elevate the shaman to a mediator between worlds. Their cries spur him on and more or less drive him into a trance. The highly intense longings of everyone present, their deep belief in the spirits, and their awe at the supernatural activity finally mount to an fever pitch of mysterious sounds, of unlocalizable noises and animal sounds. These, and the news given by the spirits, often produce an exalted state of mind, a religious ecstasy that can safely be called an altered state of consciousness. Not only the shamans but everyone present enters a state of spiritual rapture and devotion. Supported by this atmosphere, which is devoid of critical or skeptical compunctions—the assembly requires no experimental-empirical proof in our sense—the shaman can unobstructedly let all his own fears and self-doubt fall away and open himself entirely to the sublimity of the spiritual world. With its harmonious and mutually spiritual consensus, the assembly helps the shaman to a nearly superhuman concentration of all his forces and causes him to penetrate into the purely spiritual world.

If we wish to explain this kind of seance, we may say that it means freeing oneself of the fetters of the body and acquiring an impression of how the world looks from the point of view of consciousness alone. The hypertrophied emotions of the seance—fear, veneration, and sacred awe—are the most general prerequisites for altered states of consciousness. The absence of these, or the presence of only one spectator who does not share the basic cosmic outlook of the assembly, can disrupt the ceremony and lead to the miscarriage of the ritual. Trance requires a supportive mood if people are to be able to surrender the habitual experiential pattern of a causal, three-dimensional world in favor of a multidimensional, parallel transhuman world. Usually such a reformation of consciousness evokes fear, since it means the loss and even the death of the ego. Proceeding toward this voluntary death requires the encouragement of the community, a societal confirmation. Thus, a seance is a communal enterprise of a tribe or group. The absence of such cultural support in modern societies has caused the decline of altered states of consciousness and the loss of contact with the world of spirits.

The background chanting supports the ecstatic unity of everyone present. The songs are not just entertaining verses—they come from inside and express the power of the human psyche. They are utterances of an archaic union with the world. This ecstatic empathy fosters the shaman's trance. That all the participants' receptivity is communally focused on a common objective produces something that contemporary psychology has called "the experience of flowing"—movement that is in accordance with the rhythm of the collective psyche. It is not for nothing that seances and nocturnal conjurings are so popular; with a purification ritual before and a feast after, these social gatherings promise to bring contact with the beyond, where people temporarily escape the grip of everyday reality and gain access to a perfect world, purifying themselves inwardly and spiritually.

We should completely rethink all our social occasions—parties, dances, and so on—indeed, the social quest for community and togetherness, in this light. Social gatherings offer an opportunity for collective accord and harmony and, above all, for an intensity of emotion that is absent from the monotony of everyday life. Social gatherings make possible a sense of letting emotions flow that reaches a climax through dancing, rhythm, and elation—if necessary, supported by psychoactive drugs. Especially for young people, the quest for orgiastic emotion is an important motivation, one that sometimes has a foundation in a philosophical outlook.

In Western society, alcoholic inebriation is a rather hopeless attempt to overcome our compulsively mechanistic definition of humanity, one last fling at trying to regain the ecstatic, mystical side of life, to bring this element back into human existence. Although the prevailing use of alcohol leads in just the opposite direction, nevertheless, as the ecstasy of the common man, inebriation embodies the legitimate longing for an emotional peak experience, which is essentially what we have been calling an altered state of consciousness. At its inmost core, this is a state of timelessness and fusion with the world around us. In our own celebrations, as constrained as their dancing and music and singing are, survive the last vestiges of an irrepressible urge to trance and of hope for ecstatic harmony with all being that cannot be further intellectualized.

The satisfaction that arises from participating in a seance is incomparably greater than that arising from a conventional Western theatrical performance, the Russian ethnographer Shirokogoroff (1935a, 330ff.) notes. The participants themselves contribute to the success of a spirit-conjuring and approach the trance state of the shaman. Not a few Western observers of such seances have noted that it is difficult to keep from being borne along by the electrifying and infectious exaltation of these gatherings and to maintain one's intellectual objectivity. Those present can in fact enter a state bordering on mass ecstasy.

Hysteria would be another word to describe this. But its pejorative connotations leave no room for the understanding that this state is a collective healing mechanism that tribal societies naturally employ to purify themselves from restrictive, inhibitory, and delusive conditions and to reopen themselves to the all-embracing reality inherent in us, to a more multifaceted spiritual unfolding, and to a more harmonious feeling of community, free from ego-oriented motivations. Initially, the seance liberates the participants from the inhibitions and tensions of daily existence; then, through contact with a higher sphere of existence, it gives them insight and understanding into the earthly hindrances and the network of relationships in which they are embedded. Spiritual knowledge and liberation from the prison of ego-oriented emotions are the basic pillars of all healing. They lead us to a sacred way of life and are the true source of what happens in a seance.

I believe that humans possess inborn motive forces through which they can divest themselves of inveterate patterns of thought and behavior and of rigid ideas in order to heal themselves. This is true not only of individuals; whole movements motivated by a sense of freedom and human welfare—Cargo cults, as well as revivalistic and messianic religions—have, under charismatic leaders, sought happiness in a world of balanced emotion. Ecstasy, trance, and the sense of sacredness, as we must increasingly recognize, are the starting point for health and harmony. The primordial cultures recognized this and made it central to their holy and healing universe.

Not only must shamans attain a state of altered consciousness; their dramatic talents are also of decisive importance. If their performances are lacking in drama, are insufficiently true to life, or unskillful in their representations, they are incapable of carrying the audience along and are not well received. Shamanic seances are cultural occasions comparable to our society's cinematic and theatrical performances. As in these, in the seance the mundane and supramundane realms come together.

A seance need not always involve a shamanic trance and make a connection to the other world. A purely theatrical portrayal of a journey to the beyond will do. As an example, let us examine how a Siberian shaman related his journey to Erlik, the ruler of the underworld.

The shaman began by telling how he made his way southward

through the neighboring district and crossed the Chinese border and described the impression the landscape there had made on him. At last he reached Tenir Shaikha, the iron mountain, the peak of which touches the heavens. He portrayed the difficult ascent and the dangers he met, told of seeing on the side of the path the skeletal remains of shamans who had perished before him on the ascent. He breathed hard as he mimed the climb. Now on horseback he rode into "the earth's maw," the underworld. There he came to a lake, over which a thin hair was stretched. This perilous bridge had to be crossed. He simulated the balancing act he did and pointed to the fallen shamans whose bones glimmered on the bottom of the lake—only a pure soul can cross this bridge of death. Hardly was the bridge behind him when he encountered the souls of sinners who were enduring punishments that corresponded to their deeds.

At last he climbed to Erlik's dwelling. There he faced the last obstacle, the watchman before Erlik's yurt, whom he placated with gifts. He went before Erlik's throne, bowed, and explained the reason for his coming. But the khan only replied, "Those who have feathers do not fly here; those who have bones do not walk here. You, black evil-smelling beetle, what do you want?" He was dismissed, and then dismissed again. But on the third try, he succeeded in gaining Erlik's confidence and gave him gifts of wine, furs, and clothing. In exchange, Erlik Khan advised him to increase his reindeer herds and told him which females would bear males. The shaman flew back home not on his horse but on a goose, whose cries he imitated as he told the story. Then he beat the drum three times, rubbed his eyes, and pretended to awaken (Mikhailovskii 1895, 72ff.).

Whether this journey into "the earth's maw" was experienced by this shaman or only recounted by him, its features remain the same. The two cornerstones of the shamanic universe are the belief in an animating, vital, subtly material spiritual principle, or soul, and the belief in the survival of the body through the soul, which leaves the body after death, enters the realm of the dead, and continues its life there as a spirit. Without a deeper understanding of the mode of existence of the soul, the world of shamans and mediums will strike Westerners as alien and bizarre. Modern near-death research points to the existence of a life principle, although it is as yet unquantifiable and can be deduced only indirectly, as the basis of the body's life. The shaman's capability of magical flight, the object of copious speculation on the basis of false premises, today can be understood as a departure from the body through a soul or consciousness principle of some type, in the wake of empirical investigations of out-of-body states. That which makes it possible for the shaman to move about might well be an energy body that is subject to other laws than those of three-dimensional geometry and causality. For the present discussion, it is of no importance which theory is espoused in this regard. The fact remains that without the soul and the beyond, the shamanic worldview is incomplete, indeed inconceivable.

A few examples may illuminate this further. The spirit woman of Japan, *miko,* "child of god," is also called *kuchiyose,* "woman through whose mouth a god or spirit makes himself heard." She summons the souls of the dead from the beyond, for which the term *shinikuchi,* "mouth of the dead," is used. If, on the other hand, it is living persons who are summoned from a distance, *ikikuchi,* "mouth of a living one," is the pertinent term. The souls of the dead are queried concerning impending fortune and misfortune, and their healing capacities are implored. The souls of deceased relatives, spouses, and friends designate healing medicines and locate lost objects. Occasionally, the souls of the dead describe their journeys from a faraway place back to the home village, inquire about the lives of the close relations they have left behind, express their gratitude for offerings and prayers, and give information about the future.

The deceased speak through the mouth of the medium. They can be recognized by their voices, which resemble their former voices on earth; those who have remained behind use them as a basis for identification. Interrogation of the dead is undertaken at the time of memorial ceremonies, when the ritual of "summoning the dead" is performed—or in the case of those who have died violently, the ritual of "opening the way for the dead." In northeastern Japan, the questioning of the dead is also carried out in spring and fall at the time of the equinoxes, since these are general memorial holidays. In Amami-Oshima in the Ryukyu archipelago, the *tam-awase,* "meeting with the dead," is prepared after a burial. In isolated areas of

Japan (Aizu, Kawanuma District), the local shamans meet annually for the *bon* celebration, the Buddhist all-souls holiday, or on the day of Jizo, the god of the underworld, to summon the souls of the dead (Eder 1958).

The shaman's task is not only to have the souls of the dead speak through their mouths; they themselves should be able to quit their bodies and fly to the regions of the beyond. The *noaidi,* the Lapp shamans, use various symbolic aids for their voyage to Jabmeaymo, the subterranean realm of the dead. There is *saiva guelie,* the fish spirit they ride on; *saiva leddi,* the bird spirit that guides them; and *saiva sarva,* the male reindeer spirit, which fights with the spirits of hostile sorcerers when necessary. Among all tribal cultures, the psychic powers of shamans are rendered understandable in terms of motifs expressible as images. These are not, however, merely symbolic aids; behind them are real psychic powers. A shamanic symbol is always a real and effective aspect of a paranormal, transpsychic power.

The task of shamans in the underworld is to bring back the lost souls of their patients, for the cause of many illnesses is thought to be the loss of the patient's soul. Souls can be stolen or can be separated from the body in dream or sleep, or through fear or shock or mental confusion. The soul is considered the vital principle. It can wander about in the realm of the dead in the false belief that it can find its home there. The soul of the shaman chases it, and among the Lapps, it must give Kabme Akka, the mistress of the underworld, an offering to repurchase the lost soul. If other spiritual beings resist the return of the soul, the shaman must summon all his powers of persuasion to get the soul out of the realm of the dead. The process of seeking and finding the soul is described as though the spiritual world were a three-dimensional realm. The shaman attempts to discover traces of the lost soul in the landscape of this other world; or, as is customary among the Thompson Indians of British Columbia, he blocks the path of the soul that has set out for the Land of Souls (Teit 1900, 364). Shamans can remain in this land only for a short time and must hurry to catch the soul. Either they overpower the soul and bring it home, or they request the inhabitants of the region to hand the soul over to them. But they also risk having to fight with the souls there for the possession of the lost spirit body. After the seance, shamans, in such cases, display their weapons, on which blood is found as proof of the struggle.

During the seance, the Lapp *noaidi* lies there as though dead. He may be touched by no one. A group of men guards him so that no one can come too close, and a number of women sing the whole time to remind him of his task in the realm of the dead and to help him to find his way home out of the trance or the out-of-body state (Bäckman and Hultkrantz 1978).

A prerequisite of any seance is that the shaman must be able to *ilimarpoq,* as the Eskimo say—that is, to fly through the air. He must travel to heaven or to the bottom of the sea, then be able to reclothe himself in his own skin. For this reason, many cultures associate shamans with birds or with flight in general. The Sima-sima of central Ceram (in the Moluccas) call shamans *manpetua* (*manu* = bird, *petua* = fly). During seances they remove the roof of the house so that the soul of the shaman can fly out and the souls coming from the cosmic mountain can fly in.

Leaving the body by means of the soul is, as we have seen, the basis of shamanism. A psychology like ours that equates the soul with the psyche can never really penetrate into the spiritual world of the shaman. We must distinguish between the soul—the energic matrix, the etheric body that constitutes the morphogenetic or vital field of the material body—and the psyche, the product of behavior, thought, memory, emotion, and action.

11

SPIRIT-CONJURERS
OF THE ARTIC

Nowadays we do not know what to make of a term like *conjuring*. But let us realize that it is a matter not of actually conjuring up spirits, but of stimulating our own psyche. We must be placed in a receptive, trancelike state of consciousness. Conjuring is nothing more than putting oneself or a group in a state of heightened clarity of perception, alertness, and focus so that, from this heightened platform of inner vision, we can experience things or be more receptive to phenomena that are part of the shamanic universe. The spirit-conjuring, or seance, is a high point of archaic psychology. It is artfully applied group therapy and group catharsis, subtly bound up with hypnosis and suggestion. The goal is for the shaman—and also, in diluted form, for the audience—to experience an altered state of consciousness that permits them to perceive other levels of existence and relationships that are not underpinned by normal causality. Knud Rasmussen, the well-known student of Eskimo culture, describes such an event:

It was that kind of day. Growth was in the air and people were restless. . . .

Sagdlork was the greatest and oldest spirit-conjurer of the tribe, and now he had told his companions in the settlement that he intended to conjure spirits. His wife had gotten sick, and he wanted to try to cure her.

The house was built close to the sea. Therefore, the men and women gathered below at the edge of the ice. The sick woman sat on a sled in the middle of the people, and her son was standing next to her.

Above on the roof of the house, close to the window, sat the spirit-conjurer Kale, who had learned his art from old Sagdlork; for that reason, he was to be near his master. Sagdlork himself was alone in the house.

All work in the square came to a halt. No one dared to move. When I arrived, I was immediately signaled to keep still. All faces were marked with gravity and devotion.

Sagdlork was of an ancient and feared lineage. His uncle and his nephew had been killed as dangerous pirates, and Sagdlork was the only surviving person, according to his compatriots, to have inherited the wisdom of the fathers. Thus there was no other spirit-conjurer who was able to creep out of his skin and put it back on again afterwards. He could do this. Anyone who laid eyes on such a "flesh-naked" sorcerer was doomed to die, it was said. So that was Sagdlork.

It had been a long time since he had conducted a spirit-conjuring, because he had been ill. That very day he had been drawn back and forth between the houses on a sled, because his limbs were stiff with gout. And now, nonetheless, he was going to conduct a spirit-conjuring.

When I got to his house, I looked through the window at him. He was sitting alone on his cot and beating the drum. When he saw my face at the window, he stopped drumming, laughed up at me and said, "Pure tomfoolery! Stupid faking! A total tissue of lies!"

Before the beginning of the seance, it is part of decorum for a shaman to denigrate his own capabilities and to present himself as a liar and a fool—but only so that the assembly will hail him as a great spirit-conjurer and urge him to carry on with the conjuring all the same. This is not a ritual but another way to focus the shaman's power and give him self-confidence; for without a firm belief in a world of spirits, success would be impossible in this endeavor. Again and again it has proved to be the case that with the dissolution of a culture, shamanic powers also decline. The quality of being enmeshed in one's own universe, undermined by bits of modern Western knowledge, begins to fall apart.

Once again the drum sounded within the house, and all around the people stood mutely listening. Soon a humming began to mix with the drumbeats, and slowly but powerfully, the voice of the old man swelled in strength. At last the spirit chant came loud and on a sustained note from the inside of the hut.

Kale sat above on the roof of the house becoming more and more moved; involuntarily he joined in, at first only humming. From old Sorkrark, himself a spirit-conjurer, who stood in the middle of the crowd, could be heard sporadic grunts in sympathy. He had just come from cutting blubber and stood there with his sleeves pushed up and his arms covered with blood. The others all stood mute and unmoving, looking up toward the house from which the commotion was coming. Then the chanting suddenly stopped, and only the drum continued, the beat getting faster and faster. Old Sagdlork began to moan as though he lay under a great weight that made it nearly impossible for him to breathe. All of a sudden he let out a wild scream that caused the listeners to grimace with fear: "Ajornarê, ajornarê! atdlinlerpunga! ikiorniarsinga, artorssarpavssualekrisunga!" (Oh, oh! It's impossible! I'm beaten! He's lying on me! Help me! I'm too weak, I can't cope with it!) Then the screaming, driven by real terror, subsided into feeble sobs. But the drumbeat continued wilder and wilder! Old Kale up on the roof of the house had tears in his eyes and began to sing a spirit song at the top of his lungs. "Hurry up! Use your power!" (agsororsinguarit) roared Sorkrark excitedly up at the house. Then the drum stopped for a moment, and a deathly stillness pervaded the house. The suspense among the listeners grew.

But soon old Sagdlork took up his drum again, and after a few preliminary strokes to the skin, he cried out with a voice so strong that it seemed to come from a young man's lungs: "perdlugssuark, tornarss-ugssuark, kravdlunarsuit" (bad fortune—evil spirit—white men)—the words came sporadically, without logical order, but produced the desired mystical effect. Everyone waited in suspense for what would come next, but the words were interrupted by a long, drawn-out plaintive moan. Kale was shouting himself hoarse with his spirit song, and Sorkrark continued with his exhortations. It was as though Sagd-lork was getting a message from far away, as though he was struggling with an invisible being.

Then came another loud howl, and then, when the suspense had reached its climax, Sagdlork shouted out an entire sentence, which produced an actual jolt in the people who heard it: "The white people brought the bad fortune with them, they brought an evil spirit with them. I saw it myself. Lying is not found in my speech. I am not lying, I am no liar. I saw it myself." Gabriel the Greenlander got white in the face when he heard these words. "He means us!" he whispered. "He's blaming us." All the listeners turned to look at us.

Then Sagdlork explained that on the way we had encountered bad fortune in the form of a spirit, which had brushed against Harald Moltke's sled. That is why he got sick. As to the rest of us, only our dogs were infected. That is why the epidemic had broken out among the dogs.

His remarks were difficult to understand, since he often employed a special spirit language and interrupted his speech frequently with howls.

All over the world, shamans have developed their own sacred language that they use only in the state of clear consciousness. This resembles the notion of glossolalia, or speaking in tongues. Most shamanic secret languages are often no more than chattering and gibberish and new combinations of syllables, transpositions, abbreviations, and scramblings of ordinary words. Frequently, words from neighboring languages are also used, or relics of a language that the tribe spoke in a bygone era. The sacred language works like a mask behind which the speaker can hide in order to let a new identity unfold. Many shamans also hide behind the claim that this is the language of the spirits. In any case, this technique helps shamans give themselves over with less constraint to their psychic inspiration—for at that point, they are no longer responsible for what they say. Thus we may recognize in the secret language a means of penetrating swiftly into one's own unconscious or superconscious—a psychological technique of the first water, which could be adopted without further ado by modern psychotherapy.

> Pe, pe, pe, people—
> they say that people—
> ku, ku, ki, ki—
> I can't, I can't,
> I don't have enough strength, not enough strength,
> Isn't there anyone one there who wants to help me!

He might break off in the middle of a word; then he finished off with a frightful show without saying anything further. It sounded like the house was full of brawling people who were groaning under each other's powerful blows.

Kale was now just sitting there repeating the verbal play of his teacher. He was hoarse from singing. On the other hand, Sorkrark, the old bear hunter, was tireless in his exhortations: "Hurry up! Hurry up!" But as usual, only when the old man had brought the suspense to its highest point did he offer an explanation, slowly and with effort, as though he were ripping every single word from the grasp of an invisible spirit.

The white men had brought the sickness, but only the dogs would get sick. For that reason, no one should eat dog meat.

"Did Mikisork ["the little one," his wife] eat dog meat?"

"Did Mikisork eat dog meat?" Kale yelled down.

"Mikisork, did you eat dog meat?" Sorkrark asked her. The words went from mouth to mouth. The son, Agpaliguark, bent over his sick mother, and she nodded.

"Yes, just a little. I had such a craving for dog meat!" the woman answered.

"She has had some dog meat!" Kale repeated from the roof in through the window.

Then there was a wild howl from the interior of the house. And the drumming began again. "Thu, thu, thu!" was repeated endlessly with a strange forcefulness. It was like a locomotive puffing and snorting. Sagdlork was in complete ecstasy; the gouty old man was jumping around on the floor like a wounded animal. He had closed his eyes and was moving his head and trunk with a wierd circular motion in time to the drum. Then the old spirit-conjurer broke out in a long howl with other peculiar sounds in it. It was as though human laughter was blending with his plaintive wail. Then the whole thing subsided into a soft sobbing. His wife could not be saved!

Then the people separated and returned to their work, and soon the square had filled again with happy laughing people. The thought that the great summer was coming drove away all cares and worries. Who would bother thinking about the warnings of an old spirit-conjurer! Sorkrark was the only one looking inside with concern. He was in the midst of flensing four seals that his sons had brought home. "Sagdlork's getting old," he said to me. "Sagdlork has no power. His wife has to die!"

That was Sagdlork's last great inspiration. His wife died with the approach of summer. (Rasmussen 1907, 18ff.)

I would like to include one more episode of spirit-conjuring that was recounted by Rasmussen. One night, before a powerful snow-storm could overtake it, Rasmussen's small expedition reached the Agiarmiut Eskimo. On the third night of the storm, they were invited to a seance of the shaman Kigiuna, whose objective was to calm the storm.

The man who invited us was a pronouncedly blond Eskimo, bald, and with a reddish beard, as well as a slight tinge of blue in his eyes. His name was Kigiuna, "sharp tooth."

The storm seemed to have culminated. We had to walk three together in order to keep upright, and there was no knowing when one would have to build a snow house far from the place where the ceremony was to be held. We were all armed with large snow-knives, and, with heads bent almost down to the ice, we pushed our way toward the little village. Kigiuna held me by one arm, and his partner for the night by the other.

"The infant Narssuk is crying because there the wind is blowing through his diaper!" And they told me the ancient myth of the giant's son who had revenged himself upon the people who had killed his parents by flying to the skies and turning into bad weather. Now, in the course of the night, they intended to find out the cause of the child's anger to subdue the storm.

The wind took such a hold of us that sometimes we had to stand quite still and cling on to one another to keep from being blown into the pack ice that towered around about us. The tremendous gusts from the shore lashed us like whips, and after three or four strokes we were able to proceed until the next gust, followed by the screams of the storm-infant, again stopped us and almost threw us down on the ice. I think that to cross that half-kilometer took us a whole hour; how glad we were when at length we spied the warm beams of the blubber lamps in the shining ice window of the festival hall! [We passed] through waves of dogs that growled and snapped at us as we crawled in through the long passage till we reached the hall, where all the seats on the platforms were already occupied by men and women.

The hall consisted of two snow huts built together. The entrance led on to the middle of the floor, and two snow-built platforms for sleeping were opposite each other. One of the hosts, Tamuanuaq, whose name means "the little mouthful," received me cordially and conducted me to a seat. The house was four meters wide and six meters long and had such a high roof that the builder had had to reinforce it with two pieces of driftwood, which looked like magnificent pillars in the white hall of snow. And there was so much room on the floor that all the neighbors' little children were able to play "catch" around the pillars during the preliminary part of the festival.

The preparations consisted of a feast of dried salmon, blubber, and frozen, unflensed seal carcasses. They hacked away at the frozen dinner with big axes, and as the warmth of the house gradually brought a flush to all faces that had been lashed by the gale and the snow, they avidly swallowed the lumps of meat after having breathed upon them so that they would not freeze the skin off their lips and tongue.

"Fond of food, hardy, and always ready to feast," whispered Eider Duck to me, his mouth full of frozen blood.

And truly, it was not only iron stomachs that were necessary for food like this; it required strong minds to make a festival out of a snowstorm.

The shaman of the evening was Horqarnaq, or "Baleen," a young man with intelligent eyes and swift movements. There was no deceit in his face, and perhaps for that reason it was long before he fell into a trance. He explained to me before commencing that he had few helpers. There was his dead father's spirit and its helping spirit, a troll from the legends, and a giant with claws so long that they could cut a man right through simply by scratching him. Then there was a figure that he had created himself of soft snow, shaped like a man—a spirit who came when he called. A fourth and mysterious helping spirit was a remarkable red stone called Aupilalanguaq that he had once found when hunting caribou; it had a lifelike resemblance to a head and neck, and when he shot a caribou near to it, he gave it a real head-band of the long hairs from the neck of the animal. In this way he made his own helping spirit into a shaman and increased its power twofold.

He was now about to summon these helpers. He began the seance with a good deal of modest talk to the effect that he could not bring the spirits to us. All the women of the village stood in a circle around him and encouraged him with cheap prattle.

"You can, and you do it so easily because you are so strong," they said flatteringly, and incessantly he repeated:

"It is a hard thing to speak the truth. It is difficult to make hidden forces appear."

He long maintained his gravity and almost defiant aloofness, but the women around him continued to excite him, and at last he slowly became seized with frenzy. Then the men joined in, the circle around him became denser and denser, and all shouted inciting things about his powers and his strength.

Now Baleen's eyes become wild. He distends them and seems to be looking out over immeasurable distance; now and then he spins around on his heel, his breathing becomes agitated, and he no longer recognizes the people round him: "Who are you?" he cries.

"Your own folks!" they answer.

"Are you all here?"

"Yes, except those two who went east on a visit."

But he seems not to hear what is said, and repeats again and again: "Who are you? Are you all here? Are you all here?"

Suddenly his wild eyes turn toward Eider Duck and me, and he shouts:

"Who are those two, whose faces are strange?"

"Men who are traveling around the world. Men we are pleased with. Friends who also would like to hear what wisdom you can bring us."

Again Baleen goes around the circle, looks into the eyes of all, gazes ever more wildly about him, and finally repeats like a tired man who has walked far and at last gives up:

"I cannot. I cannot."

At that moment there is a gurgling sound, and a helping spirit enters his body. A force has taken possession of him, and he is no longer master of himself or his words. He dances, jumps, throws himself over among the clusters of the audience, and cries to his dead father, who has become an evil spirit. It is only a year since his father died, and his mother, the widow, still sorrowing over the loss of her provider, groans deeply, breathes heavily, and tries to calm her wild son; but all the others cry in a confusion of voices, urging him to go on and to let the spirit speak.

Baleen names several spirits of dead people that he sees in the house among the living. He describes their appearance—old men, old women, whom he has never met—and commands the others to tell him who they are.

Bewilderment, silence, then a whispered consultation among the women. Hesitatingly they start guessing, naming some departed person who would fit in with what the shaman has said.

"No, no, no! Not them!"

The men stand silent, waiting, while the women scream loudly in shrill discord, no longer at a loss but excited, trying to solve the riddle. Only the widow of the dead man who is said to be present sighs in despair and rocks her head to and fro, weeping. Then suddenly an old woman, who hitherto has remained silent up on the platform, jumps forward on to the floor and shouts the names of those whom the others had not dared to let pass their lips—a couple who have just died, a man and his wife from Nagjugtoq, whose graves are still fresh.

"Qanorme!"

"Qanorme!"

"That is just who it is!" cries Baleen in a grating voice, and an inexplicable, sinister feeling spreads over the company, because these two people were alive among them only a few days before.

Now they have turned into evil spirits—the very evil spirits that have been causing the storm. Terror spreads in the house. Life the mysterious has allowed something uncanny to sink over them all; something that no one can explain is going on, throwing everything into confusion.

Outside howls the gale. A man cannot see his hand before him, and even the dogs, which otherwise are kicked out of the house, are allowed to seek warmth and shelter among the legs of these excited people.

Two visitors, a man and wife, who live just next door but have lost their way come in now, their mouths and eyes full of snow. This is the third day of the storm. There is no meat for tomorrow, nothing to eat, nothing to make them warm, and it seems as if this menace suddenly has become alive. The storm-boy weeps, the women weep, the men murmur incomprehensible words.

The seance has lasted an hour, an hour of howling and invoking unknown forces. Then something happens that terrifies us, who have never before seen the storm god tamed. Baleen leaps forward and seizes good-natured old Kigiuna, who has just been singing a pious song to the Mother of the Sea Beasts, grips him swiftly by the throat, and brutally flings him backward and forward, to and fro in the midst of the crowd. At first both utter wailing, throaty screams, but little by little Kigiuna is choked and can no longer utter a sound. But suddenly there is a hiss from his lips, and he, too, has been seized with ecstasy. He no longer resists but follows Baleen, who still has him by the throat, and they tumble about, quite out of their minds. The men of the house have to stand in front of the big blubber lamps to prevent their being broken or upset; the women have to help the children up onto the platform to save them from being knocked to pieces in the scrimmage. And so it goes on for a little while, until Baleen has squeezed all the life out of his opponent, who is now being dragged after him like a lifeless bundle. Only then does he release his hold, and Kigiuna falls heavily to the floor.

It was the storm that was being killed in effigy. The revolt in the air demands life, and Baleen seizes Kigiuna by the back of the neck in his teeth and shakes him with all the strength of his jaws, like a dog getting the better of another.

One of the oldest means of providing support to a shaman who travels in the beyond to seek out the causes of earthly problems there is to choke and finally strangle him. Initially, Kigiuna enters a trance state resulting from oxygen deficiency; after further choking, he becomes unconscious—that is to say, his consciousness leaves his body. This characteristic sequence—first a trance state, then an out-of-body experience—represents no more than an intensification of the same basic experience:

There is a deathly silence in the house. Baleen is the only one who continues his wild dance, until in some way or other his eyes become calm and he kneels in front of the dead and starts to rub and stroke his body to revive him. Slowly Kigiuna is brought back to life, very shakily he is put on his feet. But scarcely has he come to his senses again when the same thing is repeated—the same violent grip of the throat, the same wild dance in the house, the same gasping for breath, until the poor man is again flung to the snow floor like an inanimate bundle of skins. Three times he is "killed" in this manner! Man has to display his superiority over the storm.

But when Kigiuna for the third time comes to life again, it is he who falls into a trance, and Baleen who collapses. The old seer rises up in his curious, much-too-obese might, yet rules us by the wildness in his eyes and the horrible reddish-blue sheen that has come over his face through all the ill-usage to which he has been subjected. All feel that here is a man whom death has just touched, and they involuntarily step back. Then, his foot on Baleen's chest, he turns to the audience and with astonishing eloquence announces the visions he sees. With a voice that trembles with emotion he cries out over the hall:

"The sky is full of naked beings rushing through the air. Naked people, naked men, naked women, rushing along and raising gales and blizzards.

"Don't you hear the noise? It swishes like the beats of the wings of great birds up in the air. It is the fear of naked people, it is the flight of naked people!

"The weather spirit is blowing the storm out, the weather spirit is driving the sweeping snow away over the earth, and the helpless storm-child Narssuk shakes the lungs of the air with his weeping.

"Don't you hear the weeping of the child in the howling of the wind?

"And look! Among all the naked crowds of fleeing ones there is one, one single man, whom the wind has made full of holes: *Tju, tju-u. Tju-u-u!* Do you hear him? He is the mightiest of all the wind travelers.

"But my helping spirit will stop him, will stop them all. I see him coming calmly, confident of victory, toward me. He will conquer, he will conquer! *Tju, tju-u!* do you hear the wind? *Sst, sst, ssst!* Do you see the spirits, the weather, the storm, sweeping over us with the swish of the beat of great birds' wings?"

At these words Baleen rises from the floor, and the two shamans, whose faces are now transfigured after this tremendous storm-sermon, sing with simple, hoarse voices a song to the Mother of the Sea Beasts:

Woman, great woman down there,
Send it hence, send it away from us, that evil!
Come, come, spirit of the deep!
One of your earth-dwellers
Calls to you.
Asks you to bite enemies to death.
Come, come, spirit of the deep!

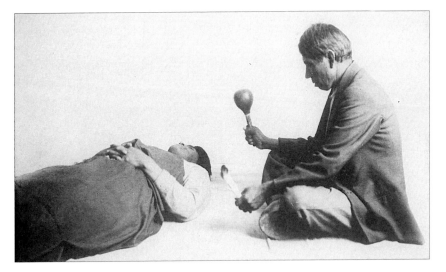

José Panco, Papago medicine specialist, treating a sick man with rattle and deer tail. San Xavier Reservation, Arizona, ca. 1920. Smithsonian Institution. (Photo 2776)

Massett shamans, Northwest Coast of Canada. Photograph by Dosseter. Courtesy of Department of Library Services, American Museum of Natural History. (Neg. 32960)

Gitskan shaman, Northwest Coast of Canada, Special Collections Division, University of Washington Libraries. (Neg. 3438)

Portrait of Kingiuna, Agia-miut shaman, Copper Eskimo, Canada. National Museum of Denmark, Department of Ethnography. (Neg. 2019)

Siberian Yakut shaman performing without his shaman costume. Photograph by W. Jochel-son. Courtesy of Department of Library Services, American Museum of Natural History. (Neg. 1983)

Siberian shaman of the Nanay, Amun River, ca. 1895. Beside him is the box for his shaman cap. Photograph by Pjotr Simkevic. Museum für Völkeskunde Berlin.

Siberian shaman holding a séance, Sachalin, late 1800s. Photograph by B. Pilsudski. Rautenstrauch-Joest-Museum, Cologne.

Burjat shamaness, East Mongolia. Archives Amelie and Holger Kalweit.

Burjat shamaness performing a purification ritual, East Mongolia. Archives Amelie and Holger Kalweit.

Burjat shamaness, East Mongolia. Archives Amelie and Holger Kalweit.

Shamaness initiating her apprentice, Western Tibet. Archives Amelie and Holger Kalweit.

When the two have sung the hymn through, all the other voices join in, a calling wailing chorus of distressed people. No one knows for what he is calling, and no one worships anything; but the ancient song of their forefathers puts might into their minds. They will have no food to give their children when next day comes. They pray for calm so that they can hunt, for food for their young ones.

And suddenly it seems as if nature around us becomes alive. We see the storm riding across the sky in the speed and thronging of naked spirits. We see the crowd of fleeing dead ones come sweeping through the billows of the blizzard, and all visions and sounds center in the wing-beats of the great birds for which Kigiuna has made us strain our ears.

With this ends the struggle of the two shamans against the storm, and, consoled and reassured, all make their way to their snow huts and compose themselves to sleep. For next day they will have fine weather.

And it comes. In dazzling sunshine and hard-blown drifts we went on next day. (Rasmussen 1946, 56ff.)

For the assembled Eskimo, the fight between the two men, carried on in genuine earnest, symbolically wiped out the power of the snow onslaught and actually brought about the end of the storm. Symbolic actions lead to real results. Rituals cause pragmatic physical effects. Shamanic ceremonies and seances show this again and again. It is only in the Western view of the world that no causal connection can exist between a symbolic microcosm and a physical macrocosm.

A fascinating account of a seance is given by another student of Eskimo life, Rasmussen's good friend Peter Freuchen. At that time, in Thule, the northernmost Greenland settlement, there lived a man named Sorqaq, an *angakok* (shaman), who had been struck by one curious misfortune after another. Now, in the midst of all his troubles, he wanted to hold a great seance and travel to the under-world to find out the cause of the problem. He fasted for several days beforehand, and during this time he frequently examined his excrement. He meditated on the coast and prepared himself to swim through rock. A large spacious igloo was constructed. Many participants appeared, among them Krilerneq, Sorqaq's friend and assistant.

Sorqaq entered the snowhouse last and, following Eskimo custom of underplaying everything, he chided those present, saying they were horrible idiots to show up to see something that contained not a shred of wisdom. The spectators, on the other hand, encouraged him, heaped praise on him, and spurred him on. Turning to Freuchen, he said:

> "This is nothing for the great white man to look at. I am a big liar, and even if these fools are stupid enough to believe me, I could never deceive you, and your presence will embarrass me. What happens here has nothing to do with the truth."
>
> "I should like to listen to your great wisdom."
>
> "Naw, naw," he said. "That goes to show you that even a white man may be born foolish."

Krilerneq now tied up his friend, who in the meantime had gotten completely undressed, and laid his drum and drumstick next to him. The lamps were extinguished except for a tiny flame. Now Sorqaq began to sing. His old voice gained in power and soon echoed from all parts of the igloo. The tempo of the drum increased, and the sealskins crackled, sometimes above the people's heads, sometimes underneath them.

> I do not remember how long this infernal din lasted. I do remember taking hold of Krilerneq's arm to see if he was helping. Apparently he was not! All of us joined in Sorqaq's song, but Sorqaq's own voice became fainter after a while; gradually it seemed to come from outside the igloo, and finally it was gone.
>
> Suddenly Krilerneq put on the lights. Sorqaq had disappeared. There was only his drum and the sealskin on the ledge. Senseless as I was from the bedlam around me, I remembered to look behind the draperies. He was definitely gone!
>
> I looked around at the audience, and I could hardly recognize the calm, quiet friends who had come down to us to trade. Their faces were ecstatic, cheeks swollen, eyes bright and unseeing. Naked from the waist up, they swayed back and forth to the rhythm of the song. In the middle of the floor, Krilerneq was writhing and twisting like a dancer, driving the men and women into a higher and higher frenzy.

Krisuk, one of the men, suddenly fell upon those present, howling like a wolf. Freuchen fended him off, but he descended on Ivalu,

ripped her pants off, and finally broke through the igloo wall into
the open. Everybody was screaming in a strange foreign language;
it was not Eskimo, but everybody seemed to understand it. During
a seance, the *angakoks* are not expected to call things by their right
names; that would bring harm to everybody. Therefore they invent
new words or change the form of the old ones.

> The song continued and tore me along with it. I lost all sense of time
> and place. Ivalu lay naked across me, and I could feel others chewing
> my hair, clawing my skin.
>
> Suddenly everything changed. Krilerneq stopped his dancing and
> proclaimed that Sorqaq was trying to return. He begged everybody to
> return to their original places and sit there and sing, concentrating our
> minds on the angakok who was at this very moment fighting his way
> up through the rock under the igloo. He—who had made the journey
> himself several times—impressed upon us what sufferings Sorqaq was
> undergoing having to swim through the rock like it was water.
>
> Krisuk returned, naked and shivering. He pressed himself down
> among the perspiring women, who screamed when he touched their
> hot bodies. Ivalu started calling him by a series of unquotable names,
> but she was cut off by Krilerneq's booming voice: "The shadow is
> ripening! The shadow is ripening!"
>
> In the seance language, "shadow" is "man," "ripen" is to "arrive."
> We listened for a few moments, and now Sorqaq's voice was heard
> faintly in the distance. Krilerneq extinguished the light completely,
> for in order to travel through the rock Sorqaq had to shed his
> skin completely, and the one who sees an angakok "muscle-naked"
> must die.
>
> Krilerneq told us that Sorqaq had trouble returning, because some-
> body had left the house and returned, which made it difficult for him
> to find it.
>
> But presently his voice grew until it almost drowned the chant from
> the audience. Again his drum made the igloo tremble, and the crackling
> sealskin flew through the air. I tried to grasp it, but received a blow
> that almost broke my arm. Hell had broken loose!
>
> Then it all stopped. Krilerneq mumbled a long tirade, and the igloo
> became quiet save for the crying of the children. In a droning voice,
> Krilerneq implored the angakok to tell what secrets he had learned in
> the underworld. Sorqaq's voice came from the ledge.

"The Great Spirits are embarrassed by the presence of white men among us and will not reveal the reason for the accidents. Three deaths are still to come. So as to avoid more tragedies, our women must refrain from eating of the female walrus until the winter darkness returns!" (Freuchen 1961, 168ff)

The seance was at an end, and all the lamps were relit. Sorqaq was exhausted. Krilerneq warned Freuchen not to touch Sorqaq, since the earth fire was still in him. As he opened his eyes and saw Freuchen, he said, "Just lies and tricks. The wisdom of our ancestors is not in me. Do not believe in any of it!"

Among the Iglulik Eskimo, before the shaman travels to the Land of Day, he is tied up. He sits with his hands tied behind his back on the sleeping platform of his igloo, clad only in his pants. When the lamps are blown out, one hears a humming and whistling in the air above, until the shaman shouts at the top of his lungs: "Halala-halalalê, halala-halalalê!" A rushing sound approaches. Everyone knows that an opening like a seal's blowhole has been formed, through which the soul of the shaman can fly to heaven. The air is now filled with sounds and voices of every description. In this way, the spirits hold the hole open.

If the shaman, or his soul, makes it safely through the hole, the inhabitants of the Land of Day receive him with great rejoicing. They think that another dead person has come to join them, but when the shaman says, "I am still made of flesh and blood," they turn away disappointed. Nonetheless, the spirits play ball with shaman's bonds, which fall away of themselves in the realm of death. When the ropes whistle through the air they take on all manner of forms, those of animals—bears, caribou, and so on. And when the shaman lands back in the igloo amid loud commotion, the loose ropes fall on the onlookers. Then the shaman recounts his experiences (Rasmussen 1930b, 129).

For the Copper Eskimo, Arnakäpsha'luk, the great evil woman, is the source of all taboos. She lives with her husband and child on the bottom of the sea, in a little air bubble in a cliff. She is the mistress of all the sea creatures.

If a taboo is broken, Arnakäpsha'luk covers the sea creatures with a cloth and hides them under her dwelling, so that they cannot go up; then human beings must endure a shortage of food. In order to propitiate her, the Eskimo assemble in an igloo built on the ice. The shaman breaks a hole in the floor, and while the others sing their songs, he keeps watch for the woman of the sea. When she finally approaches, all the men take a firm hold on the shaman, for she now enters his body and begins to speak through him. Taboo violations, she says, have taken place. Immediately the women confess everything. When the hair of the woman of the sea has finally been cleansed and combed—that is, when all of people's sins have been confessed—she again releases the sea creatures. If, however, some sins have been held back, her hair remains in wild disorder (Rasmussen 1932, 24).

In the seances of the Eskimo of eastern Greenland, the *angakok* sits on the floor of the igloo with the spectators around him on the sleeping ledges. He is tied, and his drum lies next to him. William Thalbitzer says that the shaman's feet are near where some skins are hanging, so that later he can make them rustle (1908, 458ff.). In Thalbitzer's opinion, moreover, the shaman skillfully frees himself from his bonds in order to beat the drum, then sticks his hands back into the bonds at the end. The coming of spirits from the subterranean regions, in his view, is simulated by a *makkortaa,* a small instrument made of a piece of skin that is held in the hollow of the hand. But the Eskimo believe that the drum dances and jumps on the floor and occasionally leaps against the forehead of the shaman; indeed, it plays itself. The spirit enters the *angakok* through the anus. He feels that he is sinking into the earth. From this moment on, either the spirit speaks through the mouth of the shaman or the shaman himself speaks. That is to say, there is only one soul at a time in his body.

---- 12 ----

THE SHAKING TENT

In 1879 the explorer Sir Cecil Denny visited a Blackfoot camp on the Red Deer River in Alberta. With his translator he entered the tent of a medicine man who calmly smoked his pipe, paid him no heed, and did not respond to the gifts presented to him. After they had waited in silence for a considerable time, a bell rang above them. The tepee began to shake, and it lifted a little into the air. When the jerking movements stopped, Denny went outside to see who had dared to play such a prank on him, although it seemed to him impossible that anyone could be lifting the heavy rod tent, with all the buffalo hides on it. As soon as he returned inside the tent, it began to move about even more wildly, rocking back and forth, and it rose several feet off the ground, so that it was possible to see outside. The two visitors were overcome by fear, but their host did not budge the whole time (Schaeffer 1969, 6).

Åke Hultkrantz took part in a similar seance with the Native American medicine man Mark Big Road. After the medicine man had been bound head and foot and rolled in a blanket that was fastened with straps, the lights were put out. Hultkrantz writes:

> A few minutes went by, and then it happened. The Indians later told me that they had seen blue and green sparks. I noticed nothing of that, but suddenly I had the impression that cold was stealing over my back.
>
> Voices of men, women, and animals filled the room; they seemed to come from all angles. At about a man's height above the room, a rustling sound could be heard. At the same time, I could make out the soft moaning of the medicine man, who lay on the floor in the middle of the room. The spirits had arrived. (1981, 84f.)

When the lights were lit again, Mark Big Road was sitting on his mat sweating. The belts were rolled up next to him, and the blanket in which he had been rolled had landed during the seance on Hultkrantz's companion, a woman from the Arapaho mission. (Usually this happened to someone who was skeptical of these phenomena.)

Regina Flannery experienced the shaking tent among the Montagnais in August 1938, near Rupert's House on the eastern coast of James Bay in Canada. As the news of a spirit-conjuring spread, many Montagnais quickly assembled. Soon the tent began to shake gently, and it continued through the whole seance. Wilder movements developed. A spirit made its presence known, and at that point the peak of the tepee bent over as much as a meter. Three spirits appeared in the course of the session: Mistabeo, the main spirit and the interpreter for the other spirits; Memegwecio, the lord of clawed animals; and Mistcenaku, lord of all water creatures.

On this evening, Mistabeo carried on in quite a humorous fashion and made all the Montagnais laugh, especially when he made suggestive remarks about relations between the sexes. The ceremony reached its climax when Mistabeo and the lord of clawed animals began to fight. The people could hear Mistabeo singing and Memegwecio scratching on the tent like a bear. The listeners got more and more caught up in the ceremony and excitedly took sides in the battle. They supported Mistabeo with loud cries because only if he won would it be a good year. The lord of clawed animals lost the fight, and slowly all the spirits left the tent, each departure accompanied by violent shaking of the tent (Flannery 1939, 11f.).

Mrs. Warrior, an old Gros Ventre woman, recounted stories from her childhood to Regina Flannery. In one, her father had been on the warpath and absent for a long time. Her uncle approached the female shaman Good Singer with some questions. Mrs. Warrior recounts:

> A curtain was hung across the back part of the lodge and Good Singer was bound with ropes tightly knotted, then wrapped in a blanket so only her head stuck out. She was behind the curtain and began to sing a certain song. She told us all to sing that song four times. I joined in the singing. When we finished we heard a humming sound and scraping and all kinds of noise through the opening at the top of the lodge.

The top of the lodge began to shake and all at once we heard something slide from the top down behind the curtain where the old woman
was and land with a thump. That was her spirit, that is, the spirit of
her son who had died long, long before.

As soon as they heard the thump, my uncle said: "Here is the
offering," as he handed behind the curtain the pot containing a pup
they had killed and cooked. We could hear the dishes rattling as the
spirit ate. Soon all of the bones were picked clean and the spirit tossed
them over the curtain so that they landed in our midst. The spirit then
complained that they had tied his mother so tightly, and as he untied
her we could hear the sound of the ropes as he worked at them. Then
the ropes too came over the top of the curtain. They were knotted up
in one bunch and, try as they would, they could not unravel it.
(Flannery 1944)

The existence of the shaking tent seems so suspect to Western
observers that some of them made bets with shamans, hoping to
flush out a trick. Paul Beaulieu, a half-blood and interpreter at the
White Earth Agency in Minnesota, recounted that in 1858 he made
a bet with a *jessakkid,* a shaman, for a hundred dollars—at that
time a considerable sum. Suspecting a trick, Beaulieu put together
a committee of good friends to observe. After a little birch-bark tent
had been constructed, Beaulieu tied up the shaman with a rope he
had brought himself. He bound his hands, feet, legs, and arms
together and carried the shaman, who was naked except for a
loincloth, into the tent. The committee had taken seats around the
outside of the tent. At the very moment the shaman was put in the
tent, the whole structure began to rock and shake. Loud noises were
heard, and the tent bent violently from one side to the other. A
priest who was on hand immediately left the scene, fearing machinations of the Devil. When the tumult and shaking subsided, the
voice of the shaman was heard requesting Beaulieu to go to the
house of a friend, where he would find the bonds. The bonds turned
out to be there, and they were still the way Beaulieu had tied them.
When he returned to the scene of the demonstration and looked in
the tent, there sat the shaman, comfortably smoking his pipe.
Beaulieu lost the hundred dollars (Hoffman 1891).

When a helping spirit approaches, a whistling like the wind or an owl hoot is heard. The spirit enters the tent through the smoke opening, the peak of the tent bends violently this way and that, then the whole framework shakes. When the spirit blows on the shaman, all the straps and ropes fall from him and roll themselves into a ball, which is so knotted and tangled that it is difficult to unravel. The ball is then thrown at the person who tied the shaman up, often with the sarcastic words: "You tied this man up. Now see if you can unravel this ball of rope!" Those present light a pipe and hold it up in the darkness in the direction of the spirit so he can smoke. The tobacco can be seen glowing as the spirit draws on it.

Now questions are asked. If the spirit does not have the answers immediately, he flies out. The people sing songs in the meantime and await his return. He flies as fast as thought and is soon back. Many spirits speak with a whistling sound, but with great shamans like Plenty-Try-Meat and Morning Star, the spirits spoke in normal voices. When all the questions are answered, the spirit receives something to eat. He can be heard chewing or clicking his fingernails against the bowl.

In his "Relations" of 1634, Father Le Jeune left one of the earliest eyewitness reports of the shaking tent. Although he was a very skeptical observer, he nevertheless observed key features of this seance:

> The juggler, having entered, began to moan softly, as if complaining. He shook the tent, first without violence. Then, becoming animated little by little, he commenced to whistle in a hollow tone, and as if it came from afar; then to talk as if in a bottle, to cry like the owls of these countries; then to howl and sing, constantly varying the tones . . . disguising his voice so that it seemed to me I heard those puppets which showmen exhibit in France. At first he shook this edifice gently; but as he continued to become more animated, he fell into so violent an ecstasy that I thought he would break everything to pieces. . . . I was astonished at a man having so much strength; for after he had once begun to shake it, he did not stop until the consultation was over, which lasted about three hours. (in Lambert 1956, 116f.)

Alexander Henry the elder gives us a detailed description of the shaking tent in his *Travels and Adventures in the Years 1760–1776* (1921). The Ojibwa Indians wanted to ask the Great Turtle spirit some questions regarding military problems they were having. They wanted to know whether the invitation they had received from the British was a trap and whether they should wage war against them. Hardly had the medicine man crawled into the tent as far as his head when it already began to rock and shake. Howls of dogs and wolves and human voices made a hideous concert. Then suddenly there was dead quiet; only sounds like those of a small dog could still be heard. This made the Ojibwa happy: it was the voice of Mikinak, the Great Turtle spirit, while the voices heard before that had been those of evil spirits.

Now the interrogation of Mikinak could begin. The spirit gave precise information about the whereabouts and numbers of the British. It said that the British invitation was genuine and would present no danger to a delegation. In order to gather this information, the spirit had to fly overland and observe the British troop movements; therefore it was some time before it answered the questions. Alexander Henry asked for news of his friends. The answer later turned out to be completely accurate, just as did the information about the British (Lambert 1956, 119f.).

The shaking tent is particularly used for interrogations of beings from the beyond. The shaking gives people a proof of the might of spirit beings, although it is not necessary for the seance. Whether a small one-man tent is used or a large wigwam is of no importance. I have found no observations of purely mechanical means of making the tent move anywhere in the literature. We must therefore assume that the medicine people themselves developed psychokinetic powers of extraordinary proportions or include us in the spiritistic beliefs of the Native Americans.

James W. Schultz, who lived for many years with the Piegan Indians, was told by his friend Rising Wolf of the former power of the medicine people and particularly about one named Old Sun, of whom he reported the following:

> Without a doubt this man spoke with the gods, and also a number of their mysterious powers had been conferred on him. In the dark of night, when everything was still and calm, he would sometimes invite a few of us into his tent. After everyone had taken their place, his wife covered the fire with ashes so that it became dark in the tent. Then he

began to pray, first to the sun, the creator; then to Ai-so-pwom-stan, the wind maker; then to Sis-tse-kom, the thunder; and to Puh-pom', the lightning. While he was still praying and supplicating them to come and obey his will, the tent flaps began to flutter; a draft announced the presence of a slight wind, which gradually became stronger until the tent was pitching back and forth in a gale and the tent poles were creaking and groaning. Then the thunder began to rumble, mutedly, as though at a great distance, and there were weak flashes of lightning. The storm came closer and closer until it was directly over us. The thunderclaps were deafening, and the brilliant lightning blinded us. Then this incredible man began to pray afresh, supplicating them to leave us. The wind gradually subsided. The rumbling of the thunder and the flashing of the lightning became weaker and weaker and gradually faded into the distance until we heard and saw no more of them. (Schultz 1983, 118)

This story concludes our presentation on the shaking tent. As we have seen, all the accounts concur on the essential points. But although psychokinetic or telekinetic forces have been well documented by parapsychology, how shamans could be capable of summoning such immense force as to keep a solid-framework construction in movement for hours remains unexplained.

CEREMONIES OF HEALING

The angakoq serves as an interpreter between Sila and mankind. Sila's leading qualities are those of healing sickness or guarding against the illwill of others. When a sick person desires to be cured, he must give away all his possessions, and is then carried out and laid on the earth far from any dwelling; for whoever would invoke the Great Spirit must have no possessions save his breath.
                                        —IGJUGARJUK,
                                an Eskimo spirit-conjurer
                                (Rasmussen 1927, 82)

What is a ceremony? We should stop thinking of ceremonies as fixed rituals that consist of meaningless and empty repetitions of verbal formulae, along with rigidly patterned gestures. This description might be accurate for ceremonies of the great religions, but it is not accurate for those of tribal cultures. These ceremonies are entirely different. They are intensifications of all the senses through music, chanting, dance, and movement. The attention, so diffused in normal states, focuses on a single point, the needle's eye of consciousness. Pushing it, drumming it, singing it through that hole into another dimension in which space and time, the fundamental categories of human experience of the world, possess a different quality—that is the work of the ceremony.

In addition, shamans are great actors. They combine myths, stories, current crises, and journeys to the beyond. In comparison with shamans, our modern actors are feeble figures. The self-alienated present forms of drama were developed out of the decay of spirit rituals, and they have become exercises in which the consciousness of the players is not altered and in which the spectators take no active role. Where our modern theater is personal, shamanic ritual is transpersonal, and shamanic drama a transpersonal art form. The healing or conjuring ceremony is not an entertainment for viewing, not a prelearned repetition; it is a drama of life, indeed life itself.

The psychology of the tribal ceremony is that of revivification, rejuvenation, symbolic therapy. The traditional elements of tribal cosmology are reinvigorated, ritually anchored in the unconscious. But this is not done, as is widely assumed, through mere fixed repetition and religious drill. Rather, participants or patients are drawn into a spiritual atmosphere, and their consciousness takes on trancelike qualities. And it is just in this state—on a transpersonal level of existence largely free of ego—that the archaic cosmos makes its mark on them most effectively. Shamanic learning means—when will the followers of the cult of reason realize this?—taking in data in an altered state of consciousness. By comparison, our cultural theater is a degenerated way to attain spiritual and societal identity. The dramatic, the dramaturgical structure of a ceremony is not an end in itself but is the means to an end, to evoke an altered state of consciousness in the healer, in the patient, and in the spectators. Primal drama involves a revolution in the experience of reality, a radically transformed space-time experience, a heightened, archetypally and transpersonally oriented level of perception, a reworking of cognitive conditionality to the level of a spatially and temporally elevated overview of existence. The altered state of consciousness is the crowning achievement of the dramatic-ritual, initiational-visionary process.

Ceremonies work through symbols. This might seem primitive to us, but symbols make clear the polarities, forces, and relationships of existence. Symbols remain the most effective way for humans to express the abstract forces of nature.

The attainment of inner balance, or inner purification from imbalance, from conflicting forces, brings about the restoration of health and *joie de vivre*. The inclusion of societal, ecological, and cosmological forces is indispensable for this definition of health. It may seem strange to Westerners, who note the symptoms of illness and make a corresponding diagnosis. But our spiritual horizon ends where the actual causes of illness begin. Western symptom therapy is actually a bastion of discrimination against the shamanic way of healing. Our deficiency is our narrow etiological understanding, the reduction of the illness to the immediate focal point of the illness, the concretization and reduction of disease to its material, physical manifestation. This is, generally speaking, an expression of our materialistic worldview.

Inner purification comes from sweating, the use of incense, dancing and singing over a long time, and solitude, in which the malaise of the world and its culture falls away. Becoming a shaman is, in the last analysis, nothing but an extension of inner purification. The more transparent the inner world, the more transparent the outer, and the greater the power of magic. *Purification, transparency,* and *magic* are the core words of shamanism and of the spiritual world as such. Also part of inner purification is the loss of speech, the dying away of the conceptually encapsulated world. Speechlessness is the sacred language of shamans. When we go mad and the order of our categories degenerates into schizophrenic gibberish and its meaning is lost, we become purified of external determinations due to all kinds of cultural and worldly one-sidedness. We will see that the psychotherapy of the future will be the purification therapy of "primitive" cultures. Consciousness lies at the center of this therapy. Consciousness is the *axis mundi* of the inner and outer worlds.

The supreme principle of being is the change back and forth between accumulation and emptying, between filling up and purging. All shamanic phenomena can be explained in terms of the primordial pair, space and emptiness. The greater the emptiness, the greater the shaman, the curing power. To a great extent, our culture emphasizes accumulation, enrichment, storing up; other cultures have elevated emptying to the ultimate goal. Though we may possess the discipline of getting more, others possess that of having less. There is a parallel here with the primal subatomic ground. The latest microphysical research shows that energy—that is, also matter—is apparently generated spontaneously out of nothingness, resulting in the development of the material world. Is it possible that the shaman seeks out emptiness so he can draw fresh knowledge and energy from it?

Investigations of shamanism and healing generally fail to take into account the key point: that there is a shamanic psychotherapy, and that there are successful cures. Apart from anecdotes and marginal observations, however, there still have been no ethnomedical investigations of cure results. Why not? "Shamanic therapy is pseudotherapy," we are told, or more genteelly expressed, "it is faith healing! Whoever believes in the healing process will be cured!" This is a strange piece of rationalism, but this leaves aside explanations of how, biologically and psychologically, such cures take place. The label "faith healing," an expression of helplessness, does not constitute an attempt to understand shamanism. Indeed, it is the conventional way to attempt to discredit it. Nor do concepts of social and psychosomatic healing explain anything; they too are appeasements. Faith healing is not a concept that is based on great masses of ethnological knowledge. On the contrary, behind this image is a massive absence of research. No one has yet taken the trouble to investigate shamanic healing scientifically. We remain in the anteroom of knowledge, content with academic speculations.

Shamanic healing has many facets, which we may describe as (1) sociopsychological, group therapeutic, psychohygienic; (2) suggestive, psychoanalytic, psychocathartic; (3) transpersonal, ego-transcending; and (4) paranormal, spiritistic, transmaterial. This book treats primarily the last two aspects. They represent the high point of knowledge and action in the career of shamans. In truth they are the farthest-reaching methods of therapy, and they are the ones that make shamans shamans.

But shamanic ways of healing will remain alien to us if we try to relate them to the modern concept of illness. Shamans are individualists, not academic physicians. They draw their knowledge and healing procedures from the realm of transformative experience, which is highly singular and unique. This is why many shamans have the vocation to cure only certain illnesses. Manuel Thomas of the Yuma tribe expresses this:

A doctor gets his power for one sickness specially, that power may be good to cure other things, but he will not be so good for them. The visit to Avikwame that the doctor makes when he is asleep gives him a general knowledge and power for curing. But for really great power he has to perform a cure of the disease while he is there. A few doctors have had many good dreams and are very powerful for many sicknesses. When a man is sick he gets the best doctor for his sickness that is around. If he is not so good, the doctor will send him on to another and he will get moved around until he is cured or dies. The Yuma are not angry if a doctor cannot cure, they are sorry his power is not so good and go to another. They do not try to hurt a doctor if the sick person dies unless they are sure it is witchcraft. (quoted in Forde 1931, 183)

Moreover, the intensity of the healing power, the source and working of which remain largely unknown, depends on the person of the healer. Healers use the inherited procedures of their cultures. Unlike our contemporary doctors, they are idiosyncratic people, very much self-contained, individualists and loners who draw on their own personal experience. Thomas recounts the following about himself.

I had my dreams first when I was quite young [about twelve years old] but I did not try to cure until I was an old man. I remembered them quite clearly always and never forgot anything in them.

If I hear of a sick person something tells me whether his illness is one I would be good for. This may happen even if I have not had a dream and power especially for his sickness. If I feel right I know that if they come for me I will be able to cure the man. When I have a good feeling I am very strong and light inside and any other doctor who works on the sick one usually fails. The patient and his relations know too, for I seem to draw the sick man to me. Always, I think, I have been asked to cure when I felt strong for it, and on these occasions, I am always successful. When I am called to go to the sick man I have a different (i.e., special) feeling, it is like being back on the Mountain. There is some fluid in me which I have drawn from the air and I do not mind walking a great distance. I do not know how far I have traveled. When I work on the patient it does not tire me at all and it makes me very happy. Generally I can cure very quickly then, maybe in a few hours or in a day or two. . . . But I do not always know how things are going to be. Sometimes I do not feel really good until I begin to cure. Other times, I lose a lot of strength when I start to work on the patient and it does not go well. (quoted in Forde 1931, 184)

The best-known and most widespread form of healing is sucking the harmful germs out of the patient's body. This procedure is reinforced by massage and by blowing on and stroking the body. In the course of this treatment, various disease-causing objects are drawn out of the body. Among the Australian Arunta, quartz crystals, stones, bone splinters, nails, or shards of glass appear. The shaman of the Halakwulup of Tierra del Fuego draws blood out of the body, concentrating on the painful spot. He blows on it, kneads it with his fingers, presses it with the flat of his hand, or sucks on it. He accompanies this treatment with soft humming.

The Tibetan *wangchuk dbang-phyug,* or medium, heals by sucking. A drum is held over the afflicted spot, and the harmful substance is sucked out first through the skin, then through the drum. This is done in such a way that all the spectators can see it. The harmful object is then spat out into a bowl. Usually the object is a slippery brown or gray lump of an undefinable nature (Berglie 1978, 25).

The very last shaman of the Californian Wintu tribe is Easter Flower Woman, Flora Jones. The last generation of shamans initiated her in her youth. Today she is the only shaman who performs seances and healing ceremonies and administers herbs. Flora Jones went to school in San Francisco, but curious dreams finally forced her to return home. The dreams frightened her and severely shook her personality. At the age of seventeen, she fell into a trance for the first time. She was playing cards with friends when, without warning, she experienced a ringing and burning pain in her ears: "It was like a hot bullet shot through my ear. The pain flashed through my body and I was unconscious for four days." That was her first encounter with the star spirit. When she woke up, four older shamans were sitting around her, singing and giving her medicine. Later they took her to sacred places of prayer. Her protecting spirit taught her healing chants and introduced her to the art of healing. Only years later did she begin a regular practice as a healer. Her youthful experience of being torn in two directions—on the one hand, toward being a Wintu, on the other, toward the white world—and the state of imbalance that it caused now subsided.

Since Flora Jones generally does not remember after a seance what she has said, she uses a tape recorder when no translator is present. She listens to the recording, then interprets the dialogue with the spirits for those present. Initially the spirits complain about the procedure, but soon they permit themselves to be appeased. In trance, Flora diagnoses illnesses with her hands. She moves them over the patient's body and in this way feels all disturbances. "I feel the pains, the wounds, the inflammations. When I hold my hand over the body, I feel every little muscle and every small vein. I feel the inflammation. It hurts me. If they have a heart problem, my heart beats faster. Where it hurts them, it hurts me too. I become part of their body."

Only in the case of serious illness, when the patient is near death or unconscious, does Flora Jones perform the soul dance to bring back the wandering soul of the patient. She dances to the rhythmic beat of sticks and whirls around with a tiny basket in her hand, in which she tries to catch the soul. If this succeeds, she lays the soul back on the patient's heart, the place of its origin.

Flora Jones also treats white people. Her protective spirit advised her to do so if she wanted to become a real doctor. For this, she uses a simple procedure, a short trance in which she looks at the patient's inner organs. Many of the white man's diseases she does not heal—all the ones that might be called diseases of civilization or epidemic diseases—for none of these were known to the Wintu before the appearance of the "poison people," as the Wintu call Westerners.

To those who have difficulty understanding her trance healing, Flora Jones says that they are going to "sleep spiritually" or "live with clouds before their eyes" (Knudtson 1975).

Among the African !Kung, a Bushman tribe of southwestern Africa, healing means physical, psychological, social, spiritual, and cosmic integration. The central event in the healing tradition of the !Kung is the nocturnal trance dance, which often takes place four times a month. The dance reaches its high point around midnight, when most of the participants are in trance. A second high point follows around sunrise. These dances often last more than thirty-six hours (Lee 1968, 39). The women sit at the fire and clap while the men dance. The women too can enter trance through a special woman's dance, but usually only after menopause has set in, since it is believed that trances can have a harmful effect on babies they are carrying or might carry. A third of all women have attained *!kia*, or enlightenment (Katz 1973).

The entire village takes part in such celebrations. Anyone can become a healer. The more healers there are, the better it is for the welfare of the community. The dance fosters social relationships, eliminates hostilities, and protects the village from accidents. The nocturnal dances, as the !Kung say, make "the heart happy." They are vivifying, inspiring, and joyful.

The more one surrenders oneself to the dance, the more the mysterious vital energy, *n/um*, intensifies. Thus healers call themselves *n/um k'ausi*, masters of *n/um*. *N/um* resides in the pit of the stomach or at the base of the spine. Through dancing, *n/um* is heated, turns to steam, climbs the spinal column, and ascends to the crown of the head, causing the *!kia* experience. In this state, the healer recognizes the illnesses of others and begins to cure them by pouring *n/um* into the body of the afflicted person. At this time he also sees over vast distances and possesses X-ray vision. He is insensitive to fire and travels in spirit to the villages of the gods. In the *!kia* state, the human being attains self-realization. A *n/um* master expresses this as follows: "When I make the *n/um* rise, it explodes and tosses me up into the air; I enter heaven and finally fall back down again" (Katz 1982, 7). In the *!kia* state, the !Kung say, one has the feeling of opening like a ripe pea pod. K'au = Dau, a blind healer, regularly experienced transformation when he danced. God had taken his eyes out of his head, put them in a bag, and gone back to heaven. But when he danced and entered *!kia*, God came down for that time and put his eyes back in their holes. Then he began to heal and see again. Healers speak with the sickness spirits, struggle and wrestle with them, and try to persuade them not to take the afflicted persons away (Katz 1982). The healer draws the sickness out with vibrating hands and simultaneously takes it into his own body.

The healing energy is invisible to normal individuals, and the healer perceives it only in the *!kia* state, when it has mounted and the heart is "awakened." If the *n/um* heats up too quickly, it causes pains and one no longer sees illnesses. Only when the inner eye is calm can illness be recognized.

When the healer has drawn an illness out of the body and into himself, it first enters the arms, then the neck, and finally the head. This causes pain and burns. Then, in the truest sense of the word, he shakes the illness he has drawn in out of himself, by shaking and wiggling head, arms, and legs. When the trance sets in, he yells "//Gauwa is killing me!" The atmosphere of this healing dance can be described as follows. While all the healers are dancing in a circle around the fire and the women are singing and clapping, one or another of the healers breaks out of the circle and throws himself into the fire; he scatters the coals or sticks his head in the embers so that his hair catches fire. The others, alert, pull the ecstatic out of the flames or drive away the sickness spirits, screaming loudly. In the general excitement, some of the women also jump up and begin dancing with the men, while the others continue singing and clapping heatedly. At the climax of the trance dance, the healers fall down. Some of them are taken with a cataleptic rigidity of the muscles. Some of them remain in this state for only a few minutes; others do not awaken from it for a number of hours.

A similar phenomenon is found among the Hain//om, a neighboring tribe. When the dancers have inhaled enough smoke and put themselves into a trance through rhythmic clapping, an antelope conducts them to the great tree that joins heaven and earth. They climb up on it until, in its crown, they find a thong that has been let down by //Gamab, the creator. It pulls them up into his realm. Naturally, it is not their body that climbs up but their "inmost part." Now the shaman negotiates with //Gamab over the fate of the sick (Wagner-Robertz 1976). Earlier many healers in all the tribes were capable of this; today only a few can do it. Since during this "half-dead" phase, as the !Kung call it, the healer's spirit runs the risk of being caught by //Gauwa-si, the spirits of the dead, the other healers warn him to return. They shout: "Where are you? Come back!" With the healer's rattle, they bang him over the head so as to get the attention of his spirit. They wipe perspiration from their bodies and rub it on his, thereby transferring n/um to him (Marshall 1969).

A visible manifestation of n/um is perspiration, the steam from the boiling energy. If this perspiration is rubbed on an afflicted part of the body, it has a healing effect. Perspiration is a metaphor for inner heat—that is, psychic power. This is also true for glowing coals, which the !Kung rub into their bodies as an expression of taking heat, energy, into themselves. During trance, many of them have the feeling that their stomach is boiling and that they are pervaded with vibrant energy.

After marriage takes place, between the ages of twenty and twenty-five, many !Kung earnestly pursue careers as healers. They seek out a teacher and practice the trance dance. During their first attempts at entering trance, young people frequently get out of control. They behave antisocially—they scatter coals, throw themselves in the fire, ignite the clothes of the singing women, hit and crash into other dancers, and attempt to injure themselves. People calm such beginners, pour healing energy into them, and rub their bodies with perspiration.

The first sign of trance is that the dancers can no longer be distracted by disturbing noises. Vibrations rush over their bodies, they stumble and perspire, and finally their bodies become entirely rigid. The sudden onset of trance is indicated by wild leaps; other men come to help and hold the dancers between them until they collapse. Now they lay the dancers down within the dancing area and massage them. Older, more experienced healers do not go through this "half-dead" phase. They have learned to control themselves. Some young people, determined to broaden their knowledge of trance, trek from camp to camp and take part in all the dances. In this way they learn to master their altered state of consciousness and to refine their trance techniques. If a young man has trouble attaining *!kia,* occasionally—though rarely—he is aided by the use of a drug. The drug is used to help him to overcome his fear, not to bring about the *!kia* state.

The urge to experience trance can already be seen in childhood. Entire groups of children play, emulating the adults, at *!kia* healing. They dance and let themselves fall to the ground, as if with *!kia.* A prerequisite for becoming a healer is to have a longing to drink *n/um.* For this, a person must dance until the heart opens toward *n/um.* They should also sing until their voice reaches heaven. People who experience *n/um* in themselves for the first time cry out, because it burns in their bellies like fire. The fear of the *!kia* state is great, because people are afraid of never being able to come back from it—of dying. But once beginners have learned to look death in the face, they overcome their fear—that is the breakthrough to *!kia.* As *!kia* begins to mount, fear increases. At that point, the healers rest a bit in order to "cool off." They drink a bit of water, and in this way they calm the boiling energy.

There are two types of healers. The !Kung say: "Sometimes a person grows up with *n/um,* sometimes a person makes the *n/um* grow." That is, some have an inborn *!kia* ability, while in others it is acquired. The real shamans are of course those who have the psychic energy from birth. They are also, for the most part, the ones who are able to leave the body with the soul. They possess the classical abilities of the shaman.

Here is one last example. In North America, from sunrise to sunset, the Navajo work on their sand paintings. On the smoothed earth, the medicine persons trickle sand, pollen, corn meal, and ground-root or -bark powder through their fingers. The patient is placed in the middle of these paintings of figures and signs of the Navajo cosmos made with the strewn sand and other materials. In the course of the ceremony he symbolically takes these into himself. Accompanied by sacred chants, he merges with the traditional wisdom of his tribe, the mythos of his culture, and the universal principles of existence. In this way his conflicts become situated in an appropriate framework, a framework that relativizes the conflicts, subsumes them, and removes the state of inner anarchy. At the conclusion of the ceremony, the medicine persons scatter the sand to the six directions, back to where it came from (Villaseñor 1974).

For the Navajo, healing is a harmonization of the psyche. For patients, the cosmological sand paintings bring about a balanced relationship of themselves with the universal forces. Religion, art, and psychotherapy come together, and at the apex of the unified vision of nature, earth, heaven, and humanity arises health and wholesomeness. Masked dancers, prayers, sand painting, recitation of myths, acting, drama, singing, and herbal medicines create a sense of existential unity. Myth become reality, connects patients with the source, gives them a meaning. They experience the unity of cosmos, mythos, society, and themselves. That is the prerequisite for healing—balance, abandonment of one-sided egoistic thinking. Incorporated once again in the community of the healthy, patients regain their self-esteem. Moreover, amid the endless chanting of the rituals, which last for days, the patient enters an altered state of consciousness. This in itself is psychocathartic and is the basis for healing and heightened perception and attention. The communal atmosphere also contributes: many people—relatives and friends—are present. The sacred reflection on the history of the tribe, the union with the past, with oneself, with the tribe, and the cosmos bring to the patient an intensified receptivity, which soon takes on the characteristic features of trance.

Our purely symptomatic Western therapy does not view the person as a natural being, a cosmic being. By contrast, in the Navajo ritual, the individual is transformed through identification with the abstract forces of existence into a sacred, generalized person, into a person per se. This transition to the transpersonal has a cathartic effect, since it reveals a broader horizon for one's own being. This horizon is disclosed as a microcosmic version of the macrocosmic drama of nature. Through ego clinging the creative forces are diminished; through the experience of something suprapersonal in themselves arise liberation and vast vision. But to modern people, who are rendered artificially secure through medical insurance and technology, no broader vistas are proffered. From this comes our restlessness, our self-destructive tendencies. For us, a sense of planetary and cosmic relatedness is missing.

Navajo therapy includes group therapy, hypnotic therapy, altered states of consciousness, and presumably also paranormal and parapsychological influence on the part of medicine people. The person who is sung over accedes to a special place in the family after the ritual—for was he not for a period of time the embodiment of a natural principle? Has he not absorbed the powers of the gods? That is precisely what is missing in our Western healing arts: the capability of feeling one with the forces of nature. What is magic? There is no magic, only the naturalness of life! The stages that must be gone through to reach a sense of unity may be numerous. The goal, however, remains the same: real therapy is the quest for a transpersonal connection between self, world, and God.

The unity of this trinity is the foundation of a primal sense of the world; and today we must ask ourselves: Should we not return to that? Scientific facts are accumulating to show that our mechanistic, chaotically fragmented view of the world is responsible for the destruction of the Western spirit. We have embarked upon a stage of knowledge in which we are analyzing our analyses. But analysis done in the light of the transpersonal synthesis is our real future. After Galileo demanded that we dissect nature, and after the conviction became rooted in our culture that ritual and the attitudes of faith are based on superstitious circular reasoning, the new physics is now teaching us to see relationships and connections where hitherto only fragments, antagonistic particles, eked out their anomic existence. Today physics and other sciences are increasingly revealing a picture of interrelatedness, and with that we are once again back to the spiritual rituals of tribal societies.

PART FOUR
WAYS OF POWER

. . . and whoever would be a creator in good and evil, he must first be an annihilator and shatter values.

Thus the supreme evil is part of the supreme good, but this is the creative.

—FRIEDRICH NIETZSCHE,
Thus Spake Zarathustra

14

MAY YOUR SPIRIT BE CRAZY LIKE BURSTING CLIFFS

It is not thinking, everyday thinking, driven by emotions and sudden associations, that embodies the inadvertent current of the mind. Rather, the power of absolute concentration and total dedication is the gateway to higher consciousness. For Westerners, thoughts usually remain separated from the world of action; for shamans, on the other hand, will and impulse fuse. For them, thinking is no mere symbolic expression that ekes out a pale existence in the form of language. Shamans carry thinking to the highest level of perfection, seeing in it a subtle quasi-material force that, like air, pervades the visible world.

Black magic works through maleficent thoughts that are transferred onto an enemy. Here anthropology admits at most that a power of suggestion can develop within the framework of a close-knit community. The sociopsychological aspect, however, constitutes only one facet of this phenomenon and is certainly not the key factor. The principle of a telepathic communication network and the connection of all people through a telepathic link is common to all nature peoples. The universe is understood as a pulsating unity to which everyone, especially medicine persons, can open themselves. And the principle of empathic attunement—as it existed in the primordial time when there was communication with all living beings, including stones, plants, and even heaven and earth—is a basic factor underlying human experience. There is no people that did not have this experience or that does not still possess it today. Nonetheless this approach to the world is considered by modern-day academics to be a phantasmic offspring of

nature romanticism, empty of metaphysics, and has therefore laid
a taboo upon it that one is expected to accept without objection.
This is no accident, for this way of relating to the world is the basis
of all magical-spiritual philosophies, and since the Enlightenment it
has been the intention to stamp it out.

But just through accidental maleficent thoughts or an uncon-
trolled fit of rage, a sorcerer can generate so much energy that
someone who is the object of this can die. Such is the case of John
Quinn of the Tenino of Oregon, whom his tribal brothers accused
of committing three murders. A shaman is supposed to keep his
thoughts pure, but at one point, only for an instant, John Quinn
harbored an evil thought against another man. His helping spirit
immediately understood this thought as an order to kill this person.
The spirit charged off at full speed to carry out the "order," but
collided with an innocent young girl who just happened to be going
by the door. Before John Quinn was aware of this and before any
other shaman could get there to save her, the girl died (Murdock
1965, 170).

As a rule, sorcerers use their power in a purposive and measured
fashion. Their power is subject to their will, and the better they
know how to control the power, surely the more devastating its
effect. Normal people are the slaves of a seamless, ongoing flow of
associations that jump around all over the place like monkeys, but
in the whirl of the commotion they imagine that they are masters
of this mad circus. But shamans actually direct not only their
normal powers but their parapsychological ones. Thus they are and
remain the archaic masters of consciousness.

Billy, an Australian shepherd near Kijuliji Station, was endowed
with an extraordinary ability to concentrate his thoughts. He was
given his meals in the kitchen of the station, then ate outside alone,
since he was not permitted to eat with the whites. One morning
when he got up too late, the boss threw his food out onto the
garbage heap. Billy did not say a word but walked slowly back to
his camp. Before doing this, however, he thought his 'maulwa, or
cord, out of his body and knotted it into a kind of net. Then he
threw it over the doors and windows of the boss's house. As he
walked back to the camp, he dragged the cord behind him. No one
but him could see all these lines. He then unleashed his helping

totem, lightning, which hit the house and set it on fire. When the cook wanted to put out the cookstove with water, by "singing" Billy turned the water into kerosene, which really got the fire going (Berndt 1946, 67f.). Billy's cord and his magic net may be related to a particular cultural tradition or mythological motif, but that in no way diminishes their power. While ethnologists ponder the symbolic and cultural embeddedness of magical means and metaphors, it is presently clear that the "power" behind them deserves to be the primary focus of study. For example, how did Billy set the house on fire?

Lincoln, a famous medicine man of the Winnebago, also possessed the power of thought. He repeatedly used it to take revenge for the deaths of members of his family. He told the daughters of one of his relatives they should stop crying; he would redeem the death of their father through the deaths of four others. Shortly thereafter, the four he had chosen died. He also sent the rich people in the tribe wooden snakes that came to life and bit their victims with their venomous fangs. Those afflicted then called for Lincoln's help, bequeathing him all their possessions. In this way, Lincoln's progeny were always abundantly cared for. On one occasion, Lincoln was visiting a friendly Crow tribe that always received him as a special guest and arranged a large celebration in his honor. This time, a Crow man approached him, drew a line between the two of them, and dared Lincoln to step over it. Hardly had Lincoln set his foot across it when he was knocked this way and that and finally thrown into a hole. With effort he got to his feet and said to his attacker: "I suppose you have never heard of me. Tomorrow at midday soldiers will strike you." The next day this Crow man was bitten by a snake while hunting and died. Lincoln also demonstrated to the Crow his power over birds. He pointed to some circling falcons and told the Crow who were present to keep an eye on the first of them. Then he pointed to the bird and produced a peculiar sound. It fell to the ground dead. He always advised his people, for whom he often repeated this spectacle, not to eat these birds, because they were not good (Radin 1945, 211ff.).

Shamans also use aids of various kinds, such as simulated snakes, to kill their victims, or arrowheads, as we shall see in the next example. But these serve only as vehicles of consciousness. The

imagination or "kinetic energy" of consciousness can attach itself
to them. That shamans from hunting cultures shoot with magic
arrows in altered states of consciousness is not "primitive"; it makes
logical sense, for each culture uses the external world known to it
to describe the unknown inner world.

The sorcerers of Bunan in Taiwan use their fireplace ashes, over
which they recite curses for ten days: "May your spirit be crazy like
bursting cliffs, may your spirit be easily irritable like that of a snake,
may your spirit be like poisonous grass." Then they blow the ashes
in the direction of the victim, who soon thereafter goes mad.
Another method is to say incantations over a leaf until the face of
the victim appears on it. Then the sorcerer speaks directly to the
face: "If the wind blows, your spirit will be blown away by the
wind. If a cloud floats by, your heart will float away with it. If you
see a fire, your heart and your spirit will be consumed in this fire."
If a client of a sorcerer wishes to see a thief punished, then as soon
as his face appears on the leaf, the sorcerer pierces his eyes. As a
result the thief is stricken with blindness. To cast a love spell, the
sorcerer puts some ashes or salt on a small piece of meat and
conjures it: "You two must eat together, you two must eat the meat
together." Then he must await the appropriate moment to mix the
piece of meat into the woman's food. It does not then take long for
her to fall in love with the young man. A sorcerer can also cause
a couple to start to fight. He cracks the knuckle of his index finger,
imaginarily flings a stone into the hearts of the partners, and
pronounces a curse: "You will become sick in your hearts." In this
way marital strife is kindled (Coe 1955, 186f.).

Following the same principle, the Shuswap and Carrier shamans
of British Columbia took some earth from the spot on which a man
had stood. They put it, together with the symbol of their helping
spirit, in their medicine bag. Shortly thereafter, the man would get
sick or die (Teit 1905, 613).

Among the Ainu, a person who has been put under a spell vomits
blood and with it, the object that a hostile sorcerer has projected
into him. After they are vomited, these projected objects—arrowheads for men, needles for women—are given to a shaman who is
called in. This shaman projects them back at the shaman who sent
them in the first place. In this way, the hostile shaman dies by his
own magic (Ohnuki-Tierney 1973, 20).

The great Tsimshan shaman Only One was often asked to help patients who were suffering from bewitchment. In one case, he discovered between the ribs of a man an arrowhead that had been moving closer to the heart every day and was already frighteningly near it. The bewitcher had made a likeness of his victim and stuck a thorn into its chest, which he had been pushing deeper each day in the direction of the victim's heart. To the chieftain who had brought him to heal his son, Only One explained: "I know what is the matter with your son. He is the victim of a great *halaait* who does *haldaogyet,* black magic. He possesses a representation of your son, and he is working through it. Soon this representation will fall in his magic box. Then your son will die. This man lives in another region. You must go there and ward off the harm before it is too late. This man is very jealous of your power." The chieftain journeyed immediately to the foreign *halaait,* interrogated him, removed the thorn from the figure, and burned it. At that very moment his son was cured. All his pain disappeared and he was again in good spirits. Then Only One saw that the arrowhead was no longer in his body (Barbeau 1958, 76ff.).

Almost all peoples need particular objects or at least symbolic forms and concepts to guide their psychic powers. Here is another example of this.

Among the polar Eskimo, a shaman who causes harm to others is called an *ilisitsork.* He kills his enemies with a *tupilak,* a simulated animal, usually a seal. The *tupilak* either capsizes the victim's kayak or gets itself harpooned by him. This brings about an illness in the hunter that either kills or lames him. Rasmussen was told the story of Taterark, who encountered a seal as he was returning from whale hunting with a walrus in tow. He paddled wildly after the seal and was not satisfied until he had harpooned it. Later, as he was flensing the animal on shore, he made the unfortunate discovery that it had a human rib cage. Moreover, all its bones came not from a seal but from other animals. It was undoubtedly a *tupilak.* Taterark got sick soon thereafter, took to his bed, and was incapable of doing any work. It was generally believed that the old sorcerer Krilinerk had made the *tupilak* out of peat and clotted blood and had brought it to life with a magic chant (Rasmussen 1907, 187).

It would be possible to present an endless series of such examples. Their features are alike throughout the world and across all tribal cultures. Psychically projecting arrows, maltreating figures in place of a victim, cursing by "singing," singing maleficent incantations over crystals or ashes for days on end—all these are seemingly quite different methods. But only the outside observer sees real distinctions among them. For the sorcerer who controls the psychic mechanisms, there is no difference. The same power lies behind all of these procedures and simply has need of a different symbolic vehicle or vessel in each case. As electricity requires a wire to be transmitted, psychic power requires a crystal, a little heap of earth, or the saliva of a victim to attain its desired objective. But as we have seen in several examples, thought alone can bring the same results without any symbolic vehicle. The principle behind all shamanic healing is to draw the afflicting object or the psychic energy of the hostile sorcerer out of the patient's body and neutralize it. Thus, shamanic healing occurs in an energic universe that is still completely alien to Western science.

A Shuswap shaman from Kamloops named Tcelê'sket gambled away his favorite white stallion, which he had always painted with red stripes and dots. Tcelê'sket, a powerful medicine man, had a wolf for a helping spirit, and he always wore its skin as a poncho. To intimidate the gaming rival to whom he had lost the stallion, he said, "Nobody can win my horse and get away with it." The rival became ill shortly thereafter, and stiff and lame. It was presumed that Tcelê'sket had bewitched him. Two shamans, father and son, were called in. They sang almost an entire day long and finally concluded that Tcelê'sket had caused this sickness with his unmistakable power. They continued with their ritual the following day, and the son succeeded in sucking the illness out, while the father hit the patient on the back. The son turned to all those assembled and said: "I am now holding the sickness sent by Tcelê'sket in my hand and can do with it what I like. Shall I kill Tcelê'sket or let him go?" "Kill him!" the crowd shouted. They lit a huge fire to burn up the sickness. The son remained sitting silently for a time, then said: "I have entrusted the sickness to my helping spirit, the ice diver. Next spring when the birds come, Tcelê'sket will die." At that very moment, Tcelê'sket experienced the first signs of sickness. He ran amok, sang wildly, and tried to regain possession of his own helping spirit. But nothing helped him. The next spring he died, whereas the man who now rode the white stallion regained his strength (Teit 1900, 616).

Part of the repertoire of black magic is to attack the soul of the enemy. Thus, the Shuswap of Washington state and British Columbia made use of a medicine bag in which they imprisoned a stolen soul; or they carried the soul off to the haunt of their helping spirit, who lived either where the sun rises or sets. The helping spirit then guarded the soul (Teit 1905, 613ff.).

The medicine men of the Australian Yualayi are exposed to great danger when they leave their bodies with their *dowee,* or soul. For an enemy can harm them during their journey or can even capture the soul altogether, as a result of which the soul's owner suffers illness. Some medicine men have a bag in which they keep the *dowees* of other people imprisoned (Petri 1952, 298).

The *yékamus* of the Yamana of Tierra del Fuego either sends out his own soul to catch the soul of his enemy, or he shoots an invisible arrow at him. But making use of the principle of *pars pro toto,* he can also maltreat a part from his enemy's body, such as a fingernail or a hair. Spirit animals or the most various kinds of spirit projectiles, of course, can also be used to attack a foe. Frequently the helping spirit, totem, or spirit consort takes care of the business.

Among the Unambal of northwestern Australia, it is indispensable for killing a person to know his *ungud* name—the name of his soul. Understandably, everyone keeps this name secret. A soul, or *jajaru,* may also be lured away from a person through magical practices and forced into an object or animal, such as a lizard. One then immediately burns this object or animal, hastening the victim's death. Another way of rubbing out undesirable members of the tribe is through collectively staged dream journeys. These communal flights draw extensively on the powers of the medicine man; for this reason during this journey a sacrifice must be made to his *jajaru*—it must be fed with the soul power of another person.

The men sit and sing until they enter trance. The "doctor" fetches an *ungud* snake—which is considered to be the female creator of the world, a vitality and growth principle—from the water. He has everyone take a place astride the snake, and the journey begins. They shoot so unspeakably swiftly through the air that other doctors can only get a look at the trembling tail of the snake. When they reach a faraway land, they sit in a circle around the *ungud* snake. The doctor takes his stone knife and sacrifices one of the participants, cuts him up into pieces, and feeds him to the snake. The others look on calmly, then themselves partake of the corpse. The doctor cleans the bones of the deceased, names each by name, and lays them on the ground in an unusual arrangement— that is, precisely backward. The thigh bones are put in the place of the shoulder blades, the head in that of the pelvis, and so on. The others then depart, but the doctor stays with the bones. He recites incantations over them, and they once more become covered with flesh. The deceased comes back to life. Now the doctor draws a second *ungud* snake out of his own navel, and on that the two of them fly home. When everyone awakens, no one but the doctor remembers any of what has happened. Even the sacrificial victim has no recollection of the event. Later, however, he has a *miriru* dream in which he is attacked by an *ungud* snake—and soon after that he begins to waste away (Lommel 1952, 51ff.).

In the struggle against the mighty conquering white man, the recourse to black magic was hardly crowned with success. The little evidence remains of this recourse is in anecdotal form, difficult to use here. The *xon*, the medicine men of the Selk'nam of Tierra del Fuego, tried by any and all means to kill the *kaspi*, the souls, of the white intruders, but without visible results. There were not even able to kill the animals introduced by the whites. The shaman Tenenesk explained this problem to the ethnologist Martin Gusinde in very incisive terms:

> Oh, if we *xon* had only been able to get hold of the *kaspi* of the *koliot* with our *yauater* (spirit power), we would have wiped out all those white people! At that time there were still many and powerful *xon*. Every one of them tried with the utmost effort to get to the *kaspi* of the whites, but not one was successful. How often have I tried it myself! I don't know what else to say. The *kaspi* of the whites is different from the *kaspi* of us Selk'nam. Their *kaspi* is so changeable, so wild and untamed, that it always evades our *yauater*. Otherwise we *xon* would have done in those foreigners in nothing flat! (Gusinde 1931, vol. I, 723)

In one account, the sheep of a white farmer were repeatedly being attacked by the dogs of the Selk'nam, causing him to try to shoot some of them. The Selk'nam told this to their *xon*, who immediately put himself in a trance. When the farmer shot again, no bullet came out of the barrel, and however many times he tried to shoot the dogs again, he always failed.

Tenenesk recounted a similar experience from his own life. Once when he was a boy, he was attacked by white settlers. One of them was already loading his rifle to shoot him. In this emergency, Tenenesk sent his *kaspi* against the white settler with all his force. Every time the white man tried to load, the cartridges rolled out. In this way Tenenesk was able to escape (Gusinde 1931, vol. 1, 770f.).

I would like to present the experiences of James H. Neal (1966) in somewhat more detail. Neal was chief investigation officer of the government of Ghana from 1952 to 1962. His work brought him into continuous contact with native criminals who sought out medicine people for help. The medicine people tried on a number of occasions to liquidate Inspector Neal. One evening Neal, his servant Osmani, and a friend of Osmani saw a gray snake slither over the bushes straight toward themselves. "This is an evil snake. One bite, and you die on the spot. Powerful *juju* men make snakes like that and send them out to kill." As though they were in a spell, the three men watched the progress of the snake toward them. Then, unexpectedly, it stopped. It had bumped into the protective barrier that a *malam* had set up around Neal's house for protection against attacks by sorcery. Osmani cut off its head with a kitchen knife, but there was no blood flow—a typical sign of an artificially created being.

Another time, when Neal was about to go to bed, he sensed a presence in his bedroom that evoked in him disgust and revulsion. Looking around in his overgrown garden, which bordered on the bush country, he found a poisonous snake and some insects that had gotten as far as the inside of the house. His first thought was: a snake. He returned to bed, but his thoughts kept returning to this phantasm, which gradually showed itself to be real. There was a hissing and crawling around his neck. He started with fright, got up, flicked on the light, and inspected his neck in the mirror. No wound could be detected. He looked in all the corners of the room; he could find nothing. When he returned to bed and put out the light, the crawling and nibbling sensations began again. Suddenly he felt a horrible ripping in the area of his solar plexus. His fear

increased. The situation turned into a struggle between his own iron
will, which wanted to dismiss the whole event as imagination, and
the subversive force that was taking over his body.

But Neal's will to survive was fading. The following night the
attacks got worse. Now he "saw" his attacker. He pushed this
image aside, yet the undefinable creature persisted. With its long
snout, it nibbled on his neck and coiled itself in the area of his belly.
Neal felt increasingly wretched. The beast was sucking all his vital
energy out of him and thereby reinforcing its own. It became ever
more substantial and dangerous. In order to distract himself, Neal
had himself driven to his office, where he spent the rest of the night
working on his mail.

The third night, the situation took an alarming turn. The creatures were now consuming him with full force, threatening to
hollow him out. Neal understood that they were entities created by
juju men. His body had become these creatures' toy, but his intellect attentively observed what was happening to his body. In desper-
ation, he had himself taken to a European hospital, but the doctors
were unable to help him. Neal then turned to his medicine man
friend Malam Alargi, a spiritual leader of the Muslims. Through his
prayers, Alargi destroyed the afflicting power and expelled the
attackers.

In a renewed attack, Neal felt stings in his head and on his body.
Weak in the knees, he dragged himself about in a state of exhaustion. His vitality dwindled hour by hour. The following night, he
thought he was going to die. He was helpless in the face of the
torment:

> I had the clear impression of being in the midst of an explosion, out
> of which burst an immense, brilliant light. Immediately after the
> lightning, I seemed to be standing next to the wall of my room, looking
> in a disinterested fashion at my body left behind in the bed. Then I
> walked straight through the wall, which clearly presented no obstacle
> to me. On the other side was a measureless deep blue space, and I was
> amazed to have covered such a huge distance in so short a time. Finally
> I came to another illuminated region, only to see that a yet more
> brilliantly lit passageway led out of it. Within this passageway was the
> figure of an unusually large human body. Then by some mysterious

inner prompting, I received the message that I was not yet permitted to enter this passageway, since my time had not yet come. Once again I rushed through the blue space of infinity, entered the bedroom through the wall and saw my own body lying there on the bed.

What Neal describes here is a typical near-death sequence. As a result of extreme pain, his consciousness left his body, accompanied by an explosion, out of which burst a light, the "light of the beyond." Consciousness and body were split; consciousness could now pass through material objects, fly, and cover huge distances in a short time. Obviously, Neal was traveling through a tunnel that emanated from himself. But then, as we so often read in near-death accounts, an inner voice forces him to go back; his time has not yet come.

Neal awoke and went to the hospital again. He was in great pain, but the doctors could find no cause of illness. They suspected that an unknown African virus was in his blood and held him in the hospital for observation. Three weeks later, Neal went back to work. Adjei, his first inspector, warned him that his illness had been the result of a *juju* attack.

On September 8, 1962, Neal carried out his last official duties as chief investigation officer. On Friday, the previous evening, he had thought through and precisely planned the arrest of a long-sought gang of crooks who were intending to strike next at the racetrack in Akkra. That Saturday morning he overslept. Angry that he was behind schedule, he stumbled into the bathroom and cut himself shaving in such a way that blood dripped onto his shirt.

In spite of a great deal of work at the office, Neal succeeded in getting to the stadium on time, just as things were about to start. He climbed up in the big grandstand to a point where he had an overview of the goings-on. He made out the suspects in the stands and took pleasure in seeing how skillfully his people were closing in on them. The arrest was just a moment away. But suddenly, "as I was about to climb down the stairs, I was pushed very powerfully from behind. I fell like a log, and the fraction of a second before I hit the bottom, I turned my head back to see who had done it. But there was no one there."

Everything hurt when he regained consciousness. His arms and legs had been broken in several places, and his internal injuries had been nearly fatal. He reconstructed his accident. Someone had deliberately and violently pushed him down the stairs. His inspector had also by chance seen the fall from below. But who had done it? Nobody had been near him at that moment. Neal did not believe it was a *juju* attack, but then he thought of an amulet that Malam Alargi had made for his protection. It was still lying under his pillow. Malam Alargi explained what had happened to him. A mortal enemy of Neal's had gotten a very powerful *juju* man on his side. In order to get around the protective power of the amulet, he had employed a ruse. He had turned off the alarm clock and thereby confused Neal's mind so that in his hurry, Neal forgot to bring along the protective "medicine," the amulet, to the stadium. The sorcerer then took advantage of his vulnerability and conjured up an entity to push Neal down the stairs.

Weeks later, Neal handed in his resignation. The trips into the back country and the hard work were too tiring for him, especially now that he could only walk with the aid of a cane. Uncle Tetty and Malam Alargi, his helpful medicine people, suggested to him that he leave Africa, since no "medicine" could guard him anymore. Some malicious people now wanted to kill him outright since *juju* could no longer harm him. Neal followed his friends' advice and returned to England. Looking back on his African experiences, he confessed: "I developed a critical attitude toward the Western notion that Africans are backwards. I had ample opportunity to see that in many cases the Africans are far ahead of Europeans, especially where their knowledge of the forces of nature and of the human mind is concerned" (see Schenk 1980).

Our culture prefers to concentrate on the negative aspects of other cultures. In ethnological periodicals and books, we find innumerable references to black magic, bewitchments, and sorcery. Essays on the dark side of magic are so overrepresented that the positive sides, such as healing rituals and the social, political, and religious responsibilities of shamans, often remain entirely in the background.

Through social anthropology as well, which interprets all magical phenomena as social artifacts, we gain the impression that the only magic there is is a matter of sinister machinations. The discipline of social anthropology has constructed an intellectual edifice that is entirely blind to the practical and psychological consequences of consciousness alteration. It does not comprehend that two things that are completely independent of each other in everyday consciousness can very readily have a natural relationship. Social anthropology, and indeed Western ethnology as a whole, regard what they see as acausal, synchronistic, and illogical—that is, unity-constituting—connections as representative of the intellectual backwardness of primitive cultures.

For the last few decades, it has been acknowledged that sorcerers have the power to kill through suggestion people who share their beliefs. But since the beginnings of ethnology, "suggestion" has been the catch-all idea that has made it possible to explain and categorize inexplicable phenomena. And even then, ethnology has confined itself to a theory of suggestion that is quite meager and outdated. Today, research into hypnosis and suggestion is to a great extent subsumed under research into consciousness that ascribes to the human mind and brain a far greater field of effectiveness than the theories of suggestion of the turn of the century that are still the common currency in ethnology.

Yet magic is neither a cultural fantasy of primitive people nor a complex of symbols and metaphors; rather, it is the natural means of exploration of a much more complex structure of consciousness than that currently used by the modern sciences in *their* exploration of reality. Magic is not below our present level of knowledge but beyond it. Magic is a state of cognition that psychology has yet to attain. Nevertheless, the theories that have hitherto attempted to approach the mind of magic remain interesting in that they provide data on the historical structure of Western culture. They show us how ideologies have historically been projected onto foreign cultures, tightly laid over them like a second skin. They have created an appearance for the Western mind, caught in that particular historical perspective of truths, realities, facts, and theories, while the main substance was actually nothing more than narrow colonialism and blind ethnocentrism. The history of magic is the highly informative history of Western conceptions of knowledge. It reflects our historical arrogance.

When we speak of being "bewitched" by a work of art, say, or by a wonderful piece of music, or by the beauties of nature, we are not literally thinking of a bewitcher, a witch, a sorcerer. Those figures usually have negative connotations for us, since they are capable of creating deceptions, hallucinations, and errant states of consciousness in people. In this, we have forgotten the original meaning of the word *witch,* which comes from the Old English *wicca,* meaning "wise." Modern history has not only robbed us of the ability to be "bewitched" by the natural rhythms and wonders of human existence; it has profaned the sorcerer, the witch, the real psychotherapist, the sacred magician, and turned them into their negative counterparts. Conceptually, sorcerers and magicians have been socially discredited and even degraded into representatives of primitivity and evil. At the same time they have become welcome projection screens for the inquisitorial theories of church and science. Despite the traditions of the Enlightenment on which modern theories are based, these do not take the risk of breaking out of the ruts of historical discrimination. When they do make a departure of any kind, all too often they tend to depart to the other side altogether, to a romantic glorification of the primitive natural existence or of the symbolic power of shamanic magic.

In Western fairy tales, legends, and myths, the sorcerer is predominantly associated with the dark side of magic. Similarly, in uprooted tribal cultures that have lost the wisdom of tradition and their connection to the natural cosmos, black magic takes the upper hand, while white magic, the healer, and the religious leader are being wiped out. Nowadays in Hawaiian culture, for example, most people remember only the *ana ana,* the evil sorcerer. In alliance with the ethnologists and the American conquerors, the native population now believes in the "bad" qualities of its former religion.

Ethnologists who compile the opinions of simple people and whose preconceptions about the ruined cultures are thereby confirmed rejoice in the solidity of their theoretical edifice. But the circular thinking on which their views are based goes unrecognized. First, Western culture wipes out a native tradition and wisdom and native spiritual leaders by brute force. This leaves the field to the advancing ethnologists, who in their intellectual imperialism memorialize the culturelessness and primitivity of the tribes in writing. Thus ethnologists have omitted to make precise studies of the modes of operation of magic and of the lives of sorcerers and their psychophysical techniques, let alone try these things out on themselves when needed. As a result, we receive pictures of other cultures that are as incomplete and distorted as the theories of the scientists. For this reason, we rarely find authentic descriptions worth reading of black magic and its relationship to principles of consciousness. Here, we have had to content ourselves with some of the usual anecdotes, even though they afford scarcely a glimpse of inner methods of spiritual education and the transformation of energic and psychological processes. Since ethnologists have failed to investigate underlying transpersonal principles, these reports in fact degenerate into miracle tales that veil the world of natural magic, the power of consciousness, and the laws of mental physics.

Our consciousness is neutral; it knows neither good nor evil; it is beyond human value criteria. The powers with which shamans work are neither black nor white, neither positive nor negative. They are applicable to all human objectives. In the time it takes to draw a breath, shamans can either kill or cure, can pursue life-generating or destructive aims, and occasionally even devote themselves entirely to the magic of harm. But the notion of the evil sorcerer reflects inflated unconscious fears and defense mechanisms, on the part both of ethnographers and of acculturated members of the tribal culture.

Our conception of the black magician is derived from a variety of misconceptions that may be summarized as follows.

1. Unfortunately, in their investigations of shamanism, ethnologists all too often turn to the wrong informants—that is, to ordinary tribe members rather than to the preservers of the sacred tradition themselves. Too often, they have recorded the folklore of nonshamans concerning shamans rather than direct accounts of the shamanic universe itself. They have described a painting of a landscape rather than the landscape itself.

2. Since the time of the medieval, Inquisition-fueled witch mania and Christianity's related persecution of traditional cults and ceremonies, shamanism and sorcery have been imbued with an air of the forbidden, of Satanism. Moreover, since the scientific revolution they have been disparaged as superstition, to be restrained by the

rein of reason. The Church stamped all the transpersonal wisdom out of the Western world, and science, supposedly emancipated from ecclesiastical dogma, carries on the Inquisition on the rational level with undiminished harshness and with equal ignorance and brutality. If the Church saw only heathens when it encountered highly accomplished spiritual leaders and enlightened priests, scientists now see only black magicians when faced with masters of the human mind and psychophysical self-control. The witch-hunt continues today, clothed in the mantle of science.

3. Sorcerers and witches work in alternative states of consciousness. They live with a conception of space and time that remains unfamiliar to our waking consciousness. Faced with this, do not Western defensiveness and arrogance concerning magic arise out of the Sleeping Beauty–slumber of normal consciousness?

4. The champions of mechanistic worldviews who unfold their petty greatness in the context of compulsive pushing and shoving, who cannot do without linear time lines, who entrench themselves in a universe of up and down and left and right, who misconceive space as extended time and time as extended space—none of these will ever extend their hand to the sorcerer, unless it is to lead him to the pillory.

5. Ethnologists have lost contact with current science and still cling to a turn-of-the-century view of the world. Thus, the sciences of their own culture have passed them by. Using the classical ethnology of Tylor and Frazer, they live in the dream of a material building-block universe and draw sterile gratification from the classical physics of mechanics. Their most tragic failure, however, is this: they themselves have survived and enclosed themselves in a three-dimensional world of cubic space about which any physicist would laugh with pity. Ethnologists are fossils of modern science.

—————— 15 ——————

SHAMANIC BATTLES:
SPIRITUAL DUELS

The supernatural, the metaphysical, or the transpersonal can manifest itself in the framework of life-and-death struggles and confrontations, just as normal life can. Just as in everyday life all learning processes involve tests, in paths of magical learning it has always been a tradition to set up tests of power. Tests, competitions, and public demonstrations of abilities attained are not found only at the end of shamanic education but are an integral component of it. Experienced shamans test the progress of their students, and as in every kind of education, there are those who come out better, those who come out worse, and those who do not get through at all. Moreover, shamans continually assure themselves of their own powers by testing and checking them, and as a part of this, they dare to compare their own powers with those of other shamans. Duels between shamans on a nonmaterial level are therefore a central aspect of the magical tradition. Competitions, too, are part of shamanic education and are among the unavoidable social duties of shamans. Sorcerers must always be ready to measure themselves against hostile forces, for the forces that menace them—whether they are spirits and polymorphous beings from the other world or rival shamans on the earth—are many and devious. Continuous alertness for their own sake and for that of their family and tribe elevates shamans to the level of lords over life and death, protectors of the middle dimension that hovers precariously balanced between the upper world and the lower world. The warlike aspect of shamanism is certainly also an expression of the particular living conditions of tribal society, most of which are surrounded by hostile cultures and whose subsistence is never assured because of fluctuations in game supplies and in ecological and climatic relationships.

Fights between shamans take on the most various forms, and since the laws of the transpsychic have scarcely been investigated, they are quite difficult for Westerners to fathom. Unfamiliar symbology and metaphors pose further obstacles to grasping the transpersonal element accurately. The Yamana *yékamus* of Tierra del Fuego, for example, uses his ability to blow himself up to the size of a mountain ridge to shield his patients from the attacks of hostile shamans. He interposes himself as a protective wall between an ailing person and a maleficent power. If the hostile sorcerer proves the stronger, he pushes this "spiritual mountain" aside; if he is unsuccessful at this, he must withdraw (Gusinde 1931, vol. 2). How is this symbolic presentation to be understood?

The tendency common to all cultures to mythologize and speak in mysterious terms of transpersonal events often obstructs our direct comprehension of accounts of spiritual duels between shamans. If the struggles took place a long time ago, they have taken on the character of legends and teaching examples. In our way of looking at things, they seem to be fairy tales, and we may ascribe their creation to free imagination. Shamanic fights, however, with their paranormal battle techniques certainly do not belong to the category of fairy tales; even today, they are a living and present reality. Since only adepts are familiar with the transpersonal techniques and rituals necessary for attack and defense; since normal tribe members tend to take accounts of them too literally and often regard them as taking place on the material level; and since ethnographers also adopt externalized forms of expression and as a result interpret shamanic fights symbolically or as expressions of heightened imaginative power, we remain behind a wall of silence and ignorance.

It is true that murder by voodoo has been acknowledged by a number of academics, but for the most part explanation of it has been short-circuited by recourse to theories of suggestion (Long, Winkelman 1983). A number of cases of death in shamanic duels could presumably be explained by hypnosis or self-suggestion, but this should not be assumed as frequently as it is. Just because the suggestion theory at present enjoys heightened popularity among academics does not mean that shamanic contests practiced for millennia can be exhaustively explained by it. Neither present-day, modern hypnosis hypotheses nor transpersonal investigations have sufficiently penetrated into the shamanic universe and the structure of altered states of consciousness to be able to make scientific assertions about them.

Methods of initiation and the transformations of consciousness that take place through them are real and effective. In the same way, communication between persons who are in alternative states of consciousness also seems possible. This has not as yet been acknowledged because it is so alien to our causal-mechanical outlook. But battles between shamans do take place on the spiritual level. Three types can be distinguished. First, battles can be waged in an alternative state of consciousness that is capable of calling forth physical effects at a distance. The inner workings of this process are at present by no means understood by us; certainly, however, parapsychological phenomena are in play here. Second, shamans have the ability to separate their consciousness from their bodies and attack their enemy with their spirit bodies. This is a variant of the out-of-body experience. In these cases, shamans usually block their enemies' way back into the body or "kill" them in some imaginative way so that they never revive from the out-of-body state and die. Third, of course, shamans can send out their helping spirits to accomplish tasks for them; in this case, they need not necessarily enter an alternative state of consciousness.

Large parts of the shamanic universe, if not most of it, remain closed to us, even with transpersonal science. It makes little sense to attempt to interpret culturally or symbolically the incomprehensible, bizarre, and absurd. This mistake has been made often enough in the past by theories of religion. We should, rather, let the illogical-seeming world of the shamanic battle remain intact, distorting it as little as possible with our interpretations.

A spontaneous clash between shamans was experienced by the student of Eskimo culture Peter Freuchen (1961, 165ff.). A powerful storm had forced him and his companion to take refuge in a tent on Repulse Bay, whose inhabitants he by chance happened to know. Here, quite unexpectedly, a bitter fight took place between a shaman there, Anaqaq, and an enemy shaman from Netsilik, a notorious robber of souls. The incident was as follows: A little boy who had gone outside to urinate came back frightened and horrified. He had seen something strange—an animal, a kind of snow owl, only much larger and with a terrifying glance. All activity stopped and panic took over. Anaqaq prepared himself for battle. He wound his torso in harpoon line, bound his hair into a knot, and rolled up his sleeves. Then he bit into a piece of leather and murmured strange words. Gradually he became filled with a berserk rage, and with a roar he rushed out of the tent and threw himself into the tumult of a battle in which, as evidenced by the din, several parties were taking part. Inside the tent horrible screams could be heard: it sounded as if two of the parties had each other by the throat. Freuchen wanted to go outside, but he was held back; when curiosity moved him to try to look out through a rip in the tent, he was pulled back then too. Many had lost their eyesight by catching a glimpse of incarnated spirits. The rumble of battle subsided now, and soon vigorous footsteps could be heard coming from the beach. Two men posted themselves at either side of the door so as to overpower Anaqaq when he came in. When he leaped into the tent, the women and children screamed, and only with the help of Freuchen and three men were they able to subdue the possessed man and calm him. They dragged him into a corner and covered him up. Then they asked him questions. But as always in this state the *angakok* could answer only yes or no. His hands were bloody, and there was blood running from his mouth. The enemy shaman, they now learned, had come flying through the air with the intention of devouring the little boy. A little earlier he had killed two little girls. But now he had been conquered once and for all. He had been imprisoned in a crack in the ice and could no longer cause anyone harm.

The Eskimo Samik told Knud Rasmussen the story of his grandfather Titqatsaq, who took great pleasure in leaving his body and flying through the air. On one such soul flight he met another great shaman from Utkuhikjalik, Muraoq, who was also on a journey in the sky, flitting about like a bird. But he came too near Titqatsaq, and they collided. Samik's grandfather fell and landed hard on the ice. Concerned, Muraoq flew down to him, summoned his helping spirit, and healed his friend. Hardly had Titqatsaq recovered when he rammed Muraoq so hard that he fell with a crash. Now Titqatsaq hesitated to help the other in turn; but since they were good friends and Muraoq had often stood by him, he healed him (Rasmussen 1931, 299f.).

Only One, the Tsimshan shaman from the northwestern Canadian coast, had acquired his unusual abilities in a cave. He had so much fame and success that, as often happens in tribal societies, other shamans got together and agreed to get him out of the way. They decided to lay a trap for him. They sent a number of men to him, and when the men landed in their canoe in his village, they said: "O great *halaait,* our master sends us to you to get you to help his son who has been ailing and is now dying. The other *halaaits* can do nothing, so now he is sending for you." But during this speech, Only One's spirit helper whispered to him: "These men are lying. Their chief's son is well and is just pretending to be sick so they can kill you." Despite this warning, Only One decided to go with the messengers. Along with a few of his people, he got into the canoe, and they paddled to the village of their enemies, where the chief's son was ostensibly lying sick. Only One saw instantly that the son was pretending and said to him: "I've come for nothing. You are too sick. You will never get well again, for you will soon die." At this point, a great weakness actually did come over the young man, and he became afraid. Then Only One said, "Give me water! I must have fresh water! I am very thirsty!" When water was brought, his helping spirit warned him again: "Don't drink that. It is urine mixed with a dangerous poison." Only One turned the tables and offered the feigning patient the water. The latter defended himself energetically and refused to accept the brew. But Only One insisted that he drink it, and thus the chief's son died. Victorious, Only One returned to his canoe and left the enemy village (Barbeau 1958, 76ff.).

The animosity, envy, and hatred of the other shamans toward Only One was so great that they were always trying to do him in. Once, when Only One was called upon to help an ailing shaman, it emerged that this shaman had been bewitched by ill-intentioned *halaaits.* This had been planned by the Wudhalaait, a cannibal society, and had been undertaken to lure Only One out of his village once again so he could be killed. They devised several traps and laid them along the way to the patient's house. One was an invisible magic net in which Only One was to become entangled, and another was an invisible ditch into which he was to fall. Since these traps could not be perceived by ordinary people, they were harmless for them. The traps were made especially for Only One. But he recognized the danger beforehand and was able to evade it. He accurately diagnosed the cause of his patient's illness. The other *halaaits* had wrapped up a piece of his excrement and put it into the corpse of a shaman who had recently died and been buried in a secret place. That was the cause of the illness. When Only One recognized the source of the ailment, he sent someone to the place to remove the parcel from the corpse. As soon as it had been removed, the patient immediately got better. After this success, Only One's rivals were even more enraged than they had been before and were ready to do everything in their power to get rid of him. They invited him to a great feast and offered him human flesh that would have poisoned him. But the *halaait* whose life he had saved warned him of the danger in time. Only One cut a hole in his stomach so that the meat came out again. His helping spirit smuggled it into the food of the enemy *halaaits,* who soon fell down in agony and died. In this way Only One overcame all his enemies (Barbeau 1968, 76ff.).

The *payé* of the Tukano of South America carry out their warlike confrontations under the influence of drugs. While both their bodies are lying at home in trance, the *payé* meet in the heavens, in the interior of the earth, in the water, or on a mountain. They shoot at each other with lightning bolts, change themselves into snakes and jaguars, and build around the other's heart a stone wall that makes his world smaller and smaller. As a defense measure, the attacked party can turn himself into a fly, but then the universe shrinks for him to the size of an orange and he can no longer hope to be saved (Reichel-Dolmatoff 1975, 100f.).

For the Lapps, the underworld is a place of danger. Not only are the beings that live there capable of harming shamans, but foreign shamans with hostile intentions can make them lose their way so that they must remain there forever. It is said that many shamans have fallen by the wayside in this manner. As the Yakut shamans stage wars between animal spirits every year, the Lapp shamans combat each other by confronting each other and setting their helping spirits on each other in the form of reindeer bulls or spirit birds. Among the Scandinavian Lapps, the helping spirit is called the *sueje,* or shadow. There are shadow fish, shadow reindeer, and shadow snakes, and they accompany shamans on journeys to the underworld to bring back dead or kidnapped souls. If such a shadow animal is injured in a fight, the injury is transferred to the possessor of the animal, and if the animal is killed, the shaman must die as well (Harva 1964, 284, 293). An example of this can be seen in a contest between two Lapp shamans. The hostess of a big celebration very suddenly dropped dead. A shaman who was present immediately undertook to follow the soul. With a whale, a reindeer drawing a sled, and a rowboat as aids, he chased after the soul. But after he had danced for a long time, he collapsed. He foamed at the mouth, his face took on a black color, his belly opened as though it had been slit, and he died. Then a second shaman stepped in to try to investigate the fate of the first. He was successful in bringing the hostess back to life and also in explaining the misfortune of the other shaman. The latter had swum through the sea in the form of a whale. There a hostile shaman lay in wait with a sharp pole with which he cut open its belly; this had manifested on the material level as the shaman's slit belly (Harva 1964, 294).

Edward S. Curtis (1907, 58) gives an account of another contest with the most tragic outcome. The fight was between Medicine Child and Hair-in-a-Lump. As they were smoking together, Medicine Child asked: "Are you strong?" Hair-in-a-Lump confirmed, "I have much power." Medicine Child said, "Have you ever looked at those plant stems that shake in the spring at the time of the high water? My medicine will do the same thing to you." Hair-in-a-Lump answered, "My medicine will strike you blind, and you will spend the rest of your life in darkness!" After that, each of them prepared his medicine in his tent. Pretty soon, Hair-in-a-Lump began to shake so much that he could barely hold a bowl of water without spilling it. That same day, Medicine Child lost his eyesight. When Hair-in-a-Lump could no longer bear this state, he said to his nephew: "Is that good, my son? I will never again be able to live as

I did before. I will always have to shake the way I am now. Dress me in my war dress, paint me with my medicine, and then kill me." He talked this way to his nephew until the nephew gave in: "All right. I'll kill you." He dressed the shaking man, painted him, and said: "Father, do you see my index finger? You must take it with you!" With that, he cut off the finger, laid the gun to his uncle's breast, and pulled the trigger.

Most shaman battles are fought between their souls, but transformations into material form also take place, such as transformations into animals, birds, clouds, or other people. Since tribal cultures and societies based on hunting live in close connection with the animal world, the idea of using the form of animals for shamanic battles is common. A Chukchee tale tells of such a transformation into an animal. One shaman asked another what he was going to change himself into. "Into a falcon," answered the other. "And you?" "Into the great auk!" replied the first one. Then each of them took on the form of his respective bird, and the fight began (Bogoras 1907, 443).

Among the Manchurian Tungus, according to Shirokogoroff (1935a, 371), the shamans were in a continual state of war, not only within the tribe, but between various tribes. The particularly bellicose shamans were called *bulantka*. They were a danger for other shamans, for they lay in ambush, waiting to catch souls as soon as they penetrated into the underworld. They used their ability to change into an animal—or an insect or bird—to observe their victims. And in these nonmaterial forms they used bow and arrow to hunt animals and men; their victims often died several days after a fatal arrow wound.

Shirokogoroff tells the story of a confrontation between two shamans that ended up quite harmlessly for both of them. One night a shaman was hunting in a salt marsh and saw a glittering fire moving downward. He drew his knife and made his way home. There he recounted his experience to everyone: Sanyuni, another shaman, had come, he explained. He asked everyone to remain calm, and he lay down to sleep. In his sleep he pursued the attacking shaman; he sought out his camp and found Sanyuni sitting in front of his tent. He insulted him, accused him of being a lowly menace who went around at night in the form of a fire. Sanyuni meekly admitted everything and promised never to do it again.

The Lapps make their spirit animals confront each other in combat. Their spirit animals can be their helping spirits or their own souls. When a spirit animal is defeated by another, they are afterward exhausted on the physical plane. If this alter ego of theirs is killed, they soon die (Harva 1938, 479). Stories from Finnish Lapland tell of the shamans, or *noaidit,* engaging in magical contests. For example, they abduct an enemy's reindeer herd and drive it to their own pastures.

Many stories tell of disastrous outcomes and even the death of a shaman in the course of a competition. A particularly tragic legend concerns two Yukagir shamans who were engaged in a fight on various different planes of existence. They set their helping spirits against each other—that is, they left their bodies and their souls fought each other. It is said that in such confrontations the shamans end up shooting each other, *n'eayi'nuni,* or devouring each other, *n'eleu'nununi.* One shaman said to his friend: "Let's try to dig through this rock mountain. We'll see who gets through it first." Each emanated his spirit dog to take on the job. One had a female spirit dog and the other a male. The two of them, side by side, dug through the rock until the male dog reached the center of the mountain. But then he could go no further—he had lost the contest. Now the defeated shaman proposed a flying contest. Having changed themselves into storks, they put on their cloaks, took off, and flew away. As they were flying over the beach, they saw a house below. They glided down and encountered in the house the wife of the Lord of the Ocean, Co'bun Po'gil. The woman received them kindly and served them something to eat, and when bedtime came, the shaman with the female spirit dog lay down in the corner with the children, as is customary. The other shaman got in bed with the Lord of the Ocean's wife. "It would be better for you to sleep in the corner with the children," she said to him. "I am married, and my husband wouldn't like this." But he dismissed her words of warning. The following morning, his companion found him dead. The Lord of the Ocean had slain him. The companion fled, but he soon met his own fate. He met a headless, one-eyed man whose mouth was in his armpit and spent the next night with him. On the following morning, as the one-eyed man slept, the sham took his iron boots, put them on, and climbed into the heavens. At once he heard the one-eyed man begging and pleading for him to throw his boots down to him. But the shaman's heart could not be softened, so the one-eyed man threw a glove after him. The glove tore off a bit of his cloak, which fell down to earth. The one-eyed man ate the shred of cloth, whereupon the flying shaman raised his voice in supplication—he wanted the piece of cloth back at any price and was ready to give the boots back in exchange for it. "Now it's too late; we have already harmed each other enough," the one-eyed man replied. The shaman was not intimidated by his words and shouted back: "Good. In that case you shall never leave that place, for there you will die!" But the one-eyed man was also a shaman, and when the flying shaman arrived home, he said to his family, who were happy to see him, "Do not rejoice, I will not live much longer." And as he had predicted, the following morning he was dead (Jochelson 1924, 213f.).

Many stories about shamanic duels end with the death of both rivals. This happened in the case of two Yamana shamans, brothers who had become enemies. The people became involved in their fight and took sides with the shaman they liked the best. The result was that the whole village was divided into two hostile parties and was in a state of turmoil. The time came for the two shamans to measure their power one against the other. One brother left his hut in a dream, got into his canoe, and paddled to the middle of the canal. There he met his fraternal enemy who, also dreaming, had come from the opposite bank. Each dreamed he shot a sharp *yekus,* or arrowhead, into the other's heart. Both then paddled back and continued sleeping in their huts. The next morning both brothers felt sick and miserable. Blood was flowing from their mouths and noses. Soon thereafter, both died (Gusinde 1931, vol. 2, 1392f.).

Since the weapons at a shaman's disposal are to a great extent superior to material weapons, it is natural that traditional societies make demands on shamans in all of life's situations, but particularly in war.

Among the Evenki a shaman sets up a fence made up of his protective spirits around his clan's territory. Bird spirits protect the air, fish spirits the water, and animal spirits the taiga. If a shaman wants to inflict harm on another clan, he emanates a disease spirit into the water at the mouth of his own clan's river. From there the water runs into the underworld, where all the clans' rivers meet. From the underworld the disease spirit swims up the river of the enemy clan and spreads disease, death, and cattle plagues. To do this to the enemy clan, it must overcome the immaterial fence around the clan. Naturally, the local shaman is on the alert, checks with his spirit guards, and is ready at all times for an attack (Friedrich 1955, 50).

The Hunza of northern Pakistan also draw their shamans into action in times of warlike strife. Famous was Ali Beg, a *daiyal* from Satpura, who lived about a hundred years ago and played an important role helping his people achieve victory in the war against Ladakh. When the two armies were faced off and the Ladakhis unleashed eighteen pairs of dogs against the Hunza, Ali Beg stepped forward out of the ranks of fighters and whispered something into the ear of the first beast. At once the whole pack began to follow him around like tame hunting dogs. Now the Ladakhis took recourse to another impressive war stratagem. They sent forth a sorcerer who could fly. Ali Beg mounted into the heavens and grabbed the enemy magician by the foot so that he had to give up. To make still a greater impression on the enemy and break his spirit, before the eyes of the enemy host, Ali Beg took a piece of red hot iron in his mouth. Then the Hunza gave the Ladakhis to understand that they had a number of such mighty warriors and magicians, and that Ali Beg was one of the weaker ones. At that point, the enemy army admitted defeat (Friedl 1965, 55f.).

At religious celebrations, feasts, and initiation ceremonies, competitions among shamans are put on for entertainment and amusement. In these contexts a contest seldom ends in death for the defeated party but often in illness or loss of consciousness. At least among Native Americans, however, the victor then has the duty of restoring his rival to health. Shamanic competitions are carried out not only in public settings but in closed medicine societies or secret esoteric organizations, as is customary, for example, among the Pueblo tribes.

Among the Washo, shamans stage competitions to test who has the greatest power. One form of their competition consists in seeing who can knock over the greatest number of poles, which are tightly rammed into the earth in a line, merely by pointing at them. The winner is the one who knocks over the most poles through psycho-kinesis, or psychic power working at a distance. Another form of power demonstration is to offer a pipe—or nowadays a cigarette—that is filled with power. Anyone who smokes it falls instantly to the ground unconscious. In this type of demonstration, the shaman does not emanate his power; rather, it is firmly attached to an object and injures anyone who touches it.

The Lakota have something called an elk dreamer, a *hehaka gaga*, who possesses power over women. He protects himself and other men from women's wiles and aids men in acquiring the wife they desire. At great celebrations, a *hehaka gaga* dresses up as an elk, while his young helpers dress up as deer. In these guises they perform a quite realistic drama: They fully adopt the attrib-utes of their animals. They graze and go to drink—at which point they are taken by surprise by a hunter, another medicine man. The elk dreamer draws a magic circle around himself and his companions, making them all invulnerable. Soon a fight flares up between the two medicine men, which quickly becomes bit-terly serious. Each tries to wound the other with magical weap-ons. The one who is injured must subsequently be healed by the other. Both the wounds and the healing are real, not merely simu-lated (Standing Bear 1978, 217).

Robert Lowie recounts a different kind of shamanic competition among the Crow (1951, 30). One Crow medicine man loudly pro-claimed that he could knock all his enemies in an opposing group to the ground with one movement of his hand. While he was dancing, his rivals intoned a protective chant. But when he moved his arm as though to push them all aside, they all fell over in one direction. Now a member of the opposing group got to his feet, ran four times around the fire, emitted the hoot of an owl, and suddenly disappeared. He was soon found sitting on top of a tent. He had no idea of how he had gotten there.

The famous Selk'nam medicine man Tenenesk performed the following feat for the ethnologist Martin Gusinde. He put three stones the size of cherry pits in the palm of his hand and stared at them with utmost concentration. When he blew on them, they all disappeared. Similar abilities were possessed by a Selk'nam medicine woman. She took off all her clothes, had a variety of objects put in her hand—little mushrooms, snail shells, stones, and twigs—and concentrated until all these things dissolved into the air. Then she rematerialized them all again.

Another form of competition between medicine men, one that usually ends in death, is the following Yamana test of strength. A *yékamus* throws a *yekus,* or arrowhead, at his opponent. If the latter fails to catch it, he is hit, loses his strength, and dies. If, however, the *yekus* is caught or not thrown far enough, the attacking medicine man is considered the weaker of the two.

When we see what kind of powers the medicine people of the Selk'nam and Yamana possessed, the question arises: Why did they not use their ability to kill at a distance against the invading Europeans? In fact, there was no dearth of attempts to defend themselves in this manner, but they were unsuccessful.

When two cultures that think in magical terms encounter each other, heavy battles take place between their magicians and sages. The shamans of dominant cultures often exhibit the greater power. This is shown by the example of Padmasambhava, who spread Buddhism in Tibet and defeated the native magicians of the Bon religion in great spiritual battles. In the same way, Saint Patrick gained the victory in Ireland, where he was opposed by the Druids, thus paving the way for the spread of Christianity.

Few reports of shamanic attacks against white conquerors have come down to us. Although there is scattered anecdotal evidence of victims of magic, shamans seem generally to have held themselves aloof. For example, the skepticism of the whites concerning black magic deterred the Zuñi from practicing it against them (Kalweit 1983).

Lyall Watson (1976) describes in literary form the story of Tia, an Indonesian girl who from her early years quite spontaneously developed parapsychic abilities, which were proscribed by the prevailing Islamic doctrine. The story of Tia is one of conflict between an old animistic nature religion and the severity of modern Islamic law. Tia possessed the power to heal people paranormally. Finally, she brought a drowned person back to life and set the mosque of the island on fire through her spiritual power. That was too much for the authorities. A confrontation with the imam ensued, in which, in order to demonstrate his self-mastery and the might of his religion, he gouged one of his own eyes out. After this incredible scene and continued persecution by the imam, Tia disappeared and was never seen again. A dogmatic priesthood had defeated the primal power of this shaman.

Celtic and Germanic legends and sagas of the gods are also full of supernatural battles. The tragic end of the sorcerer Merlin, teacher of King Arthur, the founder of the fabled Round Table, is well known. When Merlin encountered the beautiful virgin Ninian in the forest, he fell under her spell and let himself be drawn into teaching her his magic. Every time he saw her, she asked him to show her more. He ultimately revealed everything to her, until she said to him: "Teach me how to bind a man without bonds through the power of magic so that he can never escape unless I release him." Merlin sighed, foreseeing his own fate, but he showed her this last art as well. Once Merlin fell asleep on her lap—they had become inseparable—after leaving the knights of the Round Table, never to return. Ninian set the charm he had taught her upon him. When he awoke, he found himself in an infinitely tall tower lying on a wondrously beautiful bed. He called out: "You have betrayed me if you do not remain forever at my side, for no one else can free me from this tower." Ninian often visited him, and she would have been glad to grant him his freedom, but the the charm had become too powerful and she could no longer break it. Elfin power, love, and intoxication—these primal Celtic motifs—had once more attained the victory (Monmouth 1978).

PART FIVE
THE SHADOWS OF EVERYTHING EXISTING

The world of the physicist strikes the observer as a shadow-play performance of the play of everyday life. The shadow of my elbow is resting on a shadow table, while the shadow ink flows over the shadow paper. . . . The frank admission that physical science is dealing with a world of shadows is one of the most significant advances of recent times.

—Sir Arthur Eddington,
Nobel Prize winner in physics

—— 16 ——

THE GREATEST BLESSING COMES TO US ON THE WAY TO MADNESS

"Oh, there's nothing you can do about that," said the cat, "here everyone is mad. I'm mad. You're mad."

"But how do you know that I'm mad?" asked Alice.

"But you must be," said the cat, "otherwise you wouldn't be here."

—LEWIS CARROLL,
Alice in Wonderland

The greatest blessing comes to us on the way to madness. —SOCRATES

From time immemorial, spiritual and magical views of traditional societies have challenged the rational imagination of the Western mind. This has led to heavy-handed, even aggressive academic papers. Let us now assess the value of one of those glorious interpretations: the shaman seen as a Western psychotic. For those unfamiliar with alternate states of consciousness, psychosis, schizophrenia, and epilepsy seem highly inappropriate descriptions for this unknown potentiality of the psyche. Unknown it remains, though if a psychiatrist or psychologist were ever to have a shaman for a friend, they would doubtless understand each other very well.

The Hungarian student of Siberian culture Vilmos Diószegi portrays shamans as neurasthenic, neurotic, and mentally ill. They were often plagued by hallucinations, he says, often physically and psychologically ill; they suffered from headaches and came from neurologically impaired families that manifested a great deal of mental illness. A great number of former shamans, according to him, were afraid of people, troubled by physical defects, and were clearly to be considered abnormal. Nevertheless, in other passages Diószegi maintains that shamans were far above the average population in mental ability. The sensitivity of their nervous systems and their psychological constitutions, he says, are especially highly developed (Diószegi 1968, 314f.).

It is characteristic of academic science to find itself lying on the Procrustean bed of historical opinion. The projection of Western psychiatric concepts onto other cultures is part of this self-entrapment. The forefathers of modern psychiatry, Emil Kraepelin and Eugen Bleuler, created a definite conceptual language for psychiatric discourse. This language soon came to be used as the basis for ethnological descriptions of all outlandish phenomena that did not fit into the Western picture of rationality, linearity, ego control, anti-emotionality, and the Protestant ethic. To a great extent, the appropriation of psychopathological concepts by ethnologists has been, and remains today, an instrument for the annihilation of non-Western perceptions of the world.

Shamans in particular, with their bizarre experiences of existence, naturally appealed to all friends of the psychiatric. Thus, for Waldemar Bogoras, Chukchee shamans are all hysterical, and in their cunning, self-deceptive maneuvers, they resemble the mentally ill. Moreover, they are highly excitable and half mad. According to S. M. Shirokogoroff, many (not all) Tungus shamans are crazy, and Lawrence Krader confirms that Buryat shamans suffer from nervous disturbances. For Wilkin, the source of Indonesian shamanism is to be found in mental illness. E. M. Loeb describes the shamans of Niue as epileptic and afflicted with nervous disturbances. Paul Radin, too, draws comparisons between epileptics and hysterics and shamans. For George Devereux likewise, shamans are neurotic and psychotic. Devereux remarks that in a society of madmen, a madman will be regarded as normal, and vice versa. He even goes so far as to state that a shaman could be regarded as healthy only in an anomic culture. Curiously, in other passages he describes Mohave shamans as normal. Similarly, for psychiatrist Julian Silverman, the shaman is unequivocally a schizophrenic who is culturally tolerated.

Siberian shamans have been particularly characterized as schizophrenic. But this results from the fact that they were studied at a time when psychology's understanding of pathology was crude. Indeed, the point of departure was that shamans with these unique psychiatric features existed only in Siberia. Native American medicine people were thereby distinguished from Siberian shamans or African healers and mediums. This confusion is easily resolved the moment we realize that ethnologists equate concepts with reality: they take different concepts for different basic principles. Today we know that, no matter what name we call masters of the inner way, they are at work in all lands and among all peoples, always with the same means, the same knowledge and abilities.

But let us continue. Other concepts that were and still are associated with shamanism are feeble-mindedness, congenital psychopathy, ecological deprivation (long Arctic darkness and monotonous polar nights are thought to trigger hysteria), idiocy, delusion—almost the entire pandemonium of psychiatry has been let loose on shamans. Grotesquely, it seems that a shaman can simultaneously be a neurotic, an epileptic, and a psychotic.

Imperialistic missionary Christianity put shamans in the same category as devil-worshippers, as monstrous offspring of Satan. Here we touch upon the atmosphere of the witch-hunt—that is, the extirpation of our native European shamanism. With the replacement of religion by science, a scientific form of witch-hunt came into being, and psychiatry and psychology were the new inquisitors. A new repertoire of concepts arose that provided the Western colonizers and conquerors with an intellectual justification for all the crimes and injustices they perpetrated. As representative of many such self-justifying definitions, I will cite here that of B. J. F. Laubscher: "The master sorcerer to a great extent fits into that class of abnormal characters known in our culture as psychopaths. They manifest in their lives every shading of aberrant behavior, and it is not improbable that many are psychotic persons in a recovery phase or who have stabilized without returning to reason" (1937, 227). With a similar intention, Ruth Benedict (1934) calls the shaman "supernormal" and "abnormal by vocation." By that she means that although shamans are abnormal (to us), they are adapted to their society—which is therefore an abnormal society. The gist of this parody of science is that we, the good, triumph over the others, the evil ones. Is that ethnology? Is that science? Deve-reux expresses himself even more clearly: "Primitive religion and 'backward' primitive areas in general are 'organized schizophre-nia.'" Traditional societies understood as gigantic insane asy-lums—what a heroic victory of human thought!

Actually, shamans and psychotics do have something in com-mon. Mircea Eliade sees in the psychotic an "imitation mystic"—a person whose relationship to his experience has been disrupted and destroyed and who conveys the semblance of ostensibly genuine mystical and religious experience to the superficial observer. Here, the mentally ill person is conceived as a failed mystic. A similar view is advanced by Erich Neumann (1978, 128), who distinguishes be-tween high and low forms of mysticism. The former must be based on a strong ego that is firmly established in this world; the latter is occasioned by a fragmented, chaotic ego that is overwhelmed by the intensity of transpersonal experience and has dissolved beyond recognition. And the great student of human consciousness William James says that

> the classic mysticism and these lower mysticisms spring from the same mental level, from that great subliminal or transmarginal region of which science is beginning to admit the existence, but of which so little is really known. That region contains every kind of matter: "seraph and snake" abide there side by side. (James 1961, 326)

But this juxtaposition of high and low, as subtle as it may seem, does not bring our understanding any further. We need a more comprehensive model: a model of the spectrum of consciousness. The principle that reaches through all levels of existence is con-sciousness expansion, an increase in the perception of unity, the capacity for transmutation in all things and beings, and in some ways, a spiritual metabolism. Here, let us consider certain psycho-logical states that are found in the shaman as well as the psychotic—the difference being that the psychotic relates these experiences to the level of ego, whereas in actuality they are applica-ble only to higher levels of consciousness. The psychotic confuses self and ego, unconscious and superconscious; moreover, he does not build up a strong ego, which would be the first exercise for a shaman. Therefore the psychotic experiences ego experiences as shamanic experiences and reduces transpersonal experiences to a personal level; on the ego level, they appear as religious delusions. He interprets normal ego feelings as transpersonal revelations and thus becomes an "imitation mystic."

In this sense, psychosis is a general confusion of the levels of the consciousness, indeed, playing dice with them. The inner point of view—one's standpoint—is shorted out; the psychotic rages up and down the keyboard of levels of consciousness. He reverses the levels as in a mirror—the high tones become the low ones, and the low ones the high. The schizophrenic world is a mirror-image world, in which the writing is upside down and one reads from right to left. That is the paradox of schizophrenia. Every cognition has a back side, a shadow world, a negative image of itself: a distortion, a pathological interpretation. No step, no matter how high its aim, is secure from its own mockery, from its Janus face, the twin head that lurks everywhere, the natural shadow of all experience, the shadow of everything existing.

The psychotic is therefore no shaman, but shamans pass through psychotic episodes, venturing as they do to the edges of being's abyss—and psychotics pass sporadically through shamanic episodes, have genuine shamanic insights and glimpses into the higher world. This is why schizophrenia and epilepsy are, rightly, venerated as "sacred illnesses" by many peoples.

To what can the great number and fullness of our mental institutions be attributed? Tribal cultures do know psychosis, but it does not occur among them in the same proportions as it does with us. I think that the Western rejection of altered states of consciousness condemned to failure men like Hölderlin, Nietzsche, Van Gogh, Antonin Artaud, John Clare, Arthur Rimbaud and led to a degradation—in the literal sense of the world—of altered states of consciousness onto the ego level. It led to a "psychotic discrepancy," an intolerable compression of ego and self, of conscious and superconscious, and in this way brought about that strange inner split between angel and devil, wisdom and madness. Since our culture recognizes no higher states of consciousness, psychiatrists and society—and later even patients themselves—relate these states back to the ego, the measure of all things. Thus is schizophrenia born. How many sages, how many shaman, healers and seers, savants and saints, have been caught in the snares of psychiatry's alienation from the world and its false obsession with the ego? When will a Spartacus finally arise among the patients and throw off the chains?!

Shamans, on the other hand, are able to determine their own stations in life because of mythical and cultural models. They know what awaits them, through what euphorias and torments they will have to pass. Their predecessors have prepared the way for them and drawn up a map of inner space. The good and evil forces of the psyche have been named for them in advance. Gods, demons, and spirits—these are the street names on their journey through the realms of consciousness.

"Sacred illness" was what the ancient Greeks called epilepsy, because they believed that people stricken with it had been sought out by the gods and possessed soothsaying abilities. Today we must ask ourselves once again: Should we regard epilepsy as a disease? Epileptic fits may be provoked by various psychological influences and sensory stimuli. Moreover, the attacks take place when the brain is seeking to free itself from an imbalance of one kind or another. Could this not be regarded as a kind of biological self-healing? Would it not be more fitting to understand epilepsy, with its preceding "aura" (the feeling that predicts an oncoming cerebral discharge), as an altered state of consciousness and thus only partially as a pathological syndrome? Accounts of the psychic perceptions of epileptics during their attacks reveal many mystic and shamanic features. The descriptions of Fyodor Dostoyevsky, himself an epileptic, are classic. In *The Idiot,* he writes that during the few seconds of an attack, one feels an infinite cosmic harmony for which one would be willing to give one's whole life. I have not found any indications that shamans are epileptics, but if some of them do suffer from this disease, perhaps they have brought it under conscious control.

Adrian Boshier, a South African, was an epileptic. In his youth, he wandered through Africa on foot and was later initiated into various rites by native shamans. The tribes in the vicinity of the Makgabeng Mountains were the first to notice his ability to enter into contact with the spirit world. When Boshier wanted to travel through their hills, the elders interrogated him and refused to give him permission. At one particularly intense moment in the gathering, his old illness suddenly came over him—an epileptic fit. He was immediately recognized as a chosen one of the spirits, and his wishes were granted.

In Africa, epilepsy is considered a sacred illness that is provoked by spirits and that brings one into realms of higher knowledge. Boshier, however, was tormented by thoughts of being at the mercy of a disease so heavily stigmatized in our society, and only with difficulty was he to make friends with the "spirit world." Rrasebe the *sangoma,* a woman who became his spiritual teacher, said to him:

> You cannot fight it alone. You must let the spirits help you, instead of fighting them as well. To work, they need light. I have given you an eye, but it is still closed and there is darkness inside. . . . The spirits are angry and the sickness is their sign. Give them what they need. Let them feed alongside you. (quoted in Watson 1982, 166)

Psychotics experience a spiritually elevated world; their perceptions and emotions are hyperactive. This can lead them to a breakthrough into new creativity, into the essence of things, into the essential core of their fellow beings. They feel not only the meaningfulness of all events, the depth of whatever occurs, but also a fear that will conquer in the end and overpower the person. This is the fear of being sucked, as into a whirlpool, into all the forms and beings of existence, into the gaping maw of the truth. We need not enumerate here the many and various spiritual symptoms of psychosis. Suffice it to say that we understand this "illness" as a disturbance of the process of experience in the most general sense. We could speak of an openness to stimuli, which naturally entails the danger of loss of control. An overflow of stimuli cannot be turned off, nor can it in any way be meaningfully processed; helpless, consciousness withdraws into itself like a snail into its shell. The result is psychological retreat, physical blocks, and the loss of spontaneity.

The Russian physiologist Pavlov was of the opinion that in cases of overstimulation, a protective inhibition of the brain sets in that manifests as a mental breakdown. Other psychiatrists speak of "positive disintegration," in which the collapse is a breakthrough into new creative insights and a meaningful revivification of the personality. Psychosis would then be a reaction of the wisdom of the body to external, sickness-producing, unhealthy states.

Famous and infamous, Sigmund Freud's ethnocentric view, entirely tributary to the Western tradition, equates the child, the psychotic, and the primitive. There would be no reason to object to this if Freud had seen this equation in positive terms—that is, in terms of an ability to experience altered states of consciousness. According to psychoanalysis, however, what these three groups have in common is irrationality. Western scientists have always taken pleasure in using their vague, purely subjective knowledge of primitives as the stuff for constructing pseudo-anthropological theories of history. Primitives here are used in the service of global theories of human development. They can be called upon at any time to fill in theoretical gaps and as prototypes for heroic panoramas of evolutionary history. Ignorance of the way of life of tribal cultures is actually appropriate, since it permits the theorist to stick "primitives" into any theory wherever they are needed. In this way, "primitives" provide valuable help to psychiatrists and psychoanalysts in confirming their obscure ideas. They become metaphors for mental regression or prototypes of the schizophrenic, and as the "missing link" in evolutionary history, they are desirable objects even for biologists.

As a last example, let us turn to anthropologist Kurt Goldstein, who indulges in this unfortunate comparison with especial ambition. Here are a few glimpses into the Pandora's box of his historical delusion. Schizophrenics and primitives, he says, have in common concrete language and concrete thinking; the abstract approach is completely absent in them. Neither divides a whole into its parts; objects appear to be different to them from every perspective. Concepts and symbols lie beyond their understanding; they are incapable of distinguishing self from outer world; outer events fuse with their inner experiences; chance convergences of things, persons, and events are rashly regarded as causally connected. Both schizophrenics and primitives are extremely suggestible regarding every view and connection that is presented to them, and they cling to an idea or an object until they can no longer be separated from it. They do not distinguish imagination from real experience. They inaccurately make fringe experiences into central focal points.

What pathology this is, what prelogic, what inferiority—but whose? In response to such views as Goldstein's, a number of sincere researchers have seriously, with all the power of abstraction of civilized thinking, asked: "How could primitive races have survived under such conditions or have progressed evolutionarily to the level of the higher races if their thought and action is so unrealistic?" I find myself asking the same question. This sketch of schizophrenics and primitives, and by extension of shamans—who does it reflect? No one but the scientists themselves.

When Sir James Frazer, "the father of ethnology," was asked if he had ever laid eyes on a primitive, he cried with feeling, "God forbid!" But modern ethnologists have made no such omission; they have all personally reconnoitered and researched the remote preserves of "primitives." But what they lack still is genuine, intimate, friendly contact with shamans; what they have neglected is to truly enter into the worldview of the shaman as students of shamans. How else could they find out about their "dreams"?

Today it can be said that the attempt to defame shamans and tribal societies through the use of psychiatric terminology, to replace "hard" imperialism with a "soft" or scientific imperialism, has met with defeat. Extinction projects and genocide campaigns have found a firm support in psychiatric ideology, to be sure. But despite scientific investigations and "proofs" of their inferiority, the tribes—even though driven by deception and suffering from a confusion of self and the external world—have defended themselves with astonishing bravery against the terrorist attacks and invasions of abstractly and realistically thinking Western people.

Today a countermovement is under way, and psychotics, shamans, and children are receiving more attention. The transcendental experiences of schizophrenics are being regarded with a certain respect, shamans are being sought out as teachers, and children are ever more regarded as full-fledged members of society.

Psychologist David Cooper speaks of the rediscovery of madness as necessary for human renewal. Western society, according to him, has suppressed the "language of madness," but it is now necessary to connect again with the powers of creativity and spontaneity. For him, madness is a restructuring of alienated but habitual patterns of life. Psychosis would then be the process of perfecting this into a less alienated way of being. In traditional cultures, Cooper says, there is a greater continuity between persons and sensitive extrahuman systems, since persons in those cultures possess a more primal consciousness that is quite close to mystical consciousness. For Cooper, psychosis is a step into the world, an attempt to restore the primordial connectedness of all life. To understand the schizophrenic initiation, we need not a new method, he says, but a new attitude (Cooper 1978).

To make the relationship between psychosis and shamanism clearer, I would like to make a connection between two ideas: the idea of a continuum of consciousness and the holographic principle. Normal and alternative states of consciousness should not be regarded as two opposing types of experience. I would like to sketch here a hierarchy of levels running from normal to higher consciousness. The principle that binds the various levels is an increasing feeling of unity with the surrounding world.

1. In normal consciousness the separation between ego and external world is the greatest. At this level the unity of being is either not experienced at all or is experienced only as a mechanical exchange.

2. With a slight intensification of emotion, the sense of self connects directly with the environment, with things and beings. At this level the capacity for sympathy, empathy, and compassion develops—the ego extends itself beyond the boundaries of normalcy. In my opinion, the simple emotional state should be seen as a ground for potential expansion of consciousness. A pleasant feeling of well-being, triggered by a relaxed, warm, and friendly situation could thus be understood as a movement toward a fusion between self and surrounding world.

3. With increase in the intensity of emotion, the separation between self and environment can temporarily disappear. With greater emotional concentration, with fear or strongly conceived desire, but also with love, hate, and anger, we identify ourselves in such a way that ego consciousness is almost replaced by the object of emotion.

4. An altered state of consciousness would be seen as an extreme of strong emotion. This can result in a complete splitting off from the normal ego, so that other contents completely fill consciousness. Stanislav and Christina Grof (1986) list the following identifi-

cation phenomena: identification with the evolutionary process, with other people, with animals, with plants, with inorganic matter and with the consciousness of cells and cell tissue, or with our planet as a whole. Abraham Maslow (1973) mentions other peak-experience phenomena that could be described as experiences of unity. Included are the experience of the whole universe as a unified whole; nonevaluative, noncomparative, nonjudgmental thought processes in which figure and ground are less sharply contrasted; the experience of the world as good and worth living in, as wondrous, and as something one really understands; the resolution of contradictions and oppositions through the knowledge or the feeling of the common nature of the opposing elements; the loss of fear, inhibition, and self-supervision.

5. The next level is where the appearance of paranormal phenomena could be placed. Obviously, psychokinesis and, in connection with other people, telepathy and clairvoyance arise through a strong feeling of unity between oneself and the environment.

6. We could regard the highest level as that of unconditional consciousness, free from all concepts and human concerns.

As we see, this consciousness spectrum is organized holographically. At each level the experience of unity is realized more or less markedly. We could also speak of these levels as different levels of enlightenment, in which case normal consciousness would represent a lower stage, a miniature enlightenment. The goal of the shamanic path of initiation is to broaden and deepen the normal emotionality that we all know. Shamanism is thus not a somehow obscure or incomprehensible or mysterious magical path, but a simple heightening of the emotional experience of the world. If we want to understand shamans, we really have only to penetrate into our own emotions. What is emotion? What is experience? What is perception? This is what we have to find out. Everything else is pretty words, the vacuous battle paintings of the intellect.

What I am trying to express with this hierarchy, this continuum of emotion is that every single level of emotion aims at the realization of universal unity; each one is in itself, on its own level, a realization of unity. What we have here is a micro-macro principle: as with the greater, so with the lesser.

Shamans are thus neither psychotic nor childish creatures—it would be ethnocentrism to regard them that way. But on the other hand, if you look at it in a positive light, they have much in common with psychotics and children. In giving a positive interpretation to their common qualities, it should not be overlooked that children by their very nature live in an altered state of consciousness; and psychotics become what they are because they are unable to bear or process their altered mode of experience. Shamans, by contrast, through practice and vocation, consciously and purposively struggle their way through to another vision of the world. All three groups of people exhibit great convergences in their way of experiencing, yet they also differ decisively. Children remain unconsciously caught up in their experience; psychotics are persecuted and tortured by it. Shamans elegantly master both worlds, the normal and the altered, and are intermediaries between the two.

Children have still not developed an individual ego and presumably live and communicate on a sub- or supraconscious level. Psychotics exhibit a fragmented and confused ego structure; they do not know how they stand. Ego, unconscious, and supraconscious become muddled up with one another; one is taken for the other, and anarchy prevails. Shamans hold sovereign mastery over the worlds of ego and superego. At the beginning of their initiation phase, they naturally go through typical psychotic experiential sequences. Like nutshells on the ocean, their psyches are tossed high and low on the stormy billows; they mix up visible and invisible, living and dead. With the help of their teachers, whether earthly or otherworldly, they learn to make suitable distinctions and to look bizarre experiences calmly in the face. Once they know the difference between a vision and a normal experience, they have gone beyond the phase of pain, illness, suffering, and confusion and have learned to resist the psychotic in themselves. They are healed and are more than healthy—they are beyond sickness. They can relapse into psychotic phases, however, especially if other sorcerers put them under a spell, steal their power, muddy their clear vision from a distance through psychic obscuration, or "kill," steal, or otherwise render inoperative their helping spirits. These things occur in the context of shamanic battles, which decide who is stronger, who has better mastered the transpersonal forces; for there are greater and lesser shamans—wise, enlightened ones, and only half-developed ones with one-sided abilities. All peoples distinguish between great and minor, general and specialized shamans.

The psychotics in our clinics could also work their way up to higher knowledge with the right guidance; certainly not all of them, but at least a few. But who is to guide them—the psychologist? the doctor? Psychology has the capacity of a mere child compared with what shamans can do, and psychiatry is lost in a tangle of pure medical thought. To guide the psychotic, we need a new class of doctors and therapists who have had their own experiences, not those who traverse the corridors of insane asylums with hypodermic needles in their hands. Shamanic, transpersonal training awaits this new class of doctors and psychologists, side by side and on an equal footing with the acquisition of objective information. Their education would include not only a study of the traditional knowledge of Asiatic cultures, but all kinds of sensory deprivation serving to disable all egoistic and body-based conceptualization processes. This education would entail long periods of solitude and fasting, vision quests, and the ingestion of psychedelic drugs. It would include artificially induced out-of-body experiences and knowledge of the soul and its journey to other psychic worlds. This is the foundation of primal medicine, the source of all shamanic knowledge. The journey to other spiritual worlds in particular is an indispensable part of the psychology of the future, of genuine shamanic therapy. Without it, nothing can be attained in the area of the transpersonal.

INVERTED WORLDS: SHAMANIC PARADOXES

In this chapter let us turn again to the sources of healing. Here I shall contrast the holy and healthy as an expression of a paradoxical world with the unholy and unhealthy as an expression of our linear, Euclidean world. At the same time, I shall sketch the outlines of a new psychology.

The primal healer and the shaman live in a self-absorbed world that lies at a remove from our own and that appears to us as twisted or mad. The shaman is the fool who turns everything upside down, but he is a holy fool. He is holy because he has been healed, because he has gone beyond illness and deception. In the light of this, we may ask which world is the inverted one—theirs or ours? Should we speak of the shamanic paradox—or of the paradox of logic?

In the preceding chapters, I have pointed to a true world. But what is true is hard to grasp—better, it is totally ungraspable. In short, what we grasp, what we touch, is hardly the world—the real world remains beyond our grasp. What you have read about in these pages is the invisible world, the source of our pseudo-real facts. In fact, that world determines the visible world. Another paradox! Is it ours or the shaman's? If you were to ask: "What is a quick and easy explanation of shamanism?" I would reply, "It is precisely the opposite of us! Just turn everything in our world inside out, and the shamanic world will soon begin to shine through."

Husko, an Ainu shaman woman, declared to the Japanese researcher Emiko Ohnuki-Tierney that profound knowledge cannot be grasped in words; ultimately, the only way to learn something about shamans is to become a shaman oneself (1973, 16). A further inversion paradox: the researcher as shaman! What would they then research? The hollowness of mere researching, of not wanting to experience?

As I see it, our Western thinking has been trained for centuries to move in straight lines, from visible point A to visible point B in the material world. It has established itself with a causal explanatory model in Euclid's austere representation of existence, Newton's mechanical universe, Descartes's naive *cogito ergo sum* and "through reason to knowledge," Kant's fixed space and time constants, Luther's heartless moralism and work ethic, Marx's economic being that is supposed to determine consciousness. But all this represents only one possibility for life, only one orientation, and certainly not the best one. When are we finally going to learn this?

Shamans, on the other hand, courageously turn our naive worldview inside out—they are spiritual iconoclasts. Their secret is simple, but the realization of it goes nearly beyond human capacity—for who has the courage to experience the day as dark and the night as light? According to legend, Diogenes carried a lantern in broad daylight through the Athenian marketplace, saying "I am seeking the light." We, by contrast, live in a dark land, are on a journey through a realm of blackness. Who among us has enough boldness, enough light in themselves, to experience our lightless state completely?

The first shamanic paradox: Progress, the future, only arises through working through the categories of delusion, and through suffering. The way of suffering is at the same time the way of knowledge. The more of the former, the more of the latter. Our Western philosophy of an absence of suffering, of happiness, and of high spirits—is that not a flight from reality? If we were to try to call our most fundamental illusion by name, would it not be the quest for painless pleasure? But how do we arrive at a pleasurable existence? Presumably through pleasure. But the shaman reaches the goal through suffering.

The way of the mystic is one of suffering rather than the conceptualization of the world and the constant categorizations, circumscriptions, and determinations of the truth through proofs. Mystics long for chaos, the nonhuman state; they crave anomic pleasure.

But on our existential level, this is inverted and becomes the cause of pain. Yet if mystics rigorously work their way through the categories of illusion, they reach the pure land: joy, knowledge, equanimity, stillness—and they make a pact with nature.

We seek happiness and avoid unhappiness. This quest, by its very nature, leads us—circling through a labyrinth of obstacles—to unhappiness. Only those who acknowledge suffering gain the wisdom of the unsafeguarded life. There is only one way to enlightenment, to shamanhood—the rocky way.

Tribal cultures are aware of the hardships of shamanic education and of the despair that can plague shamanic students. For this reason, many who have a shamanic vocation refuse to travel this path; they let the germ of power be drawn out of them by other medicine people and allow their first vision to be shattered. There is fear in the face of the neophyte, deathly fear.

Western therapy and healing, by contrast, seek to arrive at the El Dorado of the mind by traveling along gentle curves in upholstered compartments through leisurely discussion. What comes of this? Soft, emotional people, introspective scholars, sensitive aesthetes. But shamans are people of nature, uncivilized, brutal toward themselves, often harsh in dealing with others, pitiless with their students, yet generous and expansive in thought to the point of self-abnegation. They have looked death in the face, they "travel" deliberately into death. they do not share our insatiable lust for life. Every day is a good day to die. There is nothing to cling to. On one side we have an artificial preoccupation with one's own psychological material; on the other side, that of the shaman, we have a primal, nature-bound existence. To put it once more in a single sentence: Self-healing means knowledge, the transformation of consciousness. This is the shamanic paradox.

While we interact with people to become more human, shamans learn humanity through solitude. Having only themselves to rely on, shut off from society, they abandon themselves ascetically to their aloneness. Because they have left others' approaches to the world behind and have become loners, they must be alone. Their new friends and companions belong to another dimension—they are spirits, the dead, personified earth or water powers, animal souls, nature beings, nonspatial entities, time beings. They have helping spirits, possibly even supramundane lovers. They relate to the departed the way we relate to our earthly neighbors. Their contacts are mental, with the quality of daydream. They speak with the soul, listen to other worlds. What we regard as dead is living for shamans. For them, the death realm is natural, overflowing life; the realm of inanimate nature is a constant conversation partner. Shamans are open and eager to relate to the whole world of the dead, as well as to that of the living. Thence their *joie de vivre,* their scintillating, fantastic nature; thence their paradoxical, inverted lifestyle! Of course, fundamentally they invert nothing—inversion is only a model for thought to help us understand them. Shamans simply communicate on a larger scale than we do.

For us, seeing means looking outward; for the shaman it means looking inward. That is another basic paradox of shamanism: seeing the world with closed eyes. We speak of an inner world, but that is only a metaphor. There is no inner and no outer. Everything lies before us: one is visible, one is invisible, depending on our outlook and knowledge. What we see, shamans see too, but more vividly, with more participation, more feeling, more clarity. From this comes their spiritual perspicacity; for this reason they see more and differently. Perception is a sensory continuum along which it is always possible to go further. Our world does not end with emotion, with concept, with genius, with orgasm, with aesthetics, with music—these are not the final boundaries, the peaks of appreciation. Where we end, the shamanic level of appreciation begins. Shamans remain alien to us because they take their first step where we dare to take our last. Their knowledge, their appreciation are boundless; their emotions border on the infinite; their perception is a true participation in an ever-expanding reality. Western culture takes the visible spectrum for the entire spectrum. What interest do we have in gamma rays or X-rays, in ultraviolet? Who cares about the subsonic? These are verbal corpses laid on white paper, bits of textbook wisdom.

Shamans do not think; they are neither primitive thinkers nor dreaming poets of the fantastic. They simply experience a vaster world. They are not inventors of refined inner worlds. With devotion, they experience that which comes to them, and they incorporate it into their culture. Shamans do not store up professional knowledge that they study. They do not sit at a desk in a classroom. They acquire their healing powers in the dimension of death, and they discover those powers through visions; personified nature powers have whispered to them. Shamans do not cram by reading piles of books; they are transformed, whether they want it or not, not by taking in intellectual knowledge but by being turned inside out psychologically, according to the principle, inmost outward. Therefore they are upside-down. They are the living embodiments of inwardness, of the hidden, the skeleton—which is why skeletons are so often depicted on shamans' drums and clothing, as symbols of their nature. The shaman is a clown, a fool, the reflection of an antimatter universe, a mirror image. Shamans are immune to every disease they know how to cure—how logical, really, but so strange to us. What doctor could assert that of himself? To what are doctors immune? I ask—to inner knowledge?

Here once again is the shamanic paradox in outline form.

Suffering as a way of knowledge—learning through pain.

From spiritual "dismemberment" to spiritual rebirth and development. Shamans die in order to live.

They enter the darkness, the inside of a mountain or the earth, in order to experience light. Darkness as light.

They must sacrifice themselves, live abstemiously, observe taboos, give in order to take later. They sacrifice themselves in order to keep themselves.

They possess double eyes, double vision; they see with the soul body.

Shamans speak, but in the archetypal, portentous speech of the spiritual world.

They do not perfect the body; they leave it and perfect the mind/spirit.

They possess two bodies: the physical body and the soul body.

They travel much. With the soul body they course parallel universes, spiritual universes.

Their friends are spiritual, invisible, of another dimension, "vibrational forms."

They must become sick in order to become healthy.

They die in order to become holy, to become healers. They die for their patients.

Self-healing comes first with them, before the healing of others.

They become healers by experiencing illness themselves and overcoming it in themselves, then later in patients. They do not cure symptoms but their origin, the "idea" of the sickness.

Ultimately, we cannot call shamans healers. They are only a reflection of nature principles, which work through them: through their openness, nature principles flow freely, because shamans embody freedom from human laws and ideas. They are the channels through which nature flows through to us, the windows into the primal world.

The shaman is the doctor's antipode. The shaman is an antiparticle, antimatter, the essence of the black hole, a spiritual counterpart to our material-mechanistic level of existence.

By virtue of all these attributes, shamans are the incarnation of paradox. What they teach us is the negative way of the fool who turns everything upside down.

18

VITAL ENERGIES, FORCES OF THE UNIVERSE

I don't blame the white people for their genius to transmit power through
their many kinds of machines. They are crude mechanical contraptions that
may break down. We Hopis don't need them. We know how to manifest our
powers—the same powers—without machines.

—Don Qochvonga,
a Hopi religious leader
(quoted in Waters 1969, 26)

All tribal cultures live in unity with nature, in unity with the
universal laws. Their sense of the world is a symbiosis of
God, world, and ego. Thus, they have a worldview for which our
"high culture" is not yet ready. If the symbiotic, synchronistic,
synergistic universe is the acme of the natural-mystical worldview
of shamanism, another high point in the natural philosophy of
natural societies is their belief that a power permeates all being.
Each tribe has its own concept of this universal energy. Pacific
peoples call it *mana;* the Crow speak of *maxpé,* the Dakota of
wakan, the Hidatsa of *xupa,* the Algonquian of *manitou,* the
Hurons of *oki,* the Tierra del Fuegans of *waiyuwen,* the African
Sotho of *moya,* the Masai of *ngai,* the Bantu of *nzmbi,* the Pygmies
of *megbe,* the Australians of *joja,* the Dajak of Indonesia of *petara,*
the Batak of Sumatra of *tondi,* the Malagasy of *hasina.* The same
is meant by the *ch'i* or the *ch'i gong* of the Chinese, the *ki* of the
Japanese, the Hebrew *ruach,* and the *prana* or *akasha* of the

Indians—*akasha,* the matrix of the universe, the *mysterium magnum,* the primordial ocean.

These concepts have many meanings. They refer to God, to being as a whole, and equally to the helping spirits who aid shamans in their penetrations into other zones of consciousness or in healing. The South American Desana call it *tulari.* Everything from physical to supernatural strength and even the seer's own "penetrating glance" is *tulari,* which more or less means mastering going into trance or magical flight, the departure from the body (Reichel-Dolmatoff 1975). In any case, it is a question of a power principle that goes beyond the mechanical-material laws of Euclidean geometry.

The Eskimo believe that a power, a spiritual essence, inhabits all stones, seas, birds, plants, or objects fabricated by man. This is called *inuat.* It is embodied in Hilap Inua, the Lord of Power. In just this sense, for the inhabitants of the Mentawai Islands of Indonesia, everything that possesses a soul emanates *bajou,* a kind of radiation. Supernatural beings and spirits possess a strong *bajou,* which can be dangerous for humans. *Bajou* can be transferred to objects; objects charged with it can become tribal fetishes (Schefold 1980). In North America the Pima call the process of acquiring psychic power *vaikita,* or "pouring in *olla.*" Students are "shot"— that is, filled with *olla* energy. The teacher coughs up white balls, which he rubs into the chests of the students. Then power begins to develop (Russell 1908, 256f.). The Australian aborigines, depending on their tribe, speak of *alcheringa,* the dreamtime, of *ungud,* or *jugur.* In spirit they return to the mythical primordial time of their tribal heroes, which is the source and origin of life. Whoever attunes himself to this past time or dimension participates in the power and abundance of life. This power is by no means understood to be symbolic, as we might expect. It is effective and visible. Thus, Helmut Petri (1962, 174) tells us of Djigal, a dream expert, who supplemented his quartz crystals with flashlight bulbs. He pressed them to his body during his dream journey and made them shine. Quite materialistically, he equated his powers with electrical energy.

According to the spiritual physiology of the Hopi, an axis runs through the earth. Along it lie several vibrational centers, where the primal tone of creation and life that resonates through the whole universe can be heard and felt. The human body is considered a reflection of the body of the earth; its vibrational centers, five in number, lie along the spinal column. The symbol of the lowest center, below the navel, is the snake, a manifestation of the earth mother who bears all life. This vibrational center regulates procreative power; it is linked to the *kopavi*, the "open door," the highest vibrational point at the crown of the head. The symbol of the *kopavi* is the antelope. Antelope and snake together are an expression of the polarity of life—of subtle and coarse materiality. When we breathe, the *kopavi*, or fontanel, moves gently up and down, as in an infant. The pulsation of the fontanel is an expression of our communication with the creator. At least that is the way it was formerly, in the preceding phase of creation. Then this spot became increasingly hardened, just as with us it hardens with increasing age. Only at the time of death does it open again, so that life, the soul, can leave the body. Below the *kopavi* is the second center, our brain or thought. With the third center, which lies in the throat, human beings produce sounds that resemble the sound of the universe and the vibrations of the planets. Therefore, with this voice, humans praise and honor the creation. The heart is the fourth center, which pulsates in harmony with the vibration of life.

Hopi medicine people hold crystals to the vibrational centers along the spinal column and look through them to see the origin of illnesses. A normal person, of course, sees nothing through the crystal; only medicine people are capable of this because of their particular gifts (Waters 1963, 272ff.).

According to the spiritual physiology of the Hindus, there are seven vibrational centers or *chakras*. The *muladhara chakra*, at the base of the spine, is symbolized by a coiled snake. It is identical with procreative power, and in the case of higher development of consciousness, it winds up the spine through the other *chakras* up to the highest *sahasrara chakra* at the fontanel. If the *kundalini* energy reaches the highest center of consciousness, the yogin attains enlightenment, or as the Hopi say, "The human being speaks with God."

The life of tribal cultures is a continually flowing spiritual experience. All aspects of nature are perceived as expressions of the nonmaterial, mysterious power of the ground of life. This energy, the blueprint of perceivable being, can be stored or tapped into; it can be transferred from one person or object to another; it can be used positively for healing or negatively for destruction—just as we use electricity. Electricity is in some ways a profane form of primal energy, an aspect of the vital energy that is narrowed down in its essence.

The quest of the shamanic student is the quest for the vital force, the universal emanation, the subtle prime matter of being. There is no distinction between this and the quest of the Western scientist. The scientist too seeks the ultimate basis of matter, "matter waves," the matrix of existence. The shaman differs from the scientist in being a psychically inspired investigator of the breath of life rather than an intellectually inspired one. In the history of science, we find repeated failed or incompletely carried out attempts to establish the existence of a vital force, a supraspatial existential field. First we have Plato's Ideas, then various alchemical notions, Hans Driesch's entelechy, Henri Bergson's élan vital, Franz Anton Mesmer's magnetism, and Harold Saxon Burr's vital field. The vital field has an ordering effect on the structure of the body; in it, symptoms of illness that have not yet manifested or the general state of health can be perceived. Interestingly, the vital field disappears before the onset of death. Burr's revolutionary and empirically well-documented discovery was, typically, never properly taken into account. A. M. Gurwitsch postulated mitogenic radiation. According to his idea, certain vibrations are diffused from one molecule to another in such a way that each cell can be understood as a minute radio transmitter. In 1944, V. S. Grischenko advocated a fifth state of matter that exists in all living organisms, called biological plasma. According to another Russian, Viktor M. Inyushin, bioplasm is composed of free electrons and protons, can be stored, and is transferable not only within an organism but to the outside, and even over great distances; according to him, it is responsible for telepathic and psychokinetic phenomena. Andrija Puharich believes that all objects, living and dead, are surrounded by a psi-plasm field. He believes that local gravitational fields of bodies can be weakened through psychological changes; this causes the psi field to spread out and reach other people, producing telepathic contacts. Perhaps, he speculates, all psi-plasm fields interact and mutually influence one another. This would mean that every person has an effect on everything existing. Puharich goes even further in supposing that this plasma remains in existence after death, yielding what he calls a "nuclear psi entity," which would be responsible, for example, for spirit phenomena (Puharich 1973).

The deeply ingrained embeddedness of the vital-energy outlook among nature peoples and great cultures of the past has been regarded by our science as an expression of extreme "primitivity." Science has not wanted to see that these were attempts at binding and unifying the fragmented world of phenomena as we experience it by means of an underlying world of essence. Even today, after the development of all the advanced models of quantum physics and paraphysics, we have still not been able to find it in ourselves to credit the "savages" with their part in the universal human search for a primal ground, for the unifying energy of being. This reveals the poverty mentality of the modern world. Not only do "primitives" not have the right to exist, their right to a capacity for knowledge is also disputed. Today, in this way, ethnocentrism, colonial arrogance, blind conversion mania, and the profound obscurity of the theory of evolution reinforce one another. This is a fatal alliance that, as we know, does not refrain from genocide.

All cultures, but especially the first small cultures, conceived of and conceive of a primal force that contains existence in an unmanifest, latent form. To dismiss this as the self-deception of magic, as a form of underdeveloped thinking—that is what I would call underdeveloped thinking. What if one day—which may not be far distant—we discover that they, the "primitives," were right all along? What will happen with them then? Well, not much, since at that point they will not be there anymore. The power of the shamans has been crippled. They now prefer to travel by gas-powered engines rather than by leaving their bodies in spirit. Even when they vaguely and confusedly recall their tribal past, they now prefer the airplane to spirit flight.

If this mysterious power is actually present in all things and beings, in thunder and lightning, in the breath and in the glance, would it not make sense to conduct ourselves in relation to natural phenomena as shamans do? Should we not feel awe toward these forces and secure their power for ourselves? The West's relationship with the holy, because of its cultural predispositions, must of necessity go by the dark way. This is the way of degeneracy, which shamans of ruined or decultured tribal societies also pursue, letting their abilities be used mostly for negative purposes.

Did Albert Einstein not try with his unified field theory to fuse together all powers known to us in a single theory? Is David Bohm's theory of the implicate order of subquantum physics not an attempt in this same direction? Is the quest of our physics for the smallest indivisible particles, quarks and so on, not motivated by the same longing to understand and express the confusing, seemingly incoherent plurality, the "particle zoo," in terms of a single formula? Is science not, I wonder, an urge ingrained in all human beings from the earliest times to find a single principle underlying all phenomena, the philosopher's stone, the one energy? For me, the modern high-energy physicists and microphysicists are the new Knights of the Round Table. What is now being asserted by the physicists would doubtless have been regarded as pure metaphysics, as shocking occultism, around 1900. In spite of all these revolutionary formulations, however, we are still incapable of perceiving our life as a cosmic ocean of energy. That kind of perception is only remotely possible in an altered state of consciousness. We could now undertake a discussion of new energy models and attempt to find points of agreement with the shamanic way of looking at things. But common elements could only be found on a superficial level, for we have not yet reached the level of knowledge of the shamans. Only later, when we have reached the their level, will there be enough genuine ground for comparison.

Here are two examples of personal relationships with power. David Jones (1972) portrays the development of Sanapia, a medicine woman of the Comanche tribe. She received her training from her mother, an uncle, her maternal grandmother, and her paternal grandfather. The climax of her period of initiation, which lasted a number of years, was the transference of power from her mother. In the first phase, her mother trickled her power into her daughter's hands and mouth, the parts of the body where the power of an eagle doctor is greatest. The mother handed her a piece of glowing charcoal, which she took without hesitation, noting with astonishment that it caused her no pain. Instead of heat, Sanapia felt cold. For the transference of power to Sanapia's mouth, her mother drew two eagle feathers through her mouth four times. The fourth time, one of the feathers disappeared. It remained in Sanapia the rest of her life. Not the feather itself, says Sanapia, but only its symbol, the power, remained in her. From that point on, she was not allowed to eat certain things.

During the second stage of transmission, the mother put an egg inside her. She could not explain how the egg disappeared from her mother's hand, but she believes in this case, too, that it was the essence of the egg, not the egg itself, that stayed in her. With this went the taboo never again to eat eggs. Later, however, Sanapia developed such an appetite for eggs that she had another eagle doctor remove the egg from her. As a result, she lost the abilities associated with it. Interestingly, after this she developed a dislike for eggs.

The third transference of power consisted of acquiring a medicine song that had originally belonged to her uncle. Sanapia uses this song, since it is very powerful, only in very serious cases. Through the song, her helping spirits, her dead mother and uncle, appear and give advice. Two taboos are connected with this. One, she is never allowed to ask anyone directly for anything. She gets around this in daily life by expressing herself in circumlocutions. The other is that she must always be alone while healing; only other eagle doctors can act as helpers.

Sanapia failed to pass her third test, in which she was to spend the night alone on a mountain. After her mother told her what she would have to face, she snuck home after dark, slept there, then snuck back out to the mountain at dawn. Sanapia believes that the many illnesses she had to undergo as a young woman resulted from this act of disobedience. Her mother had told her that beings would appear, beat her, and try to get her medicine away from her. After the transference of her power, the mother retired from her healing activities. Sanapia was expected to begin healing after she had passed through her menopause.

During her career as a healer, her power animal, an eagle, appeared only twice. He looks like an ordinary eagle but much bigger. The first time he appeared, she felt the wind of his movement; the second time, a crawling sensation in her body heralded his arrival. When the eagle appeared, everything around her faded, and as he landed in front of her, her heart beat so strongly that she nearly fainted.

Sanapia's power is not her own. It comes from her two helping spirits. She has only to make the necessary preparations and be receptive to them. Only by taking peyote, the psychedelic cactus, does she develop power of her own.

Direct connection or encounter with pure power would immediately kill a person; contact is possible only through an intermediary. The power itself is inexhaustible—it has an entirely different dynamic and mode of effectiveness from the energy forms familiar to us.

Before Sanapia begins to heal, she is taken with trembling and a cold breath passes over her body. She sings her medicine song until her uncle and mother appear as two lights. She reminds them of their promise to help her. Once these spirits have spoken with the medicine eagle, they give her a sign that she has been given the power. She describes the appearance of the eagle as follows.

> I was already tired and I cried. I sat there and saw my mother the way she was when she was alive. Suddenly, I felt a cold gust of wind pressing me down. It pressed on my head and flattened the grass all around me. I had to prop myself up with my hands; it was so violent I thought it would blow me away. My blanket was almost blown away. I held onto it tightly. . . . My hair was flying all over. I got scared and began to shake. Oh, that wind blew dust in my eyes, and as I rubbed them, suddenly everything calmed down. . . . Like a dream it was, like at night when you're sleeping. I saw the eagle . . . he was big . . . his feathers gleamed beautifully. I was silly, I began to cry again . . . like an old woman. But I heard in my head: "Go, make him healthy. You can do it!" Then I didn't see anything more. . . . I think he disappeared then. (Jones 1972)

After such experiences, the power comes over her, and she attempts to transfer it to the patient. As ritual implements for this, she uses only smoke and an eagle's feather.

The development of a shaman can be described as a continual accumulation of power. The psychic strength of every shaman is different. As soon as a shaman receives his vocation, he becomes a bearer of power, of *cuenta,* as Eduardo Calderon, a Peruvian *curandero* (healer), says. On the one hand, *cuenta* pervades the entire universe; on the other hand, it works in certain places and persons more strongly than in others. In any case, *cuenta* is indifferent to the moral values of people. It can be used for evil as well as for good. Black and white magicians make use of it in the same fashion. The notion of *cuenta* can be explained by comparison to the circulation of capital. Money can be increased, given away, bought, and lost. One person has more money than another, which makes him more powerful. One can deposit money in a bank; then this deposit possesses potential power that can be released at any time and used for the purchase of objects. The same principles apply to power.

The primary goal in the career of a *curandero* is to acquire as many power objects as possible in which *cuenta* manifests. These objects increase his healing power. They can be given by a good friend, and they can be found in holy places and known power spots near certain mountains, lakes, and caves.

Extraordinary life circumstances led Eduardo to such power objects. Dreams, as well as the psychedelic cactus San Pedro, showed him the way to power objects. All the objects he found, however, only developed their special power when Eduardo brought his own power component to bear on them as well. He started out on his healing activities with only a few power objects. His teacher, from Ferrenafe, tuned Eduardo's objects—his rattle, his dagger, and his two staffs—with his own *cuenta.* "Tuning" means that since each object has a task in the healing ceremony, its power must be directed toward a particular accomplishment. For example, a stone or a deer's foot is to be used only for love spells or bewitchments.

The healer makes use of these implements only when appropriate. If a *curandero* receives a power object as a gift that is informed with an alien *cuenta,* it necessary to "tame" it so that it obeys the healer. Eduardo found the paraphernalia of an ancient sorcerer at an excavation site. Upon finding such objects, the greatest care is in order. First their *cuenta* has to be tested. Eduardo took the things he had found home with him, because he believed he would be able to tame them.

I took them along to test them and see what kind they were. And then it happened that these objects rebelled against me. Strange animals and monstrous beasts came storming out of them, greedy and bloodthirsty. When I then put the implements on my mesa [table with all the power objects on it], they turned misshapen and black. The implements began to bleed. Beings with monstrous fangs with blood streaming from them came out of them and demanded my wife and my children. I tried to throw them out. I cleaned the objects with holy water and burned them, for beginning with the day I brought them into my house, there started to be a noise on my roof that sounded like the galloping of wild animals. And they left me no peace until I performed kabbalistic strokes with my swords to counteract these influences. . . . The implements were useless to me. They were black implements, objects of bewitchment. . . . And all this evil was preserved through the centuries just because these implements were tuned by a man of that kind of character or received their interactive predispositions from him. (quoted in Sharon 1980, 85f.)

Along with *cuenta*, Eduardo speaks of *magnetismo* when he talks about a shaman's power. "The magnetic power is something that inheres in an individual, in a person. . . . A person who directs this power, uses it cleverly and with knowledge—such a person's actions lead to a great and meaningful triumph. Most curanderos know these natural basic principles concerning the magnetic power of people and elements" (quoted in Sharon 1980, 82). The *magnetismo* comes up the left leg and goes down the right one; the same principle applies to the hands. According to Eduardo, magnetism connects people to one another, which is why *curanderos* lay on hands when they are healing.

So much for the working of the power. There are also a multitude of reports that healing energy can manifest visibly, through blue emanations, tongues of blue color and lights.

Vinson Brown describes a sweat lodge ceremony conducted by the Lakota medicine man Fools Crow. Fools Crow told him that when somebody at a ceremony has bad or skeptical thoughts, the blue lights that normally appear turn orange. In the case of a young man who some time before had taken part in such an *inipi*, orange lights appeared. Some time later, he committed suicide.

Then Fools Crow said a long prayer in Sioux, while the drum beat very softly; next he began to sing while the drum beat harder. Gradually the lights were snuffed out until we were all in complete darkness. Now the rattles seemed to float up off the floor and moved up near the ceiling, the latter about ten feet high. As they moved about rattling, a beautiful song was sung that went on and on.

Finally the rattles sank down to the floor again but continued rattling softly, and suddenly I was conscious of a light in the room. It was a very tiny blue light, like that made by a firefly, and I remember having a feeling of great exhilaration because it was blue. It danced about and soon there was another one and another one also dancing, until the room seemed full of these little lights moving about. One came within six inches of my face and seemed to hover briefly, while I breathed deeply and kept my mind concentrated on the spirit. Then I noticed that these lights would dash from the floor of the room clear to the ceiling and around to every corner. When one of them came close to the face of someone in the room, I would see that face outlined for a second in a pale ghostly glow, and especially a dark Indian face would take on a look of brooding mystery. By this time I was very happy indeed, for all lights were blue, not a single one orange, and there seemed to be great joy in the lights dancing to the beat of the drum. (1974, 159ff.)

A number of whites have seen the blue sparks during sweat lodge ceremonies. These are by no means hallucinations. Many cultures recognize favorable auguries in blue light discharges, or successful communications with the spirits, the gods, or the self. Lyall Watson (1976) reports that Indonesian tribes believe that people produce a kind of smoke around them, depending on their mood. Especially when emotions are strong, a kind of shadow develops around the body that exhibits different colors in different cases. Siberian people are acquainted with the phenomenon of blue smoke. Among the East Yakuts, the blue smoke that in their experience appears above a sorcerer is the sign of his connection with the spirits, according to Pallas. The Vogul also speak of blue smoke that forms around a shaman; it is the arriving divinity. During the chanting, according to Suew, a blue fog or smoke arises above the shaman. J. B. Müller recounts that among the chanters, at the climax of a tumultuous seance, a blue vapor appears that is understood to be the soothsaying spirit. Those present then draw away, and the shaman is thrown to the ground (authors cited in Balász 1963, 64ff.).

Perhaps the blue illumination originates in the eyes of the onlookers but is not there in reality. Changes in magnetic fields produce electric potentials, whose effect on the eye is often described as a bright blue light. These "magnetic phosphenes" arise when an alternating current of from 10 to 100 hertz flows through a person's head.

Occasionally it has been reported that the great pyramid of Cheops radiates a pale blue light. Baron von Reichenbach's "od energy" was supposed to have been blue, as was Wilhelm Reich's "orgone energy." Reich believed that the membranes of red blood corpuscles contained the orgone energy: under four-thousandfold magnification, they were seen to emit a deep blue glow. Dinshah P. Ghadiali, an Indian researcher, developed a treatment method using colored light. Inflammations and infections treated with blue light are supposed to heal faster.

In 1890 the Russian engineer Yakov Narkevich-Todko tried to make electrographic photographs using electric charges. Strange blue flames appeared to be radiating from living bodies. There have been reports of blue fireballs flying out of ovens when they are opened. The explanation for this phenomenon is that static electricity builds up in a chimney when an electric storm is nearby. The electricity collects in the oven, then comes out as a fireball. So-called synchotron rays, produced by highly accelerated particles, are harder than even the most highly charged X-rays and penetrate even the structure of molecules and atoms; these too give off a bluish light.

Whether the few examples we have adduced are related to one another is not in question here. In any case it is clear that blue light emanations, shamanism, and altered states of consciousness are somehow connected. Blue light and healing energy are perhaps one thing.

19

TRANSTHERAPEUTIC PHILOSOPHY

Son of man, thou dwellest in the midst of a rebellious house, which have eyes to see and see not; they have ears to hear and hear not. —EZEKIEL 12:2

In place of possession with God he gained a quiet conscience; in place of pleasure, ease; in place of freedom, comfort; in place of lethal heat, a pleasant temperature. —HERMANN HESSE,
Steppenwolf

Among the Wahaerama, a people of central Ceram Island (in the Moluccas), when a shaman takes possession of power, it is thanks to to Alahatala, the creator god: after the god climbs down the central pillar of the house, his shadow falls on the shaman (Röder 1948, 71).

I have entitled this last part of this book "The Shadows of Everything Existing." The first of these shadows was the "mad" world, the world of schizophrenics and shamans both. I proposed that this shadow is actually the real world; my model is a world standing on its head. The second shadow was the fool, shamans as holy fools—after all, they live in a paradoxical dimension of being, in an inside-out existence. Shamans are like antimatter, like black holes, shadow worlds that are causes of our apparently real world. The third shadow was composed of the vital energies, the invisibly moving basic ground, subtly material spiritual effects, prime matter, the *prima materia*.

Continuing to use the primal metaphor of the shadow as a

guiding image, in this final chapter we shall discuss our state of development—the state of research into the shadow—and the notion of the "healer in all of us." Let us recall J. M. Barrie's children's story of Peter Pan, who tried to catch his shadow—that is the story of the healer as well.

The shadow behind everything existing refers to our real being. What is actually the shadow is the body, life, the visible. We have unwittingly reversed core and husk to enable us to approach life in a more unencumbered and unequivocal fashion.

Healing does not come from the visible world but from the invisible shadow world. This is the world to which our subtle-material body belongs, our energy body; its visible form is the physical body. This shadow land is the homeland of shamans, where they "operate," give "shots" and "medicine." We know little of this land, the "quantum realm of the holy." The things shamans say to us about it are metaphors, images that have been run through the brain and filtered through it.

In my view, all human striving is directed toward achieving the greatest pleasure. This is not pleasure in the Freudian sense but in the sense of total freedom, enlightenment, absorption in the "radiant world." The explosion of the status quo, of normal consciousness—this is what seems to me to be the transcendent impulse in all social cults and psychological stirrings; this is the mainspring of evolution. Play, dance, song, joy, love—all these are quests for ecstasy. Ecstasy is the dissolution, the final sloughing off of all-fragmenting time, all-confining space. Ecstasy, trance, and enlightenment are an abolition of time. Time is our greatest enemy, the most damaging of all illusions.

But then, what is play, socializing, art? Every form of concentration is an inborn quest for nowness, for the moment of being there. The moment is timeless, and the attempt to extend it to eternity is trance. If one can carry this further, one arrives at enlightenment and, beyond that, reaches a point where the separate human existence itself is extinguished. The human being can be seen as a spiritual volcano, continually seething, nearing eruption. The seething and bubbling is our world, disguised forms of transcendence, apparently profane, but in truth holy and healing.

But what does holy mean? Let me say it plainly: Science or art, play or love—these are all forms of a single primal need. We could go even further. Let us look at a simple feeling, the sense of comfort. Here too we find the germ of concentration, the turning inward, life as inner peace. But this is very hard to grasp. The word cannot deliver anything at this point; it is too rigid, too pat. Here things must be intuitively felt, in a flash. Let us take devotion. This is a giving up of the self. Under the guise of devotion to science, art, or family, there is a quest for penetration. The primal form of devotion, whether we like it or not, is freedom from ego consciousness. There is a possibility of total absorption: the only obstacle is ego consciousness. The quest for freedom informs all of life's expressions. It is hidden by magic guises and confined in straitjackets; it appears as spectacles in moviehouses and theaters, as wild motorcycle rides or rocket flights storming the heavens; yes, it even appears in every kind of intoxication. Whether we like the idea or not, intoxication is free of ambivalence—there is no inherent duality of good and evil. Intoxication is a physiological principle, devoid of any valuation; it serves good and evil equally. There is only one continuum—ever-intensifying concentration. The narrower consciousness's spotlight is, the greater is the intoxication, the ego extinction, the evolutionary quality of being human, the perception—to the point of perception that is totally devoid of spatiality and temporality.

Once again, this is connected with time. Freedom from temporal sequence arises, and with it, cosmic freedom. This is the goal of being human, of every personal ambition and unfolding, whether conscious or unconscious. This is the framework for a new psychology: the knowledge that the psyche is an atemporal hologram whose every movement reflects the entirety of being and whose every action, every thought, every emotion is an attenuated expression of total experience. If we were to study human society according to this principle, we would surely arrive at a genuine transcendental anthropology and sociology. But the great that lies in the small remains hidden from us; the small always appears to us as profane in the illusory conclusion of the transcendentalists. There is no profanity, however—only sacred manifestation, only greatness.

Since the Enlightenment, developing science has denounced the indigenous and natural as primitive, and things of the past as archaic. Today, however, we are increasingly recognizing that "primitivity" is actually our foundation, that the indigenous and natural are eternal and ongoing, and that the archaic is the future. The circle of past and future has been joined. Shamanic psychotherapy is a therapy of the whole person, of the energies of the body. What shamans express in colorful images—manifestations of their life within nature—modern physics and energy research expound in curves and tables. Not that both mean exactly the same thing, for we have only just begun our journey toward equaling the shamans' rich fabric of knowledge, their journeys through countless unknown spiritual worlds. But what awaits us is breathtaking; it spells the end of our vain faith in the ultimate reality of the physical world. There are many universes, spiritual and physical in nature— ours is only one of them. The shamans' healing power derives from other spaces, other times, other energy dimensions. If we want to follow their model, we must journey to these other spaces. Still, the farther we follow the shamans, the farther ahead of us they get, always taking standpoints beyond our knowledge horizon, entirely enveloping us, overwhelming our petty ego thinking and our thirst for knowledge.

Some readers may have expected me to explain something about how shamanic healing is performed. But this is far from my aim. This book is the beginning, the foreword to a dimension of healing that has remained hidden and unnamed. To my knowledge, no one has yet touched upon it; no one has yet described it. It is the story of the primordial beginning of the world, the making of man, the development of the basic laws of being human, the origin of illness and death as recounted in the myths. Hopefully, we have here picked up the trail of real shamanic knowledge. Primordial shamans were at work at the beginning of time, when they were still demiurges and had contact with all living beings, things, and gods. Curiously enough, however, just when shamanism, mediumism, and healing power have entirely degenerated, we are arousing ourselves and making a new beginning. The modern shamans—the physicists—are grasping for the stars, for other universes, are seeking connections with the "gods." This is a process for humanity as a whole, a planetary undertaking in which our seemingly defunct culture and science are taking a major hand. The primordial shamans stood at the beginning of human development, and they will stand at the end as well, even if in the guise of the physicist. The beginning and the end will resemble each other. By technical means, through paraphysics and quantum mechanics, we are coming to grips with the paralogical, paradoxical processes of life. Ancient shamanic symbols and wisdom are coming to light in a new garb, in the framework of a culture determined by intellect.

Why is it that today archaic things are emerging from the mists of the primordial beginnings? Because having long gone astray, we are now finding our way home again. We are approaching the goal, the haven from which we first departed. We are coming home to the origin. The sails are set, the turbines are turning, driven by the power of the spirit, no longer by mechanical drive trains! Now everything is possible.

I would like to present a number of the world models of modern physics; by comparing them with the shamanic worldview, I will show how our science is coming closer and closer to shamanic thinking. When and where the two worlds of knowledge will meet and be unified is uncertain; yet it is inevitable that this will happen.

In 1975, British Nobel Prize winner Brian D. Josephson proposed the existence of parallel worlds that are nested in such a way that we are not in contact with them. According to him, we do not perceive them because they are filtered out by our normal consciousness. Certain techniques of consciousness might possibly make them visible.

Theoretical physicist Burkhard Heim envisages a six-dimensional model of the universe that takes into account both relativity theory and quantum mechanics. Things of a higher dimension that could appear in our world, he calls "syntropods," shadows of multidimensional structures.

French student of nature and philosopher Teilhard de Chardin was of the view that beyond the material universe there is a "psychic universe." This nonmeasurable universe, which lies beyond our sensory perception, makes it possible for more highly developed galactic cultures to gain access to dimensions beyond space and time.

John Archibald Wheeler of Princeton University speaks of time-neutral hyperspace, of so-called cosmic "wormholes" that are supposed to be twenty orders of size smaller than the smallest components of the atom. The entirety of space, according to this idea, is riddled with holes that connect us with the hyperspace that exists side by side with it. In the Wheelerian model of the universe, our physical world lies on the curved surface of a wheel rim. The hole in the wheel's hub represents hyperspace. This idea was anticipated by the so-called Einstein-Rosen bridges, space-warp tunnels that could bridge intergalactic distances without time lapse.

Astrophysicist John Gribbin locates our universe, on the surface of a balloon in the process of being inflated. According to him, the balloon is expanding, which is how he explains the fact that the galaxies are moving away from their midpoint nearly at the speed of light. As a mirror image to the outer skin of the balloon, where we are located, there is an anti-universe on the inner skin of the balloon, differentiated from ours by oppositely charged particles and a time arrow pointing in the opposite direction.

Nikolai Kozyrev, one of the most important Soviet astrophysicists, also assumes the existence of worlds that are related to us in the manner of a mirror image but in which causality remains fully intact. Beyond this, Kozyrev believes he can show experimentally that time possesses a certain quality of an objective, not subjective, nature. He speaks of temporal density, temporal intensity, and an energic quality of time. If he is right, this quasi-material time would influence material structures. Physical structures would exist not in time but with the help of time. All things would influence one another through time. Time would be further extended or newly formed through every material interaction, as Kozyrev hopes to prove with his experiments. He concludes that time is extended by causes and accelerated by effects. Thus exchanges of information between systems take place through time itself, indeed, with no time lapse. According to his view, psi phenomena such as telepathy and precognition can be explained this way. A similar view is held by Charles Musès, an American theoretical physicist, who postulates that time is the cause of all energy release.

In short, "on that day when science begins to investigate non-physical phenomena, it will make greater progress in a decade than in all the centuries it has existed." These are the words of Nikola Tesla, perhaps the greatest genius among all physicists. This is precisely the point at which shaman and physicist will come face to face.

The most consequential paradigm produced by the Western mind, the idea of human evolution, will be entirely dispelled by a philosophy of the future. Friedrich Nietzsche understood man as being the bridge and not the end; Dogen, the great medieval Japanese Zen master, expressed this even more unequivocally: "You have climbed to the top of a hundred-meter-high pole—now go further." When we have, according to Nietzsche, crossed the bridge—that is, man—or according to Dogen, when we have come to the end of the pole, the first stage of enlightenment, where shall we go? For Nietzsche, the next place to go is the superman; for Dogen, into the "air," the immaterial.

I say that evolution is a historical paradigm. The idea of evolution as a three-dimensional concept fails when we leave the realm of the observable, of the senses. For the idea of evolution is based on one time, on a really existing single time that pervades the entire universe. The naïveté of this idea was exposed as early as Lewis Carroll, when he made Alice experience a great temporal paradox:

> "Well, in our country," said Alice, still panting a little, "you'd generally get to somewhere else—if you ran very fast for a long time as we've been doing."
>
> "A slow sort of country!" said the Queen. "Now, here, you see, it takes all the running you can do, to keep in the same place. If you want to get somewhere else, you must run at least twice as fast as that." (Carroll 1960, 210)

Shamans go back and forth between this world and the upper world. They are people of two worlds. Their cartography and sketches of upper space remain imaginal, very human. By contrast, modern physics is becoming more concrete—but at the same time it is less susceptible to observation, hardly accessible anymore to everyday understanding. The universe that physics offers us after we have left Dogen's pole is breathtaking, shocking; it relativizes everything human. Shamans and physicists come nearer to each other at this point. Arthur C. Clarke, scientist and science-fiction author, expresses it this way: "Every adequate advanced technology is indistinguishable from magic." And the great psychologist Carl Rogers notes that "the peak of scientific knowledge is like a mystical peak experience."

The idea of evolution is a product of three-dimensional thought and a one-dimensional concept of time. It is doubtless a naive theory. In contradistinction to it, mathematics and physics, as well as the shamanic outlook, offer multidimensional parallel universes and a holographic cosmos in which evolution represents only one possibility among many. Involution, other-time universes that are subject to other temporal conditions—these are further possible real worlds.

Ralph Waldo Emerson once said: "We live in orders, in subdivisions, in parts, in particles. At the same time, the soul exists in man: wise silence, universal beauty for which all parts and particles are related to each other in the same way." And in a letter of March 21, 1955, Albert Einstein said: "For us believing physicists this division between past, present and future is no more than an illusion, albeit an especially stubborn one." Oxford physics professor Roger Penrose asked: "Could it be that the things for which time really passes by are something like outgrowths of a deeper level of reality in which in a certain sense time stands still for all things?" (quoted in Temple 1982, 244). According to Penrose's view, the normal state of the universe is masslessness—initially everything was massless, while derivative, secondary things were encumbered with mass. Here, matter is understood as a shadow of more-real worlds.

This universe seems to be more like a dream than like the "hard facts" that we are used to thinking about. "We do not possess our dreams, our dreams dream us," opines David Cooper, the anti-psychiatrist. And in a conversation, Niels Bohr remarked, "Well, yes, one could also say that we are not sitting here drinking tea, but that we're dreaming all that" (quoted in Weizsäcker 1971, 424). And Alice said:

> "So I wasn't dreaming after all," she said to herself, "unless—unless we're all part of the same dream. Only I do hope it's my dream, and not the Red King's! I don't like belonging to another person's dream,"

she went on in a rather complaining tone: "I've a great mind to go and wake him, and see what happens!" (Carroll 1960, 293)

The universe seems to be more fantastic than we can imagine; therefore I might say to you, with Kekulé, who discovered the formula for the benzene ring in a dream, "Let us dream, gentlemen!"

Time paradoxes and dream worlds—these lie beyond rigidly defined ego states and the linear theory of evolution. For this reason, Einstein remarked, "Fantasy is more important than knowledge," and his colleague Freeman Dyson added: "For a speculation that does not seem mad at first glance, there is no hope!" And David Cooper pointedly remarked: "The future of madness is its end," to wit, its "transformation into universal creativity, and this is also its lost place of origin" (1978, 132).

So what is healing, where does it begin, where does it end? Are we really only trying to get rid of physical ailments and to balance psychological deficiencies? Or are we looking for more? Is it really the case that all that needs to be healed is what is labeled illness in the hospital and the psychiatrist's office? Certainly the first stage of healing is the healing of body and mind. But the second stage is healing the "ego condition." Here we open ourselves to a transpersonal, transtherapeutic level. On this level, healing is an expansion of perception and of communication. The cosmos that now unfolds is characterized by the existence of many worlds and different kinds of beings, a holographic existential matrix, parapsychic energies.

Not only do shamans convey to us ways of healing; they are models for humanity as a whole, for every one of us. They embody the unused potential of everyone. Making their abilities and their perception of the world accessible to everyone is the task of the psychology of the future. How that is to be achieved must, to a great extent, be left open at the beginning. I have nevertheless set down a few ideas here on this point.

In contrast to our own notions, healing in tribal cultures has a completely different dimension. For shamans themselves, healing means transformation, not curing some sort of an ailment. A fundamental reversal of the existential poles is their goal. Thus healing for him is what Nietzsche called a "transvaluation of all values," on the way to the "superman."

The prerequisite for healing is disentanglement of the conceptual complications of our thinking; what I mean is that the goal is to experience the world without concepts. Belief in the reality of concepts, imagining that they are things or that things are what the concepts say, is the first illusion to be dispelled. The experience of the "speechless world" is a basic part of shamanic psychology. As Immanuel Swedenborg, certainly the greatest of all Western visionaries and "shamans," said, "I am now for the first time in such a state that I know nothing and all my preconceived opinions have eluded me, which is the beginning of all learning, that is, one must first become a child again and then receive knowledge infused into one from one's nurse, just as is happening to me now" (quoted in Dusen 1974, 49). The extent to which we are attached to words and their meanings remains to a great extent hidden from us. It is impossible for us to perceive the world other than through concepts, but it is a matter of total indifference which word is filled with which content. Humpty Dumpty, one of the bizarre figures Alice meets in the land beyond the looking glass, says on this point: "When I use a word, . . . it means just what I choose it to mean—neither more nor less" (Carroll 1960, 269). But Alice's meeting with the Fawn expresses the problem best:

> "Please, would you tell me what you call yourself?" [Alice] said timidly. "I think that might help a little."
>
> "I'll tell you if you come a little further on," the Fawn said. "I can't remember here."
>
> So they walked on together through the wood, Alice with her arms clasped lovingly round the soft neck of the Fawn, till they came out into another open field, and here the Fawn gave a sudden bound into the air, and shook itself free from Alice's arm. "I'm a Fawn!" it cried out in a voice of delight. "And, dear me! you're a human child!" A sudden look of alarm came into its beautiful brown eyes, and in another moment it had darted away at full speed. (Carroll 1960, 226–27)

SUMMARY OF THE PHILOSOPHY OF THE SHADOW

1. The *prima materia* casts shadows. What we call substance and life are actually the shadows of the world of a higher dimension. They are reflections, footprints, echoes of the boundless. Thus, like the shaman, we define life as the quest for the essentially real. This is the initiation process of the primal healer. That is the primordial paradox of the shaman.

2. As the body is the expression of genetic material and as the husk is an expression of the core, life is an expression of a striving to reach home. We find ourselves far from home. We are "off-spring" of our real world. We are stranded on the shores of an illusion. Put another way: An inborn drive and instinct of human beings seeks ecstasy and intoxication, seeks to be filled with effervescent energy, seeks symbiosis, synesthesia, synergy, seeks the altered state of consciousness, seeks shamanic initiation. That is our way of recalling "the homeland." Shamans are thus the real people who discover their real potential. We are forgetful shadow beings who repress the thought of the homeland.

3. There is a continuum, a hierarchy of consciousness. This is the micro-macro principle, the cosmic hologram principle: As with the great, so with the small. Every mental stirring, every sensation, is a miniature expression of a universal resonance. Emotions are diluted cosmic harmony. Shamanic therapy intensifies this participative perception and thereby brings us nearer to the transmaterial communication with all forms and beings that is shamanic existence.

4. The primal therapy of the shaman is the future therapy of the modern world. Modernity will be archaized, and that which is primally indigenous and natural will be modernized. Subatomic physics, energy research, and the immediate shamanic perception and feeling of unity will transcend institutionalized, bureaucratized, culturalized religion and the technology of mechanical "iron" technology. In this way a psychophysics of life will be founded. The principles of shamanism will be highly modern, whereas mechanical technology will be out of date. The aspects of both of them that fit the future will converge.

5. Shamans experience a universe made up of many worlds. They

communicate with beings from other spheres and travel on levels of existence that are quasi-material in nature. Similarly, modern physics speaks of parallel worlds, antiworlds, mirror worlds, energy dimensions. In subatomic and macrophysical dimensions the mind-matter duality so passionately adored by mechanical materialists crumbles—mind and matter seem not really to be distinct from each other. "Matter is frozen energy," said Albert Einstein, and Isaac Newton asked in his *Opticks*, "Is it not conceivable that matter and light change into each other?" We must relativize ourselves; we are in the midst of a Copernican Revolution. The earth is not the midpoint, nor is the sun the midpoint, nor is any distant galaxy the midpoint—the midpoint is everywhere! Seen in the framework of the many-worlds hypothesis, man is nothing, yet he possesses the potential for everything. And it is the shamanic consciousness that deciphers the genetic material of the spirit and opens the gates to other cosmoses.

6. Time seems to be the golden key, the *mysterium magnum.* We are speaking here of time conceived of as quasi-material, as being itself, as a binding medium that holds everything together. Time is not without a nature of its own; indeed, it is life itself. There is nothing but time. We are time beings, time travelers. "Clever people," says the time traveler in H. G. Wells's *The Time Machine,* "know quite precisely that time is only a kind of space"—and vice versa. The psi phenomena with which shamans work are presumably temporal phenomena. The shaman manipulates time. The question of time is a primal question that will decide the future of humanity.

7. Evolution is a myth, a speculation, that ends in the cul-de-sac of three-dimensional thinking. Straight lines, linearity, Euclidean geometry, causality—perhaps these all do really exist, but only—who knows?—as local phenomena, as a local illusion. In any case, the idea of evolution has few prospects in a universe with many worlds. The aversion of tribal cultures to linear thinking and behavior is both famous and infamous; it has brought them the label "primitive." Today the tables are turning. We are the primitives, the ignorant ones.

Since Chronos is the master of all, there may exist universes in which time runs backward; there may exist temporally "more expanded" or "more contracted" universes than ours. Perhaps everything exists that is thinkable, and even everything that is unthinkable.

8. Our dreams dream us, as I said. Who is the dreamer and who the dream figure? Who is realer? Nobody knows, for as Søren Kierkegaard said: "Before God, man is eternally in the wrong." We cannot arrogantly decide what is hallucination and what is reality. Only naive materialists permit themselves that. When shamans enter an altered state of consciousness, many cultures speak of "dreams." In the near future, our dreams will intensify and take on bizarre forms.

9. What we need is neither a stay in a hospital nor conventional psychotherapy: we need shamanic schools, medicine societies, initiation paths, transtherapeutic methods. The future of therapy—as we learn from shamans—is the transformation of consciousness, which promises direct healing. And that in turn means making contact with other levels of being, other existences, with death, with the beyond, with superspace. Every conscious being can change, and so everyone can become a healer, everyone can learn to see the holy. Healing means comprehending holiness, letting it work through oneself—nothing else. Only because it is so simple do we find it so hard.

10. Healing is enmeshed in the course of history, moreover, in the destiny of this planet. This is beyond the control of any individual, but it is what confers on the individual his measure of integrity, health, and wholesomeness. That is the metaperspective of healing, under which all normal healing procedures are subsumed. This dimension eludes the grasp of experience. Only by voyaging in hyperspace have shamans gained knowledge of it. Myths of origin make a big point of the current degeneration of humanity. According to them, we are in the midst not of an evolution but of a regression—holiness is on the decline. And today, with the final annihilation of tribal cultures and the neglect of shamanic power, we may be at the terminal point of history—the spiritual power has almost melted away. Now many peoples are awaiting the demise— that is, the rebirth—of humanity, for the nadir of culture produces a fresh renewal. Traditional peoples and shamans expect this rebirth

to come through suffering, catastrophe, planetary destruction—a new age of the world is at hand. What we must anticipate is worldwide chaos, crisis—or depending on one's point of view—purification, inner and outer.

EPILOGUE

The history of science is the history of a mutilated vision.

—MICHAEL MURPHY (1976)

THE WHITE MAN HAS,
THE BLACK MAN IS

The unleashed power of the atom has changed everything but our way of thinking; and so we are headed for an unparalleled catastrophe. . . . A new type of thinking is indispensable if mankind is to survive and develop further.

—ALBERT EINSTEIN
(quoted in *The New York Times*,
May 25, 1946, p. 13)

We are still stuck in the same mental husks. We move gothically or in the baroque style or romantically or scholastically or gnostically or impressionistically or expressionistically in a world that has long since begun to demand an entirely different style of thinking and approach.

—WILHELM MÜHLMANN
(1964, 45)

Knowledge, for the Western mind, is unknowingly bound up with rational knowledge. Indeed, knowledge is considered a synonym for rationality. Irrationality is rationally conceivable; what remains inconceivable and ungraspable for us is the irrationality of rationality. Long before the scholar dissects the "primitive" mythos, the civilized mythos has appropriated it, vivisected it, decorated it with rubrics of its own. I am reminded here of Bertrand Russell's brain surgeon, who sees in his patient's brain only what is happening in his own brain. Could it be that the ethnological cerebral cortex sees only "primitive" because it itself is primitive?

A theory or worldview that neglects to look for its own negation in a metatheory of higher dimensions, that considers it superfluous to investigate its own cultural consciousness, becomes increasingly distant from the sense and purpose of science. Does science really produce *scientia,* knowledge? we must ask. Or does it produce only what it needs for its own self-confirmation?

The greatest revolution of this century has been the consciousness revolution. Future researchers will surely be amused by our struggle over this most self-evident of all knowledge, yet we are just at the point of catching a glimpse of our own consciousness. We are just beginning to pull ourselves out of the bog by our own hair, the bog being the historical paradigm that sets us against the investigation of consciousness.

A profound criticism of our anticonsciousness attitude based on transcultural comparison has yet to emerge; and the anti-ethnocentrism that has existed up until now has not helped much. It has condemned the obvious depredations of colonialism and the theory of evolution, but it has failed to examine the sources of our ethical behavior closely, and at present there exists not even a vague idea about our own cultural expression. Our own nature remains completely veiled to us, and the idea of a cultural self-analysis remains unknown.

It is not as if our investigators dismiss or entirely ignore the magical world. It is has received a treatment like other things—but under the rubric of pseudo-facts, of unreal prescientific knowledge, an archaic mentality. As late as 1978, in their book *Magie: Die sozialwissenschaftliche Kontroverse über das Verstehen fremden Denkens* (Magic: The Controversy in the Social Sciences Concerning the Understanding of Alien Thinking), Hans G. Kippenberg and B. Luchesi opine: "It becomes the task of the ethnologist to resolve the confusions of primitive thinking." Still intact, the tendency to identify alien thinking with false thinking prevails today. Even researchers who possess the ability to approach alien mentalities sympathetically and empathetically might well not reach the point of speaking of an alternative mode of thought. Lévi-Strauss remarked of "primitive" thought: "It of course remains something different from scientific thought and also lags behind it in certain respects" (1980, 29).

Myths are also readily used to characterize the awkwardness of the thinking of nature societies, as for example when Lévi-Strauss sees in myth the possibility for the "primitive" to gain power and control over the environment but then in the next breath dismisses this as an understandable illusion and finally shows how it entirely contradicts scientific thinking. Just as we used the discovery of Tahiti as a welcome occasion to develop a critique of our own sexual pietism but in the process had very little interest in Tahiti itself, today the myth of primitive thinking is a welcome guest in the house of science. Who does not gladly recognize the aberrations of others? They are so helpful as a basis for one's own pompous self-elevation. It is hardly a mark of strength, however, that our science requires an undeveloped predecessor to put itself in the limelight of evolution. The contrived duality between primitive and civilized, magic and science, is reminiscent more of kitschy film romances with good and evil heroes than of a sound basis for anthropological research.

We believe that it is impossible for us to emulate the other kind of thought. Indeed, we find even the use of the term *thought* for "primitive" thought a rather generous, progressive, or even theoretically refined acknowledgment. In point of fact, "primitive" thought is no stranger than our own—it is only that its contents and relations are different. Thus there is no such thing as magical thought, only a magical worldview, which is the one that pervaded all of antiquity and the Middle Ages and is still present in many a spiritualistic philosophy of today. Scholars' bizarre search for "primitive" thought in traditional societies, if looked at closely, is nothing but a search for failures and lapses in the Western system of thought. In essence there is hardly any difference between the mode of thought in tribal cultures and that of modern Western cultures. Differences, however, do appear in the religious outlook toward the world, for with us religion as a factor in power and survival has been lost, replaced by economic and materialistic approaches to life. The myth of another kind of thinking is basically an expression of the degeneracy of our outlook and our inability to experience nature as an animated whole. Anyone who can no longer do that will obviously have to take exception to "primitives." Discrimination against this "other kind of thinking" is therefore not a matter of ethnocentrism, but rather the reaction of a denatured culture to contact with a natural one. Hatred of nature and love of nature collide with each other; alienation from life and intensity of life find themselves face to face.

In contrast to theories of "primitive" thought, transpersonal anthropology reveals regions of consciousness with which we have been increasingly losing touch since the Enlightenment and that appear to be completely lost in the current phase of our civilization. I am speaking of states of consciousness that for us smack of irrationality, hysteria, pathology, and myth but that other cultures regard as vivifying and existentially important.

Transpersonal anthropology sees itself as a science that studies features of the human mind hitherto neglected by classical theories with new, more farsighted methods. It affirms that the human being possesses a capacity for consciousness that cannot be adequately accounted for by theories of behavior or psychoanalysis or depth psychology. Transpersonal science no longer advocates the Western-inspired monopsychology that believes it can fathom the depths of all cultures by using Victorian and mechanico-behavioristic models. The two heuristically valuable concepts of transpersonal anthropology are "alternative state of consciousness" and the "transpersonal." The transpersonal means transcending the sphere of ego, the personally centered existence, and entering into areas of consciousness that—spatially, temporally, and materially—permit a broader range of experience. In our society, most people experience only an ego confined to a miniature private universe. In nature societies, by contrast, there exists, beyond the ego sphere, an intensive contact with metapersonal entities and transpsychic forces of the higher self. For so-called primitive people the space of reality is comparatively greater and has more dimensions than that of Western people.

Transpersonal anthropology creates an entirely new kind of relationship to the suprapersonal realm. It does not see it as merely a symbolic world, nor does it make use of a culturally relative system of interpretation in working with it. It considers the transpsychic realm to be as real and as relevant for our survival and our sense of reality as our ordinary, everyday repertory of behavior and experience. It does not regard traditional societies' claims to be able to activate higher forms of consciousness as metaphors, as cultural circumscriptions, but shows that modern research into consciousness has in many areas come up with the same results. A new generation of researchers represent the fabulous experience of the world that is part of magic as an alternative state of consciousness that opens up latent psychic functions. What we previously regarded as fantastic or primitive, we are now discovering is the primitivity and lack of imagination of a self-curtailing methodology and theory of knowledge.

We can safely say that modern science, after long theoretical errancy, has now decided on the basis of neuropsychological knowledge to broaden its investigations to those areas of consciousness that have been familiar to the traditional mentality for thousands of years. Today it is no longer appropriate merely to record the strange customs and ideas concerning magic to which particular peoples adhere but to show their real and pragmatic value for living, in the light of the latest research into the potentials of consciousness. This undertaking cannot but impiously burst the bonds of anthropological neutrality and bring anthropology into accord with the level of development current in the other sciences. The ethnology of religion, which as a result of its standoffish attitude toward modern consciousness research is in a particularly antiquated state, is particularly in need of revivification. A similar situation exists with regard to the political engagement of traditional ethnology; its stiff and frozen scientific "objectivity" makes it impossible for it to go so far as to make judgments and undertake appropriate action. Armchair ethnology combined with periodic sojourns in the field is obsolete. Ethnology must now practically participate in the struggles of threatened tribal societies, both to protect those cultures from ourselves and to regenerate ourselves and our civilization through new models for living.

The approach of transpersonal anthropology is the reverse of that of traditional anthropology. Classical ethnographers looked at shamans from the outside, used them as informants, recorded their rituals and their external body movements during trance; present-day ethnographers are faced with a much harder undertaking. They must not only fulfill the usual tasks, they must also attempt to penetrate into the inner psychic universe, into the alternative state of consciousness of the spiritual person who lives with spatiotemporal criteria completely different from those that the normal scientific consciousness of the researcher is capable of dealing with.

The problems that have hitherto arisen for anthropology in interpreting magical thought appear today as communication problems between two different modes of mental functioning. Our consciousness is not exhausted by a Euclidean-Newtonian structure of experience. This represents only a special state that has been hypertrophied and inordinately overgeneralized in the West.

The psychic laws of the alternative state of consciousness are so spectacularly opposed to those of the normal state of consciousness that we may be inclined to think of the two as mutually exclusive rather than as mutually complementary. At present, scarcely any descriptions of alternative states of consciousness in shamans exist in the literature because the new psychological knowledge has not yet reached the field of ethnology. So far, Western society has limited itself in its research into psychological areas almost entirely to normal consciousness, and states not compatible with it with have been relegated to the special department of psychopathology. Thus we may speak of an imperialism of normal consciousness that dominates and suppresses other forms of consciousness. Whereas in tribal societies several forms of consciousness are accessible, the Western world has restricted itself to a minimal range of the mental spectrum.

For this reason I have repeatedly stressed that our level of discrimination has not yet reached the point where it can cope with the psychic realm of medicine people. Medicine people use a broader spectrum of consciousness forms, in relationship to which the normal Westerner and Western science are mere psychic stepchildren. Our present scientific hedonism possesses no special authority in this area, and its claims to predominance in the realm of the psyche remain unfounded. Thus in the future we will have no choice but to pay homage to shamanic consciousness. Transpersonal science is in the process of broadening our ideas and our range of experience and calling upon us to tread in the footsteps of the shamans.

Only through the development of the materialistic worldview did higher forms of human consciousness fall into disrepute; then the conflict between science and magic ran its fruitless course. The confrontation between normal scientific consciousness and magical consciousness is increasingly less vehement. In the meantime the research pioneers have catapulted themselves into the precincts of the traditional cognition of the world. Past and future are proving to be identical. It is now a question of documenting in detail the fact that humanity has made use of alternative states of consciousness to better its chances of survival from the very beginning.

The rational investigative style itself is now giving birth to a knowledge of the necessity of another mode of investigation. As classical physics transformed itself into a relative physics, today normal consciousness is recognizing its own limitedness and sees itself as just one stage on the way to more comprehensive forms of consciousness. In an act of self-abandon, it is presently calling for a new level of knowledge. The rational mode is pushing its thought potential to its high point, arriving in a border area of experience, and at the point of no return is finally deciding on its own destruction.

A state of consciousness maintains its stability by discrediting deviant perceptions and perceptions that create doubt. Every state of consciousness attempts to maintain a state of balance, strives for maximal clarity of its own principles, and suppresses disturbing perceptual forms. And as every state of consciousness requires for its transformation a series of consciousness-altering measures, our stable paradigm of consciousness, the prevailing scientific theory, is destroyed only when enough destabilizing alternative data are present. And we are just now reaching that point. We are on the verge of another Copernican Revolution, a global revolution of consciousness.

What mark does the experience of alternative states of consciousness leave on normal consciousness? The memory of transpersonal symbols, paranormal contacts, communication with nonhuman entities, and so on, remains intact, but it characteristically translates itself into the normal state of consciousness. People cling to spiritual revelations and try to experience them anew through rituals. Out of this, religions with all their institutions come into being. Religion and magic—and magic is nothing but the experience of a transpersonal dimension—have their origin in altered states of consciousness. The laws of magic are the laws of a higher realm of consciousness. Our ethnology attempts to come to grips with the magical sphere through the means of normal intellect. This undertaking is doomed to failure, for an invisible methodological wall and the experience of the world as filtered by normal consciousness prevents it from entering the realms of other consciousnesses and forces it to invent a magic that functions entirely according to the laws of its own rational-causal thinking. The study of religious phenomena therefore remains a pseudoscience, enclosed in the autistic world of ordinary understanding.

The critique of Western culture inherent in the "primitive" worldview has previously had no chance to be expressed openly. To be sure, certain sociophilosophic traditions use other cultures as the basis for a critique of civilization; but they have hardly dared to present the magico-religious worldview as a model to the mechanico-materialistic mentality. Nonetheless, that is our goal here—astonishingly enough, with the help of Western science itself. This paradox has come about only because our modern psychological and physical knowledge has unexpectedly taken on an increasing resemblance to the view of traditional societies. Now that the microphysicists have begun to speak of the unity of physics and consciousness, transpersonal science is taking the final step and laying out a wide-ranging spectrum of consciousness running from the simple ego state to the mystical experience of unity with everything existing. The general characteristic of alternative states of consciousness is that they further unity, whether by psychotropic plants and mushrooms, by prayer, dance, and meditation, or by ascetic techniques like fasting, sleep withdrawal, and self-castigation. The result is always an increase in the spiritual connections and exchanges within the world of things that otherwise seems so isolated from us. Between simple changes in consciousness, perhaps provoked by psychedelic drugs, and mystical experiences of totality, the only difference is in their intensity; what remains constant is the principle of unification that characterizes all levels of transpersonal consciousness. The experience of unity arises amid a process of increasing integration and increasing knowledge of the universal interaction and the mutual influence of all aspects of existence. Our science began with the naive idea of a push-pull type of interaction between things, according to the mechanical Newtonian planetary model; today in the new physics we are finding confirmation that all elementary particles influence one another mutually and are mutually interdependent. On the macrocosmic level, we are also recognizing the unity of the plant, animal, and human domains as well as the necessary unity of all the races and cultures of our planet.

In discussing alternative states of consciousness, my intention has been to show that our relationship with the environment has been characterized by a rational-linear mentality whose one-sided emphasis has failed to establish harmonious contact with the outside and with what is other or different, because it perceives the world exclusively as a random collection of individual factors. The cultural, ecological, and psychological crisis of Western civilization hardly needs to be pointed out. Because Western science refuses to subject its own paradigmatic models to critical examination, we are in the midst of an escalating catastrophe today. The cause for this lies essentially in the relationship we have defined to our own human and natural qualities. In point of fact, our ignorance of alternative styles of thought and modes of experiencing the world have entangled us in an unprecedented state of circular thinking. Ethnology, from which we might have expected a contribution toward solving this problem, presented other cultures not as positive alternatives but as repellent and unfruitful or primitive approaches to life from which we can learn nothing. In this way it contributed to perpetuating the process of tautological self-confirmation.

The deification of the machine has been seen as the acme of our civilizational effort. Yet at the same time it is an expression of our increasingly poverty-stricken inner world. We have placed all our energy in the machine, and now our emptied psychic husks are dependent on the world of machines: hollow within, we must enter into a symbiosis with the cybernetic robots we have created. We have degenerated into cyborgs, cybernetic-organismic hybrids, characters in a schizophrenic tragedy. The power of our psyche has lost its function; instruments of all kinds, from X-ray apparatuses to telescopes, have taken priority over the psyche. In the competition of the mind against the world of apparatus, the machines have

out-trumped their own inventors, have made themselves autonomous, and today are turning en masse against their creators.
Human beings, reduced to helpless replacement parts for their own
creations and blind to their inner powers, passively permit themselves to be rotated by the turbines.

Magic, on the other hand, generated entirely out of its own mind,
sees itself as interwoven in the "great machine of natural forces."
Nevertheless, through attunement to and harmonization with natural movement, it succeeds in assuring that these forces do not direct
themselves against it. Real magic is nothing but real life, a life with
which ethnologists in their scientist's coats have lost touch, a life
whose delicious fruits they never taste. Real magic is the total
coherence of life, of all facets of life, the intensely experienced, felt,
and sensed movement of nature. In our model of the universe,
ideologies of the exploitation and destruction of nature and of the
reduction of man to an isolated ego are so closely interwoven that
we are no longer able to bring culture and nature, ego and nature,
in touch with each other. Our instrumental, goal-oriented action
and thought is what we regard as effective. By contrast, the kind of
thinking that attempts to empathize, to work purely on the basis
of feeling, we regard as archaic and undeveloped.

The key to magic, as to modern physics, is the relationship of
matter and consciousness. For both, consciousness is the nucleus
around which our existence revolves. This is quite the opposite of
the generally held view of science, which has subscribed fully to the
primacy of matter. Today, both traditional natural philosophies and
microphysics recognize an inseparable unity of consciousness and
matter. In some way that we cannot yet gauge, the gap between
these two sciences will be bridged.

If ethnographers were to analyze themselves courageously and
selflessly, their mental and spiritual self-alienation would quickly be
revealed—alienation from themselves, from their work, from the
products of their work, from their fellow human beings, from
nature, and from the cosmos. What they would be left with would
be a social robot devoid of all sentience. The real processes of nature
have been lost to them through their all-explaining and all-disman-
tling science. Real integrity—that is, intensely experienced connectedness with natural processes and with the stages of the human life

cycle—that they now study in other peoples, hardly strike them as other than primitive. For the concepts of individualism, objectivism, and materialism have rendered them incapable of penetrating into the wealth of connectedness of traditional societies. For ethnographers, whoever makes inadmissible connections is primitive; by contrast, whoever recognizes inadmissible connections, then creates that famous-infamous favorite toy of the Western mind, the mechanical building-block universe, is modern and is describing the truth.

In saying, in the title to this chapter, "the white man has," I am not referring merely to our industrial buildings overflowing with manmade wares but also and especially to our intellectual way of appropriating the world. The rational expression of normal consciousness is oriented toward possession; it attempts to wrap the world in handy little packages and make it mechanically manipulable. The Westerner analyzes being and in the same moment destroys it, for his form of analysis is limited and reduces the infinite wealth of the connectedness of existence to mere formulas and artificial concepts. Nevertheless, this analysis leads faithfully to its own self-dissolution and self-transcendence, at which point it changes from a caterpillar to a butterfly—a butterfly that we seem to want to teach how to fly.

The omega point of analysis to which I am referring is the advance of physics into areas in which matter is converted into energy and in which individual particles reveal themselves to be events more than rigid structures, events that are indivisibly bound up with one another and cannot be analyzed isolatedly. But this requires a new epistemological methodology. And this methodology is somehow connected with the researcher's own consciousness, for consciousness and the object of research form a unity, albeit one that we are unable to precisely define. And *unity* is the magic word upon which the future of our scientific research will be founded. Transpersonal experience and alternative states of consciousness move on a more holistic and integrative level of knowledge than the researchers' reason. That is why I say "the black man is," for nature peoples do not do research into alternative states of consciousness. Rather, these are part of their ceremonies, part of their magico-religious experience of the world.

BIBLIOGRAPHY

Abt, Paul. 1927. *Im Banne des Zauberers: Unheimliche Erlebnisse in der Südsee.* Stuttgart.

Ackerknecht, Erwin H. 1971. *Medicine and Anthropology.* Bern.

Agapitow, N. N., and M. N. Changalow. 1887. "Das Schamanenthum unter den Burjäten." Translated by L. Stieda. *Globus* 52: 286–88, 299–301, 316–18. Brunswick.

Akerman, K. 1979. "Contemporary Aboriginal Healers in the South Kimberley." *Oceania* 50: 23–30. Sydney.

Amiotte, Arthur. 1976. "Eagles Fly Over." *Parabola* 1, no. 3: 28–41.

Angoff, Allan, and Diana Barth. 1974. "Parapsychology and Anthropology." *Proceedings of the International Conference* (1973). New York: Parapsychology Foundation.

Anisimov, A. F. 1963. "The Shaman's Tent of the Evenks and the Origin of the Shamanistic Rite." In *Studies in Siberian Shamanism,* edited by Henry N. Michael. Toronto.

Arbman, Ernst. 1963–70. *Ecstasy and Religious Trance.* 3 vols. Uppsala.

Bäckman, Louise, and Åke Hultkrantz. 1978. "Studies in Lapp Shamanism." *Stockholm Studies in Comparative Religion,* no. 16.

Bahr, Donald M., Juan Gregorio, et al. 1974. *Piman Shamanism and Staying Sickness (Ká:cim Múnkidag).* Tucson: University of Arizona Press.

Balász, János. 1963. "Über de Ekstase des ungarischen Schamanen." In *Glaubenswelt und Folklore der sibirischen Völker,* edited by Vilmos Diószegi. Budapest.

Barbeau, Marius. 1958. "Medicine Men of the Pacific Coast." Bulletin No. 152, Anthropological Series No. 42. Ottawa: National Museum of Canada.

Barnouw, V. 1942. "Siberian Shamanism and Western Spiritualism." *Journal of the American Society for Psychical Research* 36: 140–68.

Beattie, J. H. M. 1964. "Rainmaking in Bunyoro." *Man* 64: 140–41.

———. 1967. "The Ghost Cult in Bunyoro." In *Gods and Rituals: Readings in Religious Beliefs and Practices,* edited by John Middleton. Garden City, N.Y.: Natural History Press.

Belo, Jane. 1960. *Trance in Bali.* New York.

Benedict, Ruth. 1922. "The Vision in Plains Culture." *American Anthropologist* 24 (n.s.): 1–23.

———. 1934. "Anthropology and the Abnormal." *Journal of General Psychology* 10: 59–79.

Berglie, Per Arne. 1976. "Preliminary Remarks on some Tibetan 'Spirit Mediums' in Nepal." *Kailash: A Journal of Himalayan Studies* 4, no. 1: 85–108.

————. 1978. "On the Question of Tibetan Shamanism." In *Tibetan Studies*, edited by M. Brauen and P. Kvaerne. Zurich: Völkerkundemuseum.

Bergman, Robert L. 1973. "A School for Medicine-Men." *American Journal of Psychiatry* 130, no. 6: 663–66.

Berndt, R. M. 1946–47, 1947–48. "Wuradjeri Magic and 'Clever Men.' " *Oceania* 17: 327–65, and 18: 60–86. Sydney.

Bischko, Johannes. 1970. *Einführung in die Akupunktur.* Heidelberg.

Black, A. K. 1934. "Shaking the Wigwam." *Beaver* (December). Winnipeg.

Blacker, Carmen. 1975. *The Catalpa Bow: A Study of Shamanistic Practices in Japan.* London.

Bleibtreu-Ehrenberg, Gisela. 1983. *Der Weibermann.* Frankfurt am Main.

Blodgett, Jean, ed. 1978. *The Coming and Going of the Shaman: Eskimo Shamanism and Art.* Winnipeg: Winnipeg Art Gallery.

Boas, Franz. 1964 (1888). "The Central Eskimo." *6th Annual Report of the Bureau of American Ethnology, 1884–1885.* Washington, D.C.: 399–669.

Bogoras, Waldemar. 1907. "The Chuckchee." *The Jesup North Pacific Expedition, 1904–1909*, vol. 7, no. 2. *Memoirs of the American Museum of Natural History.* Leiden and New York (1904).

————. 1929. *Asia* 29, no. 4 (April).

————. 1956. "Schilderungen zweier schamanischer Séancen der Küsten-Tschuktschen (Nordsibirien)." *Abhandlungen und Aufsätze aus dem Institut für Menschen- und Menschheitskunde.* Augsburg.

Boisen, Anton. 1936. *The Exploration of the Inner World.* New York: Harper.

Boshier, Adrian K. 1974. "African Apprenticeship." *Parapsychology Review* 5, no. 4: 1–3, 25–27.

Bourguignon, Erika. 1970. "Hallucination and Trance: An Anthropologist's Perspective." In *Origin and Mechanism of Hallucinations*, edited by Wolfram Keup. New York: Plenum Press.

Bowers, Malcolm B., and Daniel X. Freedman. 1975. " 'Psychedelic' Experiences in Acute Psychosis." In *Psychiatry and Mysticism*, edited by Stanley R. Dean. Chicago: Nelson-Hall.

Boyer, L. B. 1961. "Notes on the Personality Structure of a North American Indian Shaman." *Journal of the Hillside Hospital* 10: 14–33.

Boyle, John Andrew. 1972. "Turkish and Mongol Shamanism in the Middle Ages." *Folklore* 83: 177–93.

Bozzano, Ernesto. 1975. *Übersinnliche Erscheinungen bei Naturvölkern.* Freiburg.

Bramly, Serge. 1978. *Macumba: Die magische Religion Brasiliens.* Freiburg i. Br.

Brown, Joseph Espes. 1970. "The Unlikely Associates. A Study of Oglala Sioux Magic and Metaphysic." *Ethnos* 1–4: 5–15.

————. 1976. "The Roots of Renewal." In *Seeing with a Native Eye*, edited by W. H. Capps. New York.

————. 1979. "The Wisdom of the Contrary: A Conversation with Joseph Espes Brown." *Parabola* 4, no. 1: 54–165.

————. 1980. "The Question of 'Mysticism' within Native American Traditions." In *Understanding Mysticism*, edited by Richard Woods. New York: Image.

Brown, Vinson. 1974. *Voices of Earth and Sky: The Vision Life of the Native Americans and Their Culture Heroes.* Harrisburg, Pa.: Stackpole Books.

———. 1987. "Ein Regenbogen im Morgengrauen." In *Heilung des Wissens,* edited by Amelie Schenk and Holger Kalweit. Munich.

Browning, Norma Lee. 1970. *The Psychic World of Peter Hurkos.* New York.

Buck, Peter H. 1970. *Regional Diversity in the Elaboration of Sorcery in Polynesia.* New Haven, Conn.

Bunzel, Ruth. 1929–30. "Introduction to Zuñi Ceremonialism." *47th Annual Report of the Bureau of American Ethnology.* Washington, D.C.

Burgesse, J. A. 1944. "The Spirit Wigwam as Described by Tommie Mair, Point Bleue." *Primitive Man* 17, no. 3–4: 50–53.

Burney, C. 1952. *Solitary Confinement.* London.

Burr, Harold Saxon. 1972. *Blueprint for Immortality: The Electric Patterns of Life.* London.

Butt, A., S. Wavell, and N. Epton. 1967. *Trances.* London.

Campbell, Joseph. 1985. *Lebendiger Mythos.* Munich.

Carroll, Lewis. 1960. *The Annotated Alice,* edited by Martin Gardner. New York: Bramhall House.

———. 1963. *Alice im Wonderland.* Frankfurt am Main. Originally published as *Alice in Wonderland.*

———. 1981. *Alice im Spiegelland.* Munich. Originally published as *Through the Looking Glass.*

Cartwright, Sarah. 1884. "Magnetism Clairvoyantly Discussed." *Human Dimensions* 5, no. 1–2.

Cerutti, Edwina. 1975. *Mystic with the Healing Hands: The Life Story of Olga Worrall.* New York.

Chadwick, Nora K. 1936. "Shamanism Among the Tatars of Central Asia." *Journal of the Royal Anthropological Institute of Great Britain and Ireland* 66: 75–112. London.

Chaumeil, Jean-Pierre. 1983. *Voir, Savoir, Pouvoir: Le Chamnisme chez les Yagua du Nord-Est Péruvien.* Paris.

Chesi, Gert. 1974. *Voodoo: Afrikas geheime Mächte.* Wörgl.

Clements, Forrest E. 1932. "Primitive Concepts of Disease." *University of California Publications in American Archaeology and Ethnology* 2. Berkeley, Calif.

Coe, Mayne Reid. 1957. "Fire-Walking and Related Behaviors." *Psychological Record* 7: 101–110.

Coe, Michael D. 1955. "Shamanism in the Bunun Tribe, Central Formosa." *Ethnos* 20, no. 4: 181–98.

Cooper, David. 1978. *Die Sprache der Verrücktheit.* Berlin.

Cooper, John M. 1944. "The Shaking Tent Rite Among Plains and Forest Algonquians." *Primitive Man* 17, no. 3–4: 60–84.

Counts, D. A. 1983. "Near-Death and Out-of-the-Body Experiences in Melanesian Society." *Anabiosis: The Journal for Near-Death Studies* 3, no. 2: 115–37.

Csikszentmihalyi, M. 1975. "Play and Intrinsic Rewards." *Journal of Humanistic Psychology* 15, no. 3: 41–63.

Curtis, Natalie. 1907. *The Indian's Book.* New York.

Cushing, Frank Hamilton. 1983. *Ein Weisser Indianer: Mein Leben mit den Zuñi,* edited by Holger Kalweit. Olten.

Cutten, G. B. 1927. *Speaking with Tongues: Historically and Psychologically Considered.* New Haven, Conn.

David-Néel, Alexandra. 1931. *Heilige und Hexer.* Leipzig.

Davis, E. Wade. 1983. "The Ethnobiology of the Haitian Zombi." *Journal of Ethnopharmacology* 9: 85–104.

Dean, Stanley R. 1972. "Shamanism versus Psychiatry in Bali, 'Island of the Gods.' " *American Journal of Psychiatry* 129: 59–62.

————, and Denny Thong. 1975. "Transcultural Aspects of Metapsychiatry: Focus on Shamanism in Bali." In *Psychiatry and Mysticism,* edited by Stanley R. Dean. Chicago: Nelson-Hall.

Densmore, Frances. 1918. "Teton Sioux Music." Bureau of American Ethnology, Bulletin no. 61. Washington, D.C.

Deren, Maya. 1975. *The Voodoo Gods.* St. Albans.

Derlon, Pierre. 1976. *Unter Hexern and Zauberern: Die geheimen Traditionen der Zigeuner.* Basel.

————. 1981. *Die geheime Heilkunst der Zigeuner.* Basel.

Devereux, George. 1945. "The Origin of Shamanistic Powers as Reflected in a Neurosis." *Revue Internationale d'Ethnopsychologie Normale et Pathologique* 1: 19–28.

————. 1961. "Shamans as Neurotics." *American Anthropologist* 63, no. 5: 1088–90.

————. 1967. *Angst und Methode in den Verhaltenswissenschaften.* Munich.

————. 1974. *Normal and Anormal.* Frankfurt am Main.

————. 1978. *Ethnopsychoanalyse.* Frankfurt am Main.

DeWoskin, Kenneth J., trans. 1983. *Doctors, Diviners, and Magicians of Ancient China: Biographies of Fang-Shih.* New York: Columbia University Press.

Diószegi, Vilmos. 1961. "Problems of Mongolian Shamanism (Report of an Expedition Made in 1960 in Mongolia)." *Acta Ethnographica* 10: 195–206. Budapest.

————, ed. 1963a. *Glaubenswelt und Folklore der sibirischen Völker.* Budapest.

————. 1963b. "Zum Problem der ethnischen Homogeneität des tofischen (karagassischen) Schamanismus." In *Glaubenswelt und Folklore der sibirischen Völker,* edited by Vilmos Diószegi. Budapest.

————. 1968a. *Tracing Shamans in Siberia: The Story of an Ethnographical Research Expedition.* Translated from the Hungarian by Anita Rajkay Babo. Oosterhout, Netherlands.

————. 1968b. "The Origin of the Evenki Shamanic Instruments (Stick, Knout) of Transbaikalia." *Acta Ethnographica* 17, no. 4–5: 265–311. Budapest.

Dobkin de Rios, Marlene. 1978. "A Psi Approach to Love Magic, Witchcraft and Psychedelics in the Peruvian Amazon." *Phoenix: Journal for Transpersonal Anthropology* 2, no. 1: 22–28.

Donner, Kai. 1954. *Among the Samoyed in Siberia.* Translated by Rinehart Kyber. New Haven, Conn.

Dorsey, J. Owen. 1894. "A Study of Siouan Cults." *11th Annual Report of the Bureau of American Ethnology, 1889–1890.* Washington, D.C.: 361–549.

Drury, Nevill. 1982. *The Shaman and the Magician: Journey between the Worlds.* London.

DuBois, Constance Goddard. 1908. "The Religion of the Luiseño Indians of Southern California." *University of California Publications in American Archaeology and Ethnology* 8, no. 3. Berkeley, Calif.

Dusen, Wilson van. 1971. *The Natural Depth in Man.* New York.

————. 1974. *The Presence of Other Worlds.* New York.

Dusenberry, Verne. 1961. "The Significance of the Sacred Pipes to the Gros Ventre of Montana." *Ethnos* 26, no. 1–2: 12–29.

Eaton, Evelyn. 1982. *The Shaman and the Medicine Wheel.* London.

Eccles, John C. 1980. *Gehirn und Geist.* Munich.

Eder, Matthias. 1958. "Schamanismus in Japan." *Paideuma* 6, no. 7 (May): 367–80. Bamberg.

Edsman, Carl Martin, ed. 1967. *Studies in Shamanism.* Stockholm.

Eliade, Mircea. 1970. *Zalmoxis: The Vanishing God.* Translated by Willard R. Trask. Chicago: University of Chicago Press.

Elkin, Adolphus Peter. 1938. *The Australian Aborigines: How to Understand Them.* Sydney and London.

———. 1977. *Aboriginal Men of High Degree.* New York. Originally published in Sydney (1946).

Elwin, Verrier. 1955. *The Religion of an Indian Tribe.* London and New York.

Endicott, K. M. 1970. *An Analysis of Malay Magic.* Oxford.

Erdoes, Richard. 1972. *The Sun Dance People.* New York.

Fabrega, Horacio, and Daniel B. Silver. 1973. *Illness and Shamanic Curing in Zinacantan.* Stanford, Calif.: Stanford University Press.

Feraca, S. E. 1961. "The Yuwipi Cult of the Oglala and Sicanu Teton Sioux." *Plains Anthropos* 6, no. 13.

Fichte, Hubert. 1976. *Xango: Die afroamerikanischen Religionen in Bahia, Haiti, Trinidad.* Frankfurt am Main.

———. 1976–77. "Ketzerische Bemerkungen für eine neue Wissenschaft vom Menschen." *Ethnomedizin* 4, no. 1–2: 171–81.

Findeisen, Hans. 1953. "Schamanentum im tungusischen Kinderspiel." *Zeitschrift für Ethnologie* 78, no. 2: 307–308. Berlin.

———. 1956. "Der Adler als Kulturbringer im nordasiatischen Raum und in der amerikanischen Arktis." *Zeitschrift für Ethnologie* 81. Special Issue. pp. 1–13; 70–82. Berlin.

———. n.d. "Die vier Visionen des Schamanen Kinggät." (unpublished manuscript).

Flannery, Regina. 1939. "The Shaking-Tent Rite Among the Montagnais of James Bay." *Primitive Man* 7: 11–16.

———. 1944. "The Gros Ventre Shaking Tent." *Primitive Man* 17: 54–84.

Fletscher, Alice C. 1884. "The Shadow or Ghost Lodge: A Ceremony of the Oglala Sioux." *Reports of the Peabody Museum of American Archaeology and Ethnology.* Cambridge, Mass.

———, and Francis La Flesche. 1911. "The Omaha Tribe." *27th Annual Report of the Bureau of American Ethnology, 1905–1906.* Washington, D.C.

Forde, C. Daryll. 1931. "Ethnography of the Yuma Indians." *University of California Publications in American Archaeology and Ethnology* 27, no. 4. Berkeley, Calif.

Fornander, Abraham, and Thomas G. Thrum. 1919. *Fornander Collection of Hawaiian Antiquities and Folk-lore.* Honolulu.

Frank, Walter A. 1980. "Paranormal Healing in Africa and Asia." *Journal of Transpersonal Anthropology* 4: 54–60.

Frazer, James G. 1966 (1915). *The Golden Bough.* London.

Freuchen, Peter. 1961. *Book of the Eskimos.* Greenwich, Conn.: Fawcett.

Frick, Johannes, and Franz Eichinger, eds. 1985. *Schamanismus in Nordwest-China: Aufzeichnungen von Steyler-Missionären in Tsinghai und Kansu.* Bonn: St. Augustin.

Friedl, Erika. 1965. "Träger medialer Begabung im Hindukush und Karakorum." *Acta Ethnological et Linguistica,* no. 8.

Friedrich, Adolf. 1939. *Afrikanische Priestertümer.* Stuttgart.

————. 1955. "Das Bewusstsein eines Naturvolkes von Haushalt und Urspring des Lebens." *Paideuma* 6, no. 2 (August): 47–53. Bamberg.

————, and Georg Buddruss. 1955. *Schamanengeschichten aus Sibirien.* (Translation of *Legendy i rasskazy o shamanakh u yakutov, buryat i tungusov* by G. V. Ksenofontov, 2nd ed., Moscow [1930]). Munich.

Fuller, John G. 1975. *Arigo: Surgeon of the Rusty Knife.* Suffolk: Bungay.

Funke, Friedrich W. 1969. *Religiöses Leben der Sherpa.* Innsbruck.

Furst, Peter T. 1973. "An Indian Journey to Life's Sources." *Natural History* 82, no. 4: 34–43.

————, and Marina Anguiano. 1976. " 'To Fly as Birds': Myth and Ritual as Agents of Enculturation among Huichol Indians of Mexico." In *Enculturation in Latin America: An Anthology,* edited by Johannes Wilbert. Los Angeles.

Galanti, Geri-Ann. 1982. "Psychic Consciousness: Inside Views." Presentation to the Congress of the Southwestern Anthropological Association, Sacramento, Calif.

Gallagher, H. G. 1974. *Etok: A Story of Eskimo Power.* New York.

————. 1982. "Over Easy: A Cultural Anthropologist's Near-Death Experience." *Anabiosis: The Journal for Near-Death Studies* 2, no. 2: 140–49.

Garett, Eileen J. 1968a. *Adventures in the Supernormal.* New York.

————. 1968b. *Many Voices: The Autobiography of a Medium.* New York.

Garfield, Charles A. 1977. "Ego Functioning, Fear of Death, and Altered States of Consciousness." In *Rediscovery of the Body,* edited by A. Garfield. New York.

Gatheru, R. Mugo. 1960. "The Medicine-Man as Psychotherapist." In *Exploring the Ways of Mankind,* edited by Walter Goldschmidt. New York: Holt, Rinehart and Winston.

Gellhorn, Ernst, and W. F. Kiely. 1972. "Mystical States of Consciousness: Neurophysiological and Clinical Aspects." *Journal of Nervous and Mental Disease* 154, no. 6: 339–405.

Goldstein, Kurt. 1960. "Concerning the Concept of 'Primitivity.' " In *Primitive Views of the World,* edited by Stanley Diamond. New York.

Goodman, Felicitas D. 1972. *Speaking in Tongues.* Chicago.

Greenlee, Robert F. 1944. "Medicine and Curing Practices of Modern Florida Seminoles." *American Anthropologist* 46: 317–28.

Greschat, Hans-Jürgen. 1980. *Mana und Tap: Die Religion der Maori auf Neuseeland.* Berlin.

Grey, George. 1979. "The Two Sorcerers." In *Reader in Comparative Religion,* edited by W. A. Lessa and E. Z. Vogt. New York.

Grinnell, George Bird. 1919. "A Buffalo Sweatlodge." *American Anthropologist* 21: 361–75.

Grof, Stanislav. 1978. *Topographie des Unbewussten: LSD im Dienst der tiefenpsychologischen Forschung.* Stuttgart. Originally published as *Realms of the Human Unconscious: Observations from LSD Research.* New York: Viking, 1975.

————, and Joan Halifax. 1980. *Die Begegnung mit dem Tod.* Stuttgart. Originally published as *The Human Encounter with Death.* New York: E. P. Dutton, 1978.

————, and Christina Grof. 1986. *Jenseits des Todes: An den Toren des Bewusstseins.* Munich. Originally published as *Beyond Death: The Gates of Consciousness.* New York: Thames and Hudson, 1980.

Gushiken, José. 1977. *El Curandero.* Lima.

Gusinde, Martin. 1931–74. *Die Feuerland Indianer.* 3 vols. Vienna.

Gutmanis, June. 1976. *Kahuna La'au Lapa'au.* Honolulu.

Haaf, E. 1978. "Heilende Kirchen in Ghana." *Curare* 1, no. 2: 73–84.

Halifax-Grof, Joan. 1977. "Hex Death." In *Frontiers of Healing,* edited by N. M. Regush. New York.

————. 1981. "The Sacred Way of the Wounded Healer." *Laughing Man* 2, no. 4.: 8–12.

————. 1982. *Shaman: The Wounded Healer.* London.

Hallowell, A. Irving. 1936. "The Passing of the Midewiwin in the Lake Winnipeg Region." *American Anthropologist* 38: 32–51.

————. 1942. *The Role of Conjuring in Salteaux Society.* Philadelphia.

Hammond, Sally. 1973. *We Are All Healers.* New York.

Hargous, Sabine. 1976. *Beschwörer der Seelen.* Basel.

Harner, Michael, ed. 1973a. *Hallucinogens and Shamanism.* Oxford.

————. 1973b. "The Sound of Rushing Water." In *Hallucinogens and Shamanism,* edited by Michael Harner. Oxford.

Harrer, Heinrich. 1966. *Sieben Jahre in Tibet.* Frankfurt am Main.

Harva (formerly Holmberg), Uno. 1938. "Die religiösen Vorstellungen der altaischen Völker." *Folklore Fellows Communications* 52, no. 125. Helsinki.

————. 1964. *Finno-Ugric [and] Siberian [Mythology].* Vol. 1 of *The Mythology of All Races,* edited by C. J. A. MacCulloch. New York. Originally published in Boston and London (1927).

Hecht, Elisabeth-Dorothea. 1977a. "Krankheit und Heilkunde bei den Somali." *Saeculum* 28: 169–90.

————. 1977b. "Krankheit und Heilkunde bei den Amhara." *Saeculum* 28: 191–222.

Heim, Albert. 1892. "Notizen über den Tod durch Absturz." *Jahrbuch des Schweizer Alpenclub* 27: 192–327.

Henry, Alexander. 1921. *Travels and Adventures in the Years 1760–1776.* Chicago: R. R. Donnelley and Sons.

Hermanns, Matthias. 1956. "Eine Myth über den Ursprung der Bhil-Zauberei (Indien)." *Anthropos* 51.

————. 1970. *Schamanen—Pseudoschamanen, Erlöser und Heilbringer.* 3 vols. Wiesbaden.

Hoffman, W. J. 1891. "The Mide'wiwin or 'Grand Medicine Society' of the Ojibwa." *7th Annual Report of the Bureau of American Ethnology, 1885–86.* Washington, D.C.

Holm, Gustav. 1914. "Ethnological Sketch of the Angmagsalik Eskimo." In *The Ammassalik Eskimo: Contributions to the Ethnology of the East Greenland Natives,* edited by William Thalbitzer. Part 1: 1–147. Copenhagen.

Holmer, Nils M., and S. Henry Wassén, eds. 1958. "The Complete Muu-Igala in Picture-Writing." *Etnologiska Studier* 21. Göteborg.

Honko, Lauri. 1959. "Krankheitsprojectile: Untersuchung über eine urtümliche Krankheitserklärung." *Folklore Fellows Communications* 72, no. 178. Helsinki.

Hoppal, Mihály, ed. 1985. *Shamanism in Eurasia.* 2 vols. Göttingen.

Horse Capture, G., ed. 1980. *The Seven Visions of Bull Lodge*. Ann Arbor, Mich.

Howitt, Alfred W. 1887. "On Australian Medicine Men or Doctors and Wizards of Some Australian Tribes." *Journal of the Royal Anthropological Institute of Great Britain and Ireland* 16: 23–59. London.

Huard, Pierre. 1969. "Western Medicine and Afro-Asian Ethnic Medicine." In *Medicine and Culture*, edited by F. N. L. Poynter. London.

Huhm, Halla Pai. 1980. *Kut: Korean Shamanist Rituals*. Elizabeth, N.J.: Hollym International.

Hultkrantz, Åke. 1967. "Spirit Lodge: A North American Shamanistic Séance." In *Studies in Shamanism*, edited by Carl Martin Edsman. Stockholm.

―――. 1981. "Ritual and Geheimnis: Über die Kunst der Medizinmänner, oder Was der Professor night gesagt hat." In *Der Wissenschaftler und das Irrationale*, edited by H. P. Duerr, vol. 1: 73–97. Frankfurt am Main.

―――. 1987. "Geistige Verwandtschaft." In *Heilung des Wissens*, edited by Amelie Schenk and Holger Kalweit. Munich.

Hungry Wolf, Adolf. 1977. *The Blood People*. New York.

Hung-Youn, Cho. 1982. *Koreanischer Schamanismus*. Hamburg: Hamburgisches Museum für Völkerkunde.

Huxley, Aldous. 1952. *The Devils of Loudun*. London.

―――. 1963. *The Doors of Perception; and Heaven and Hell*. New York: Harper and Row.

―――. 1977. *Moksha: Writings on Psychedelics and the Visionary Experience (1931–1963)*, edited by M. Horowitz and C. Palmer. New York: Stonehill.

Itkonen, Toivo Immanuel. 1960. "Der 'zweikampf' der lappischen Zauberer (Noai'di) um eine Wildrentierherde." *Journal de la Société Finno-Ougrienne* 62: 27–76. Helsinki.

James, William. 1907. *Die religiöser Erfahrung in ihrer Mannigfaltigkeit*. Leipzig. Originally published as *The Varieties of Religious Experience*. New York: Longmans, Green, 1911.

―――. 1962. *Essays on Faith and Morals*. Cleveland: World.

Jay, Robert. 1969. "Personal and Extrapersonal Vision in Anthropology." In *Reinventing Anthropology*, edited by Dell Hymes. New York.

Jensen, G. 1973. *The Doctor-Patient Relationship in African Tribal Society*. Assen.

Jilek, W. G. 1971. "From Crazy Witch-Doctor to Auxiliary Psychotherapist." *Psychiatric Clinic* 4: 200–20.

―――, and Louise Jilek-Aall. 1978. "The Psychiatrist and His Shaman Colleague: Cross-Cultural Collaboration with Traditional Amerindian Therapists." *Journal of Operational Psychiatry* 9, no. 2: 32–39.

―――, and N. Todd. 1974. "Witchdoctors Succeed Where Doctors Fail: Psychotherapy among Coast Salish Indians." *Canadian Journal of Psychiatry* 19, no. 4: 351–56.

Jochelson, Waldemar I. 1926. "The Yukaghir and the Yukaghirized Tungus." *The Jesup North Pacific Expedition*, vol. 9. Memoirs of the American Museum of Natural History. Leiden and New York.

Johnson, Frederick. 1943. "Notes on Micmac Shamanism." *Primitive Man* 16, nos. 3 and 4: 53–80.

Johnston, Basil. 1979. *Und Manitu erschuf die Welt*. Cologne.

Jones, David Earle. 1972. *Sanapia: Comanche Medicine Woman*. New York.

————. 1980. "Face the Ghost." *Phoenix: Journal of Transpersonal Anthropology* 4, nos. 1 and 2: 53–57.

————. 1987. "Die Lehrer." In *Heilung des Wissens,* edited by Amelie Schenk and Holger Kalweit. Munich.

Kalweit, Holger. 1981a. "Alles ist eins." *Esotera* 5: 402–409.

————. 1981b. "Transpersonal Anthropology and the Comparison of Cultures." *Phoenix: Journal of Transpersonal Anthropology* 5, no. 2: 97–105.

————. 1982a. "Die Entfesselung des Bewusstseins." *Psychologie Heute* 7: 54–60.

————. 1982b. "Das Paradox ist unser Barometer für Erleuchtung." *Psychologie Heute* 8: 46–53.

————. 1983a. "Der Trickster: Ein Nachwort zu 'Castaneda.' " *Curare* 6: 91–92.

————. 1983b. "Gewiss, es gehört immer zum Wesen der Anthropologie, die Dinge von aussen zu betrachten." *Curare* 7: 203–208.

————. 1984. *Traumzeit und innerer Raum: Die Welt der Schamanen.* Munich.

————. 1985. "Formen transpersonal Psychotherapie bei nicht-westlichen Kulturen." *Integrative Therapie* 3, no. 10: 253–62.

————. 1987. "Himalaya-Orakel." In *Heilung des Wissens,* edited by Amelie Schenk and Holger Kalweit. Munich.

————. In press. *Maximum Life.*

Karajalainen, K. F. 1927. "Die Religionen der Jugra-Völker." *Folklore Fellows Communications* 20, no. 63. Helsinki.

Katz, Richard. 1973. "Education for Transcendence: Lessons from the !Kung Zhü/twäsi." *Journal of Transpersonal Psychology* 5, no. 2: 136–55.

————. 1976. "Education for Transcendence: !Kia-healing with the Kalahari !Kung." In *Kalahari Hunter-Gatherers,* edited by Richard Lee and Irven DeVore. Cambridge, Mass.

————. 1982. *Boiling Energy: Community Healing among the Kalahari Kung.* Cambridge, Mass.: Harvard University Press.

————. 1987. "Heiler sprechen." In *Heilung des Wissens,* edited by Amelie Schenk and Holger Kalweit. Munich.

————, and Megan Biesele. 1980. "Male and Female Approaches to Healing among the !Kung." Paper presented at the Second International Conference on Hunting and Gathering Societies, Quebec (September).

Keen, Sam. 1970. *Voices and Visions.* New York.

Kelly, Isabel T. 1936. "Chemehuevi Shamanism." In *Essays in Anthropology: Presented to A. L. Kroeber.* Berkeley, Calif.: 129–42.

Kelsey, Theodore. 1980. "Flying 'Gods of Hawaii.' " *Full Moon* 1, no. 3/4: 1.

Kemnitzer, Luis S. 1970. "The Cultural Provenience of Objects Used in Yuwipi: A Modern Teton Dakota Healing Ritual." *Ethnos* 1–4: 40–75.

Kiev, Ari. 1968. *Curanderismo: Mexican-American Folk Psychiatry.* New York.

Kilson, Marion. 1968. "A Note on Trance Possession among the Ga of Western Ghana." *Transcultural Psychiatric Research* 5 (April).

Kim, Kwang-Iel. 1973. "Shamanist Healing Ceremonies in Korea." *Korea Journal* 13: 41–47.

Kippenberg, Hans G., and B. Luchesi. 1978. *Magie: Die sozialwissenschaftliche Kontroverse über das Verstehen fremden Denkens.* Frankfurt am Main.

Kluckhohn, Clyde, and L. C. Wyman. 1940. "An Introduction to Navaho Chant Practice." *Memoirs of the American Anthropological Association,* no. 53. Menasha, Wis.

Knudtson, Peter H. 1987. "Flora, Medizinfrau der Wintu." In *Heilung des Wissens,* edited by Amelie Schenk and Holger Kalweit. Munich.

Kohl, J. G. 1859. *Kitschi-Gami oder Erzählungen vom Oberen See.* Vol. 2. Bremen.

Krader, Lawrence. 1975. "The Shamanist Tradition of the Buryats (Siberia)." *Anthropos* 70: 105–44.

Krippner, Stanley. 1975. *Song of the Siren: A Parapsychological Odyssey.* New York.

———, and Alberto Villoldo. 1976. *The Realms of Healing.* Millbrae, Calif.

———, and Michael Winkelman. n.d. "Ein Besuch bei Maria Sabina" (unpublished manuscript).

Kroeber, Alfred Louis. 1935. "Walapai Ethnography." *Memoirs of the American Anthropological Association,* no. 42. Menasha, Wis.

———. 1940. "Psychotic Factors in Shamanism." *Character and Personality* 8: 204–15.

———. 1965. *The Nature of Culture.* London.

Kroeber, Theodora. 1961. *Ishi in Two Worlds.* Berkeley, Calif.

Kruger, Helen. 1974. *Other Healers, Other Cures: A Guide to Alternative Medicine.* New York.

Kuhlenbeck, Ludwig. 1909. "Der Okkultismus der nordamerikanischen Indianer." In *Geschichte des neueren Okkultismus,* edited by Karl Kiesewetter. Liepzig.

Kuhn, Thomas S. 1967. *Die Struktur der wissenschaftlichen Revolution.* Frankfurt am Main. Originally published as *The Structure of Scientific Revolutions.* Chicago: University of Chicago Press, 1962.

Kunze, Gerhard. 1982. *Ihr baut die Windmühlen—den Wind rufen wir.* Munich.

———. 1987. "Die kleine Geisterfrau." In *Heilung des Wissens,* edited by Amelie Schenk and Holger Kalweit. Munich.

La Barre, Weston. 1970. *The Ghost Dance: The Origins of Religion.* Garden City, N.Y.: Doubleday.

Lambert, R. S. 1956. "The Shaking Tent." *Tomorrow* 4, no. 3: 113–28.

Lame Deer, John (Fire), and Richard Erdoes. 1972. *Lame Deer: Seeker of Visions.* New York: Simon and Schuster.

Lamp, Bruce F. 1981. "Wizard of the Upper Amazon as Ethnography." *Current Anthropology* 22, no. 5: 577–80.

Lang, A. 1900. *The Making of Religion.* London.

Lantis, Margaret. 1946. "The Social Culture of the Nunivak Eskimo." *Transactions of the American Philosophical Society* 35: 3.

Larsen, Stephen. 1978. "Shamanism and Psychotherapy." Paper presented at the Symposium for Indigenous Healing Practices, Toronto.

Larson, T. J. 1980. "Sorcery and Witchcraft of the Hambukushu of Ngamiland (Southwest Africa)." *Anthropos* 75, no. 3–4: 416–32.

Laski, Vera. 1959. *Seeking Life.* Austin, Tex.

Laubscher, B. J. F. 1975. *The Pagan Soul.* London.

Lechner-Knecht, Sigrid. 1965. "Reisenotizen über Zauberhandlungen in Mexiko." *Zeitschrift für Ethnologie* 90: 247–59.

Leclerc, Gérard. 1973. *Anthropologie und Kolonialismus.* Munich.

Lee, Richard B. 1958. "The Sociology of !Kung Bushman Trance Performances." In *Trance and Possession States,* edited by R. Prince. Montreal.

Leh, L. L. 1934. "The Shaman in Aboriginal American Society." *University of Colorado Studies* 20.

Lehtisalo, Toivo V. 1924. "Entwurf einer Mythologie der Jurak-Samojeden." *Mémoires de la société Finno-Ougrienne,* no. 53, Helsinki.

Leighton, A. H., and D. C. Leighton. 1949. "Gregorio, the Hand-trembler: A Psychobiological Personality Study of a Navaho Indian." *Papers of the Peabody Museum of American Archaeology and Ethnology,* no. 40.

Leiris, Michel. 1977. *Die eigene und die fremde Kultur.* Frankfurt am Main.

LeShan, Lawrence. 1976. *Alternate Realities.* New York.

Levett, Carl. 1974. *Crossings: A Transpersonal Approach.* Ridgefield, Conn.

Lévi-Strauss, Claude. 1972a. *"Primitive" und "Zivilisierte": Nach Gesprächen aufgezeichnet von Georges Charbonnier.* Zurich.

————. 1972b. *Rasse und Geschichte.* Frankfurt am Main. Originally published as *Race and History.* Paris, 1952.

————. 1974. *Traurige Tropen.* Cologne. Originally published as *Tristes Tropiques.* Paris, 1955.

Lewis, T. H. 1977. "Therapeutic Techniques of Huichol Curanderos with a Case Report of Cross Cultural Psychotherapy (Mexico)." *Anthropos* 72: 709–16.

Lindig, Wolfgang. 1970. "Geheimbünde und Männerbünde der Prärie- und der Waldlandindianer Nordamerikas." *Studien zur Kulturkunde* 23. Wiesbaden.

————, and Mark Münzel. 1976. *Die Indianer.* Munich.

Loeb, Edwin Meyer. 1929. "Shaman and Seer." *American Anthropologist* 31 (n.s.), no. 1 (January–March): 60–84.

Lommel, Andreas. 1951. "Traum und Bild bei den Primitiven in Nordwest-Australien." *Psyche* 5, no. 3: 187–209.

————. 1952. "Die Unambal: Ein Stamm in Nordwest-Australien." *Monographien zur Völkerkunde* 11. Hamburg: Hamburgisches Museum für Völkerkunde.

————. 1980. "Shamanism in Australia." *Festschrift für T. G. H. Strehlow.* Adelaide.

Long, Joseph K. 1972. "Medical Anthropology, Dance and Trance in Jamaica." *Bulletin of the International Committee on Urgent Anthropological and Ethnological Research* 14: 17–23.

Long Lance Buffalo Child. 1976 (1928). *Long Lance: The Autobiography of a Blackfoot Indian Chief.* New York.

Lopatin, Ivan A. 1946–49. "A Shamanistic Performance for a Sick Boy." *Anthropos* 41–44: 365–68.

Lowenstein, Tom. n.d. *The Shaman Aningatchaq: An Eskimo Story from Tikiraq, Alaska.* London.

Lowie, Robert H. 1951. "Beiträge zur Völkerkunde Nordamerikas." *Mitteilungen aus dem Museum für Völkerkunde in Hamburg* 23. Hamburg.

————. 1979. "Shamans and Priests among the Plains Indians." In *Reader in Comparative Religion,* edited by W. A. Lessa and E. Z. Vogt. New York.

Luckert, Karl W. 1979. *Coyoteway: A Navajo Holyway Healing Ceremonial.* Tucson, Ariz.

Luna, Luis Eduardo. 1983. "The Concepts of Plants as Teachers among Four Mestizo Shamans of Iquitos, Northeast Peru." Paper presented at the 11th International Congress for Anthropological and Ethnological Sciences. Vancouver, B.C.

————. 1985. "The Healing Practices of a Peruvian Shaman." *Journal of Ethnopharmacology.*

————. 1987. "Erfahrungen mit den Mestizen-Schamanen von Iquitos." In *Heilung des Wissens,* edited by Amelie Schenk and Holger Kalweit. Munich.

Madsen, William. 1955. "Shamanism in Mexico." *Southwestern Journal of Anthropology* 11: 48–57.

Mails, Thomas. 1979. *Fools Crow.* New York.

Marshall, Lorna. 1969. "The Medicine Dance of the !Kung Bushmen." *Africa* 39: 347–80.

Maslow, Abraham H. 1964. *Religions, Values, and Peak-Experiences.* New York.

————. 1971. *The Farther Reaches of Human Nature.* New York.

————. 1973. *Psychologie des Seins.* Munich.

————. 1977. *Die Psychologie der Wissenschaft.* Munich. Originally published as *The Psychology of Science.* New York: Harper and Row, 1966.

McElroy, W. A. 1955–56. "Psi Testing in Arnhem Land." *Oceania* 26: 118–26. Sydney.

Meek, George W., ed. 1977. *Healers and the Healing Process.* Wheaton, Ill.

Melville, Leinani. 1969. *Children of the Rainbow.* Wheaton, Ill.

Mendelson, E. Michael. 1965. "Los Escándalos de Macimón." *Seminario de Integración Social Guatemalteca* 19. Guatemala City.

Messner, Reinhold. 1978. *Grenzbereich Todeszone.* Cologne.

Métreaux, Alfred. 1944. "Le Shamanisme chez les Indiens de L'Amérique du Sud tropicale." *Acta Americana* 2, no. 3: 197–219; and 2, no. 4: 320–41. Mexico.

Michael, Henry M., ed. 1963. *Studies in Siberian Shamanism.* Toronto: University of Toronto Press.

Middleton, John, ed. 1967. *Magic, Witchcraft and Curing.* London.

Mikhailovskii, V. M. 1895. "Shamanism in Siberia and European Russia, Being the Second Part of *Shamanstvo.*" Translated by Oliver Wardrop. *Journal of the Royal Anthropological Institute of Great Britain and Ireland* 24: 62–100, 126–58. London.

Miller, Kaspar. 1979. *Faith-Healers in the Himalayas.* Kritipur: Center of Nepal and Asian Studies.

Moisés, Rosalio, and Jane Holden, et al. 1971. *A Yaqui Life: The Personal Chronicle of a Yaqui Indian.* Lincoln, Neb.

Monmouth, Geoffrey von. 1978. *Das Leben des Zauberers Merlin.* Amsterdam.

Moray, Ann. 1965. "The Celtic Heritage in Ireland." *Horizon* 7, no. 2 (Spring): 33–39.

Morgan, William. 1931. "Navaho Treatment of Sickness: Diagnosticians." *American Anthropologist* 33: 390–402.

Mühlmann, Wilhelm E. 1964. *Rassen, Ethnien, Kulturen: Moderne Ethnologie.* Berlin.

Münzel, Mark. 1977. *Schrumpfkopfmacher? Jibaro-Indianer in Südamerika.* Frankfurt am Main: Museum für Völkerkunde.

Murdock, G. P. 1965. "Tenino Shamanism." *Ethnology* 4: 165–71.

Murphy, Jane M. 1964. "Psychotherapeutic Aspects of Shamanism on St. Lawrence Island, Alaska." In *Magic, Faith and Healing,* edited by Ari Kiev. New York.

Murphy, Michael. 1976. *Golf in the Kingdom.* Pine Brook, N.J.

Myerhoff, Barbara G. 1966. "The Doctor as Cultural Hero: The Shaman of Rincon." *Anthropological Quarterly* 39: 60–72.

Nadel, S. F. 1979 (1946). "A Study of Shamanism in the Nuba Mountains." In *Reader in Comparative Religion*, edited by W. A. Lessa and E. Z. Vogt. New York.

Neal, James H. 1966. *Ju-Ju in My Life*. London.

Nebesky-Wojkowitz, René de. 1948. "Das tibetische Staatsorakel." *Archiv für Völkerkunde* 3: 136–55. Vienna.

———. 1956. *Oracles and Demons of Tibet: The Cult and Iconography of the Tibetan Protective Deities.* The Hague.

Neumann, Erich. 1978 (1953). *Kulturentwicklung und Religion.* Frankfurt am Main.

Newcomb, Franc J. 1964. *Hosteen Klah, Navaho Medicine Man and Sand Painter.* Norman, Okla.: University of Oklahoma Press.

Nioradze, Georg. 1925. *Der Schamanismus bei den sibirischen Völkern.* Stuttgart.

Noyes, Russell, and R. Kletti. 1976. "Depersonalisation in the Face of Life-Threatening Danger: A Description." *Psychiatry* 39: 19–27.

Ohnuki-Tierney, Emiko. 1973. "The Shamanism of the Ainu of the Northwest Coast of Southern Sakhalin." *Ethnology* 12: 15–29.

———. 1981. *Illness and Healing among the Sakhalin Ainu: A Symbolic Interrelation.* Cambridge, Mass.

Oppitz, Michael. 1981. *Schamanen im blinden Land.* Frankfurt am Main.

Ott, Theo. 1979. *Der magische Pfeil.* Zurich.

———. 1981. "Der Medizinmann als Arzt und Priester." In *Prana: Jahrbuch für Yoga,* edited by Rocque Lobo. Munich.

Park, Willard Z. 1934. "Paviotso Shamanism." *American Anthropologist* 36 (n.s.) (January–March): 98–113.

———. 1938. *Shamanism in Western North America: A Study in Cultural Relationships.* Northwestern University Studies in the Social Sciences 2. Evanston and Chicago.

Pelletier, Kenneth R., and Erik Peper. 1977. "The Chutzpah Factor in Altered States of Consciousness." *Journal of Humanistic Psychology* 17, no. 1: 63–73.

Peper, Erik. 1974. "Voluntary Pain Control: Physiological and Psychological Correlations." In *Alterations in Awareness and Human Potentialities,* edited by T. X. Barber. New York.

Peter, Prince of Greece and Denmark. 1961. "The Traces of a Tibetan Oracle." *Folk* 3.

———. 1976. "Tibetan Oracles." In *The Realm of the Extra-Human: Agents and Audiences,* edited by A. Bharati. The Hague.

Peters, Larry. 1978. "Psychotherapy in Tamang Shamanism." *Ethnos* 6, no. 2: 63–91.

———. 1981a. "An Experimental Study of Nepalese Shamanism." *Journal of Transpersonal Psychology* 13, no. 1: 1–26.

———. 1981b. *Ecstasy and Healing in Nepal.* Los Angeles.

Petri, Helmut. 1952, 1953. "Der australische Medizinmann." *Annali Lateranensi* 16:159–317, and 17:155–227. Vatican City.

———. 1962. "Australische 'Medizinmänner' am Rande der technischen Zivilisation." *Die Umschau in Wissenschaft und Technik* 62: 171–74.

———. 1971. "Traum und Trance bei den Australiern." In *Naturvölker unserer Zeit* (DVA). Stuttgart.

———. 1984. (unpublished manuscript).

Pfeiffer, Wolfgang M. 1966. "Versenkungs- und Trancezustände bei indonesischen Volksstämmen." *Der Nervenarzt* 37: 7–18.

———. 1972. "Besessenheit, normalpsychologisch und pathologisch." In *Ergriffenheit und Besessenheit*, edited by J. Zutt. Bern.

Pfund, Kurt. 1984. *Ich, Waibadi, Regenmacher, Zauberer und König.* Munich.

Powers, W. K. 1982. *Yuwipi: Vision and Experience in Oglala Ritual.* London.

Prem Das. 1978. "Initiation by a Huichol Shaman." In *Art of the Huichol Indians*, edited by Harry N. Abrams. The Fine Arts Museum of San Francisco. New York.

———. 1987. "Die singende Erde." In *Heilung des Wissens*, edited by Amelie Schenk and Holger Kalweit. Munich.

Prince, Raymond H. 1976. "Psychotherapy as the Manipulation of Endogenous Healing Mechanisms: A Transcultural Survey." *Transcultural Psychiatric Research* 8: 115–33.

———, ed. 1982. "Shamans and Endorphins." *Ethnos* 10, no. 4.

Puharich, Andrija. 1973. *Beyond Telepathy.* New York.

Radin, Paul. 1945. *The Road of Life and Death: A Ritual Drama of the American Indians.* Bollingen Series, no. 5. New York.

Rasmussen, Knud. 1907. *Neue Menschen: Ein Jahr bei den Nachbarn des Nordpols.* Bern.

———. 1908. *The People of the Polar North: A Record.* Edited by G. Herring. Philadelphia.

———. 1926. *Rasmussens Thulefahrt: Zwei jahre im Schlitten durch unerforschtes Eskimoland.* Edited by F. Sieburg. Frankfurt am Main.

———. 1927. *Across Arctic America.* New York: G. P. Putnam's Sons.

———. 1930a. *Intellectual Culture of the Hudson Bay Eskimos. Report of the Fifth Thule Expedition, 1921–1924*, vol. 7. Copenhagen.

———. 1930b. *Intellectual Culture of the Iglulik Eskimos.* Translated by William Worster. *Report of the Fifth Thule Expedition, 1921–1924*, vol. 7, no. 1. Copenhagen.

———. 1930c. *Observations on the Intellectual Culture of the Caribou Eskimos. Report of the Fifth Thule Expedition, 1921–1924*, vol. 7, no. 2. Copenhagen.

———. 1931. *The Netsilik Eskimos: Social Life and Spiritual Culture.* Translated by W. E. Calvert. *Report of the Fifth Thule Expedition, 1921–1924*, vol. 8, no. 1–2. Copenhagen.

———. 1932. *Intellectual Culture of the Copper Eskimos.* Translated by W. E. Calvert. *Report of the Fifth Thule Expedition, 1921–1924*, vol. 9. Copenhagen.

———. 1946. *Die grosse Schlittenreise.* Essen.

———. 1952. *The Alaskan Eskimo.* Copenhagen.

Reichel-Dolmatoff, Gerado. 1975. *The Shaman and the Jaguar.* Philadelphia.

———. 1976. "Training for the Priesthood among the Kogi of Colombia." In *Enculturation in Latin America: An Anthology*, edited by Johannes Wilbert. Los Angeles.

Ridington, Robin. 1978. *Swan People: A Study of the Dunne-za Prophet Dance.* Ottawa: National Museum of Canada.

———, and Tonia Ridington. 1978. "Das innere Gesicht von Schamanismus und Totemismus." In *Über den Rand des tiefen Canyon: Lehren indianischer Schamanen*, edited by D. and B. Tedlock. Cologne.

Ring, Kenneth. 1985. *Den Tod erfahren—das Leben gewinnen.* Munich.

Rock, Joseph F. 1935. "Sungmas, the Living Oracles of the Tibetan Church." *National Geographic* (October): 4475–85.

———. 1959. "Contributions to Shamanism of the Tibetan-Chinese Borderland." *Anthropos* 54: 796–818.

Röder, Josef G. 1948. *Alahatala: Die Religion der Inlandstämme Mittelcerams.* Bamberg.

Rodman, Julius S. 1979. *The Kahuna: Sorcerers of Hawaii, Past and Present.* Hicksville, N.Y.

Rogers, Spencer L. 1982 (1905). *The Shaman: His Symbols and His Healing.* Springfield, Ill.

Rose, Lyndon. 1951. "Psi Patterns amongst the Australian Aborigines." *Journal of the American Society for Psychical Research* 45, no. 2: 71–75.

Rose, Ronald. 1952a. "Experiments with ESP and PK with Aboriginal Subjects." *Journal of Parapsychology* 16: 219–20.

———. 1952b. "Psi and Australian Aborigines." *Journal of the American Society of Psychical Research* 46, no. 1: 17–28.

———. 1957. *Living Magic.* London.

Rosen, D. 1975. "Suicide Survivors: A Follow-up Study of Persons Who Survived Jumping from the Golden Gate and San Francisco–Oakland Bay Bridges." *Western Journal for Medicine* 122: 289.

Russell, Frank. 1908. "The Pima Indians." *26th Annual Report of the Bureau of American Ethnology, 1904–1905.* Washington, D.C.

Sandner, Donald F. 1978. "Navaho Medicine." *Human Nature* 1 (July): 54–62.

———. 1979a. "Navaho Indian Medicine and Medicine Men." In *Ways of Health,* edited by David S. Sobel. New York.

———. 1979b. *Navaho Symbols of Healing.* New York.

Schaefer, Hermann. 1978. *Hunza: Ein Volk ohne Krankheit.* Düsseldorf.

Schaeffer, Claude E. 1969. "Blackfoot Shaking Tent." Occasional Papers, no. 5. Calgary, Alberta: Blenbow-Alberta Institute.

Schebesta, Paul. 1936. "Eine Schamanenbeschwörung auf Sumatra." *Ciba Zeitschrift* 4, no. 38: 1313–16.

Schefold, Reimar. 1980. *Spielzeug für die Seelen.* Zurich: Museum Rietberg.

Schenk, Amelie. 1980. "JuJu, tödlicher Zauber in Afrika." *Esotera* 8: 713–21.

———. 1987a. "Ein Medizinmann erzählt." In *Heilung des Wissens,* edited by Amelie Schenk and Holger Kalweit. Munich.

———, and Holger Kalweit, eds. 1987b. *Heilung des Wissens.* Munich.

Schlesier, Karl H. 1974. "Action Anthropology and the Southern Cheyenne." *Current Anthropology* 15, no. 3: 217–238.

Schlosser, Katesa. 1972. *Zauberei im Zululand: Manuskripte des Blitz-Zauberers Laduma Madela.* Kiel.

Schultz, James W. 1983. *Sucht mich in der Prärie: Mein Leben als Indianer.* Munich. Originally published as *My Life as an Indian: The Story of a Red Woman and a White Man in the Lodges of the Blackfeet.* Williamstown, Mass: Corner House, 1973.

Schuster, Meinhard. 1960. "Die Schamanen und ihr Ritual." In *Völkerkunde,* edited by B. Freudenfeld. Munich.

Schüttler, Günter. 1971. *Die letzten tibetischen Orakelpriester.* Wiesbaden.

Seabrook, W. B. 1931. *Geheimnisvolles Haiti: Rätsel und Symbolik des Wodu-Kultes.* Berlin. Originally published as *The Magic Island.* New York: Literary Guild, 1929.

Sharon, Douglas. 1976. "Becoming a Curandero in Peru." In *Enculturation in Latin America: An Anthology,* edited by Johannes Wilbert. Los Angeles.

————. 1980. *Zauberer der vier Winde.* Freiburg. Originally published as *Wizard of the Four Winds: A Shaman's Story.* New York: Free Press, 1978.

————. 1987. "Der gescheiterte Schamanenschüler." In *Heilung des Wissens,* edited by Amelie Schenk and Holger Kalweit. Munich.

Shirokogoroff, Sergei M. 1935a. *Psychomental Complex of the Tungus.* London.

————. 1935b. "Versuch einer Erforschung der Grundlagen des Schamenentums bei den Tungusen." *Baessler Archiv* 18, part 2: 41–96. Berlin. (Translation of article in Russian published in Vladivostok [1919].)

Siiger, Halfdan. 1963. "Shamanism among the Kalash Kafirs of Chitral." *Folk* 5: 295–303.

Siikala, Anna-Leena. 1978. "The Rite Technique of the Siberian Shaman." *Folklore Fellows Communications,* no. 220. Helsinki.

Silverman, Julian. 1967. "Shamans and Acute Schizophrenia." *American Anthropologist* 69: 21–31.

————. 1975. "On the Sensory Bases of Transcendental States of Consciousness." In *Psychiatry and Mysticism,* edited by Stanley R. Dean. Chicago: Nelson-Hall.

Simmons, Leo W. 1976. *Sun Chief: The Autobiography of a Hopi Indian.* New Haven, Conn.

Singer, Philip, and Kate W. Ankerbrandt. 1980. "The Ethnography of the Paranormal." *Phoenix: Journal of Transpersonal Anthropology* 4, no. 1: 19–34.

Speck, Frank. 1919. "Penobscot Shamanism." *Memoirs of the American Anthropological Association* 6, no. 4. Menasha, Wis.

Spencer, Baldwin, and F. J. Gillen. 1899. *The Native Tribes of Central Australia.* London.

————. 1969. *The Northern Tribes of Central Australia.* Oosterhout, Netherlands. Originally published in London (1904).

Spranz, Bodo. 1961. "Zauberei und Krankenheilung im Brauchtum der Gegenwart bei Otomi-Indianern in Mexiko." *Zeitschrift für Ethnologie* 86, no. 1: 51–67. Berlin.

Standing Bear, Luther. 1978 (1933). *Land of the Spotted Eagle.* Lincoln: University of Nebraska Press.

Stefánsson, Vilhjálmur. 1913. *My Life with the Eskimo.* New York.

Steiger, Brad. 1974. *Medicine Power.* New York.

Sternberg, Leo. 1935. "Die Auserwählung im sibirischen Schamanismus." *Zeitschrift für Missionskunde und Religionswissenschaft* 50: 229–52 and 261–74. Berlin.

Stevenson, Matilda Coxe. 1904. "The Zuñi Indians: Their Mythology, Esoteric Fraternities, and Ceremonies." *23rd Annual Report of the Bureau of American Ethnology, 1901–1902.* Washington, D.C.

Stewart, H. 1976. "A Pilot Study of the Afro-American Healer." *Psychoenergetic Systems* 1: 131–34.

Stöcklin, Werner. 1978. "Archaische Zauberdoktoren im Gesundheitsdienst?" *Ciba-Geigy Magazin* 1: 33–35.

Stone, R. B., and L. Stone. 1980. *Hawaiian and Polynesian Miracle Health Secrets.* New York.

Storl, Wolf-Dieter. 1974. *Shamanism among Americans of European Origin: A Case Study in Diffusion and Convergence.* Bern: self-published.

Sturtevant, William C. 1960. "A Seminole Medicine Maker." In *In the Company of Man,* edited by J. B. Casagrande. New York.

Swanson, Guy E. 1973. "The Search for the Guardian Spirit: A Process of Empowerment in Simpler Societies." *Ethnology* 12: 359–78.

Swanton, John R. 1908. "Social Condition, Beliefs, and Linguistic Relationship of the Tlingit Indians." *26th Annual Report of the Bureau of American Ethnology, 1904–1905.* Washington, D.C.: 391–485.

————. "Contribution to the Ethnology of the Haida." *The Jesup North Pacific Expedition, 1905–1909,* vol. 5, no. 1. *Memoirs of the American Museum of Natural History.* Leiden and New York.

Taksami, C. M. 1978. "The Story of a Nivkhi Shamaness as Told by Herself." In *Shamanism in Siberia,* edited by Vilmos Diószegi and M. Hoppál. Budapest.

Taube, Erika, and Manfred Taube. 1983. *Schamanen und Rhapsoden: Die geistige Kulture der alten Mongolei.* Leipzig.

Tedlock, Dennis. 1976. "In Search of the Miraculous in Zuñi." In *The Realm of the Extra-Human: Ideas and Actions,* edited by A. Bharati. The Hague.

Teit, James. 1905. "The Shuswap." *The Jesup North Pacific Expedition, 1900–1908,* vol. 2, no. 7. *Memoirs of the American Museum of Natural History.* Leiden and New York.

Temple, Robert K. G. 1982. *Götter, Orakel und Visionen.* Frankfurt am Main.

Thalbitzer, William. 1910. "The Heathen Priests of East Greenland (Angakut)." *Proceedings of the 16th International Congress of Americanists* (1908): 447–64. Vienna and Leipzig.

Torrey, E. F. 1969. "The Case for the Indigenous Therapist." *Archive of General Psychiatry* 20: 365–73.

Underhill, Ruth M. 1969. *Papago Indian Religion.* New York.

Villaseñor, David. 1974. *Mandalas im Sand: Vom Wesen indianischer Sandmalerei.* Obernhain.

Wagner-Robertz, Dagmar. 1976. "Shamanismus bei den Hain//om in Südwestafrika." *Anthropos* 71: 533–54.

Walker, Steward E. 1967. "Nez Percé Sorcery." *Ethnology* 6: 66–96.

Walter, V. J., and W. Grey Walter. 1949. "The Central Effects of Rhythmic Sensory Stimulation." *Electroencephalography and Clinical Neurophysiology* 1: 57–86.

Wapnick, Kenneth. 1969. "Mysticism and Schizophrenia." *Journal of Transpersonal Psychology* 1 (Fall): 49–68.

Warner, W. Lloyd. 1958. *A Black Civilization.* New York.

Wassilyewitsch, G. M. 1963. "Erwerbung der Schamanenfähigkeiten bei den Ewenken (Tungusen)." In *Glaubenswelt und Folklore der sibirischen Völker,* edited by Vilmos Diószegi. Budapest.

Waters, Frank. 1963. *Book of the Hopi.* New York.

————. 1969. *Pumpkin Seed Point.* Chicago.

Watson, Lyall. 1974. *Die Grenzbereiche des Lebens.* Frankfurt am Main. Originally published as *The Romeo Error: A Matter of Life and Death.* London.

————. 1976. *Gifts of Unknown Things.* Kent: Sevenoaks.

————. 1982. *Lightning Bird.* London.

Weil, Andrew. 1977. "The Marriage of Sun and Moon." In *Alternate States of Consciousness,* edited by Norman Zinberg. New York: Free Press.

Weizsäcker, Carl Friedrich von. 1971. *Die Einheit der Natur.* Munich.

White, John, and Stanley Krippner, eds. 1977. *Future Science.* New York.

White, Rhea A., and Michael Murphy. 1983. *Psi im Sport.* Munich.

Whiting, B. B. 1950. "Paiute Sorcery." *Publications in Anthropology* 15, New York.

Willoya, William, and Vinson Brown. 1976. *Im Zeichen des Regenbogens.* Obernhain.

Worrall, Ambrose, and Olga Worrall. 1965. *The Gift of Healing.* New York.

Wyman, Leland C. 1936. "Navaho Diagnosticians." *American Anthropologist* 38: 236–46.

Zaretsky, Irving I., ed. 1974. *Trance, Healing and Hallucination.* New York.

Zerries, Otto. 1964. *Waika.* Munich.

Zimmerly, David. 1969. "On Being an Ascetic: Personal Document of a Sioux Medicine Man." *Pine Ridge Research Bulletin* 10: 46–71.

Zuccarelli, Hugo. 1983. *Brain-Mind Bulletin* 8, no. 17 (October 24).

APPENDIX: LOCATION OF TRIBES

Agiarmiut Eskimo—Northwest Territories
Ainu—northern Japan (Hokkaido, southern Sakhalin, and Kurile islands)
Algonquian—northeast of the Great Lakes
Arunta—central Australia, near Alice Springs
Badyaranke—Senegal
Bantu—central Africa and South Africa (collective name for many peoples)
Batak—Indonesia, northern Sumatra, Lake Toba
Birartchen—northeastern Siberia (northern group of the Tungus)
Blackfoot—upper Saskatchewan to Missouri, Montana
Bunan—Taiwan
Buryat—Siberia, around Lake Baikal
Carrier—British Columbia
Chant—western Siberia, upper and middle Ob
Chukchee—northern Siberia, Chukchee Peninsula
Comanche—northwestern Texas
Copper Eskimo—Northwest Territories
Crow—Montana
Cuna—Panamanian islands
Dajak—Indonesia, Borneo
Dakota—North and South Dakota, Montana
Desana—northeastern Peru and southeastern Colombia (subgroup of the Tukano)
Dieri—Australia
Dunne-za—California
East Yakuts—western Siberia, upper and middle Ob
Evenki—northeastern Siberia (northern group of the Tungus)
Forrest River Tribes (Yeidji)—northwestern Australia, on the Forrest River
Gitksan—northwest coast of Canada
Gros Ventre—Montana
Haida—British Columbia

Hain//om—southwestern Africa

Halakwulup—Tierra del Fuego

Hidatsa—northwestern Montana, North Dakota

Hopi—Arizona

Huichol—Mexico

Hurons—north of Lakes Huron and Ontario

Iglulik Eskimo—Northwest Territories, Baffin Island

Kakadu—Australia, Northern Territory, Arnhem Land

Kulin—Australia, New South Wales, Victoria coast

!Kung—Kalahari Desert, Botswana

Kuni—Sudan

Kurnai—Australia, New South Wales, Victoria coast

Lakota—North and South Dakota

Lapps—northern Scandinavia

Luiseño—southern California, Mexican border

Magar—Nepal

Malagasy—Madagascar

Mandan—northwestern Montana, North Dakota

Maori—New Zealand

Masai—southern Kenya and northern Tanzania

Menomini—north of Lake Michigan

Micmac—Nova Scotia, New Brunswick, and Newfoundland

Mohave—southwestern Arizona (subgroup of the Yuma)

Montagnais—north of the St. Lawrence River to Labrador

Mossi—Sudan

Nasleg—Siberia

Navajo—Arizona

Netsilik Eskimo—

Nez Percé—Idaho

Oglala—North and South Dakota

Ojibwa—north of the Great Lakes

Papago—Arizona, Mexican border

Passamaquoddy—Maine

Paviotso—Nevada

Penobscot—Maine

Piegan—between upper Saskatchewan and Missouri; Montana (subgroup of the Black-foot)

Pima—southwestern Arizona, Mexican border

Ponca—eastern Montana

Pygmy—central African rainforest area

Selk'nam—Tierra del Fuego

Seminole—Florida

Shuswap—British Columbia

Sotho—South Africa, Bechuanaland (subgroup of the Bantu)

Tenino—Oregon

Thompson—British Columbia

Tsimshan—northwest coast of Canada

Tukano—northeastern Peru and southeastern Colombia

Tungus—northeastern Siberia

Unambal—northwestern Australia

Ungarinyin—northwestern Australia, Walcott Inlet

Vogul—Siberia, northwest Urals

Wahaerama-Tanabaru Group—Indonesia

Washo—California, Pyramid Lake

Winnebago—western side of Lake Michigan

Wintu—northern California

Worora—Australia

Wurajeri—Australia, New South Wales, Victoria near Melbourne

Yamana—Tierra del Fuego

Yualayi—Australia

Yukagir—northeastern Siberia

Yuma—southwestern Arizona

Zulu—South Africa, Natal Province

Zuñi—Arizona

INDEX